hamlyn

# the creative art of bonsai

*Isabelle & Rémy Samson*

# CONTENTS

The advice that is contained on the following pages is the result of almost thirty years' experience of growing bonsai, and we wrote this book because we wanted not only to share our passion for these small plants but also to share our knowledge. We would be among the first to admit that there is still much to learn, however. The guidelines given for each plant should, of course, be adapted to suit your own climate, seasonal variations, local conditions and each individual plant. There must always be room for intuition in the growing of bonsai as in all other aspects of gardening.

The second part of the book contains advice on growing, pruning, propagation and caring for the trees that are most often grown as bonsai. The plants are arranged in alphabetical order of botanical name, and there is an index of common names at the end of the book so that you can find the plants that interest you. Those plants that can be grown outdoors are on pages with a green background; those that can be grown indoors are on pages with a blue background; those that will benefit from being grown in a conservatory are on pages with a cream background. These are not hard-and-fast rules, and you may find that plants that are hardy in our garden will be tender in your own.

First published in France in 1986 under the title *Comment Créer et Entretenir vos Bonsai* by Isabelle and Rémy Samson

© Bordas, Paris, 1986

This revised edition first published in France in 1999

© Larousse Bordas/HER 1999

Photographs © Alain Draeger, Isabelle Samson, Christian Pessey and Jeanbor
Illustrations of pests and diseases by Danièle Molez
Other illustrations by Valerie Ducugis

First published in Great Britain in 2000 by Hamlyn a division of Octopus Publishing Group Ltd, 2–4 Heron Quays, London E14 4JP
Translated by Derek Hanson and Judith Hayward in association with First Edition, Cambridge.

English text © Octopus Publishing Group Ltd 2000

ISBN 0 600 60180 3

Produced by Toppan
Printed in China

# TREES SUITABLE FOR TRAINING AS BONSAI

# GENERAL PRINCIPLES

# WHAT IS A BONSAI?

A bonsai is a miniature tree that is grown on a tray or flat container. The word bonsai itself is Japanese and is derived from the contraction of the words *bon* (meaning 'tray') and *sai* (meaning 'planting').

*A Japanese print by Andó Hiroshige (1797–1858), showing a landscape contained in bowl.*

## HISTORY

To grow a bonsai is to create a work of art, but, unlike other art forms, this one can never be brought to completion. It is a living form, and the work of shaping it will last a lifetime, with the artist's hand visible, for good or for ill, in every inch of its growth. A bonsai has the potential to become a perfect work of nature, with the result that man is transformed into a creator.

Growing bonsai requires a great deal of time and can be achieved only with the utmost patience. It is a two-way process, for the tree exercises an influence on its grower just as the grower exercises an influence on the tree. In Chinese poetic thought the tree is regarded as providing a link between heaven and earth. Whatever its size, the tree is the vehicle of a spiritual meaning, for the equilibrium that it is intended to represent is a means of restoring the harmony of nature, which a bonsai embodies in a symbolic form, and although this is frequently beyond the grasp of the western intellect, it is a symbol that has a profound cultural significance.

The first mention of the art of bonsai dates from the period of the Ch'in dynasty in the third century BC in China. Then, in the tomb of Zhang Huai, the second son of the Empress Tang Wu Zetian, there was found a figure of a woman carrying a bonsai in both hands. During the Tang dynasty (which ruled China from 618 to 907) and the later Sung dynasty (960–1279) public records refer to a man who 'had learned the art of creating the illusion of immensity enclosed within a small space and all this contained within a single pot'. At the same time, between the tenth and the twelfth centuries, Buddhist monks are said to have carried *p'en-tsai* (trees taken from the natural surroundings and replanted, just as they were, in ornamental pots) throughout the Far East.

During the Sung period many Chinese artists painted pictures of trees that, through the action of the forces of nature, had been reduced to dwarf size and had been subsequently replanted in ornamental pots. But it was only in the twelfth century, during the Southern Sung dynasty, that, after much hard work and many modifications to the process (resulting from trial and error), there gradually appeared the idea of bonsai that we know today. At this time the art was the exclusive preserve of the rich, for whom it provided relaxation. During the Yuan dynasty (1206–1368) an official is said to have fled from the rule of the Mongols and gone to live in Japan, taking with him some *p'en-tsai* and a number of texts describing the art, and this is, so the story goes, how they were introduced into Japan.

Under the Ming (the imperial dynasty that ruled from 1368 to 1644) great importance was placed on highly ornamental pots containing trees that were left untouched. Observers would almost inevitably find in the landscape of China those meanings that architecture had imposed on it: sand would evoke water, the well-spring of life, and rocks would remind onlookers of mountains, the framework of the earth. These elements stood for the creative power of the soil, but thought was entirely mutable, just like life. It was the task of trees to hint at these truths, and in every garden there was one particular plant that embodied the idea of wisdom. In China, as subsequently in Japan, this role was taken by bamboo.

From the Sung period onwards (960–1280), artists begin to represent dwarf trees that had been miniaturized through natural causes. These are shown growing in pots, which rival each other in the splendour of their ornamentation.

During the Tsing dynasty (which held sway after the Ming), creating *p'en-tsai* ceased to be a pastime enjoyed only by the nobility and became accessible to everyone. At the same time, a number of *p'en-tsing* (complete landscapes of dwarf trees) were also planted in China.

## BONSAI IN JAPAN

Between the early twelfth century and the middle of the fourteenth century – the period of the first shogunate in Kamakura (1192–1333) – the first references to bonsai began to appear in Japan. There is, for example, the well-known scroll of the Buddhist monk, Honen, which is decorated with bonsai and which dates roughly from the twelfth century. Later, Seami (1363–1444) created a drama based on the story of the Regents of Kamakura, Hojo Tokiyori, for whose benefit a poor man called Tsuneyo had burned three bonsai, which represented the sum total of his earthly goods.

The Edo period (1615–1867) coincided with a growth in interest in highly wrought, colourful trees grown on trays. The *bonkei* were both whole landscapes on trays and bonsai trees grown in pots. In the former it is possible to find the essential elements of nature (water, mountain, sand and vegetation). In the latter, the foreground is occupied by 'being' (that is, the world of creatures). The upper classes in Japan gradually formed an attachment for bonsai, and the trees they succeeded in growing took pride of place in their homes.

From that point onwards the cultivation of bonsai became a pastime that spread slowly throughout the various social strata, the last to adopt the hobby being the poorest people, who began the cultivation of these trees only a century or more after they had become popular with the upper classes. But today the cultivation of bonsai is practised throughout the whole of Japan.

## BONSAI IN EUROPE

Bonsai appeared in Europe in the fourteenth century, introduced by travellers who were discovering the Orient and were beginning to make eastern art fashionable. Booklets, with a certain amount of unconscious humour, dealt with the art of bonsai in a rather naïve way, but not without poetry. They bore titles such as 'Japanese Curios', 'Essays on Japanese Horticulture' and 'Japanese Gardens'.

Then the art became all but forgotten. During the eighteenth century it was revived to some extent by sailors coming back from the colonies with plants ordered by collectors, apothecaries or gardeners. Bonsai became a curiosity, and for a short period they were all the rage, but the fad did not last long – it was a momentary whim of the pampered rich.

In the nineteenth century bonsai were rediscovered, and serious essays began to appear on the means employed by the Japanese to obtain dwarf trees. Both in Britain and France an interest developed in the art, which seemed to be something completely new for Westerners. Hypotheses were formulated, which proved to be sound. In 1889 J. Vallot wrote an article published in the *Bulletin de la Société de Botanique de France* on 'the physiological causes which bring about the stunting of trees in the Japanese cultivation of plants'. While he was French ambassador in Japan, Paul Claudel was surprised, overwhelmed and fascinated by the sight of a forest of maples wrought into

*The first collections of bonsai to be exhibited in Europe appeared at the World Exposition in Paris in 1878.*

the form of bonsai. As he contemplated these trees, with their highly coloured autumn leaves, he said that he could not help imagining himself in one of those maple woods, and, in imagination, could even hear the chirping of the birds on the branches.

Between the two world wars, a Parisian florist, André Baumann, brought a number of bonsai to Paris to satisfy the demands of the people who had been attracted by Far Eastern culture. Japan was once again in fashion, but the revival was short lived. Today, every country of Europe is familiar with all forms of bonsai.

*A servant carrying a p'en-tsai. A Chinese mural dating from the Tang period (eighth century), found in the tomb of Zhang Huai at Xian.*

# MINIATURE TREES

Like all trees, bonsai belong to the world of living things. They grow and change according to the amounts of sun and water they receive, the soil in which they are grown, and the climate in which they are kept. Because of the way their development is constrained by their being grown in containers, these plants will never grow as freely as their counterparts in the wild or in the garden. They have to be watered and fed by hand, and they must be pinched out, pruned and repotted regularly. Their needs when it comes to sun, shade, fresh air, watering and soil type are major considerations in their well-being.

## ROOTS

The roots make all the difference between a well-grown bonsai and a failure, for they regulate a plant's growth by the way in which they absorb nutrients from the growing medium (the compost) and make them available to the plant. The root system also anchors a plant in the ground.

Plants need water, of course, and also what are known as macro- and micro-nutrients or minerals, which are present in the soil (see page 27), and the roots are the means by which these nutrients are transferred from the growing medium to the plant's tissue. The main root or tap root grows straight down into the ground

*Left: Acer palmatum 'Deshôjô': 70 years old; 80cm (32in) high; Neijikan style. Photographed in mid-spring. In spring the new leaves are a beautiful red. They are bright green in summer before turning orange, purple and red in autumn.*

*Below: Pinus parviflora var. pentaphylla (Japanese white pine): 180 years old; 80cm (32in) high; Fukinageshi style. Photographed in midwinter. Snow has fallen on the branches and should be removed.*

before it forms branches. From these lateral roots a network of fine, fibrous roots develops. At the end of these roots are the delicate root hairs, which are responsible for absorbing nutrients and water from the soil. In the garden a root system may grow far wider than the canopy formed by the branches above ground, as roots spread out in search of moisture and nutrients. When a plant is grown within the confines of a container, its roots have only a limited amount of soil from which to take up the minerals, moisture and oxygen.

## BARK, TRUNK AND BRANCHES

The trunk and branches might be regarded as the bones of a tree, and it is their structure, achieved by pruning and wiring, that creates the overall appearance of a well-balanced and well-proportioned bonsai.

The bark, continuing the analogy, might be equated with skin. It is, in fact, a layer of corky but dead cells, which serves to protect the trunk and branches from predators and helps to minimize water loss. The bark expands as the plant grows, the upper layer splitting, while a new layer is formed beneath it. Wood itself is made up of lignin, the substances that are deposited in the cell walls, making them rigid. The wood of the trunk and branches consists of heartwood and sapwood.

The wood of woody plants is made of a tissue known as xylem, which is composed of conducting cells and supporting tissues, transporting minerals from the roots to all parts of the plant. The cells die when they mature. The cambium layer lies under the bark and is formed of dividing cells, which cause the increase in the girth of trunks and branches through the additional growth of vascular tissue and cork. These tissues are formed by the meristem, the growing tip and tissue of a plant. The meristem consists of actively dividing cells. The phloem is the softer

*Malus x micromalus (syn. Malus spectabilis 'Kaido'): 30 years old; 40cm (16in) high; Neijikan style. Photographed in mid-autumn.*

part of the vascular bundle by which nutrients are transported in sap within a plant. The vascular bundles (with xylem on the inside and phloem on the outside) eventually join to form a band.

## FOLIAGE

Photosynthesis is the process by which light energy is used to convert water and carbon dioxide into simple carbohydrates. It makes plants the main source of atmospheric oxygen, which is released as a by-product. The chief of the light-absorbing pigments is chlorophyll, the green colouring matter in vegetation.

Transpiration is the evaporation of water from the surfaces of the leaves and stems of a plant. Its rate depends on factors such as light, temperature and humidity, and it is largely controlled by the cells of the stomata. The stomata are minute openings in the epidermis of leaves and stems (mostly the undersides of leaves) through which gases are exchanged, and they open and close partly in response to changes in the humidity of the atmosphere. The process helps to cool and prevent damage to the leaves in very hot weather. In addition, it helps to draw up water from the roots to the other parts of the plant. The leaves are, therefore, vital to the survival of plants. The leaves of conifers are needle-shaped and covered with a tough layer that helps to minimize water loss, which is particularly important in winter when the roots may not be able to find sufficient water in frozen ground, and to cut down the effects of cold, drying winds. The larger leaves of deciduous trees fall as light levels and temperatures fall in autumn, but in spring they reappear as fresh green shoots to begin the process of photosynthesis again.

# CLASSIFICATION

Some Japanese masters believe that there are five classes of bonsai; others maintain that there are only three, for the intermediate classes are really not very much different from the others. Some specialists say that the maximum height should be 1.2m (4ft), but this is hotly disputed, not least because if you are lucky enough to be invited to the Imperial Palace in Tokyo you can admire bonsai that exceed that height. People in Japan also speak of a minuscule size, known as Keshitsubu. Special pots are made for bonsai of this size, but the plants are extremely rare.

In the present volume we shall consider only the three main classes of bonsai – mini, classic and great – as these are the most widely grown.

Mini-bonsai can be held in one hand, and they range in size from 5 to 15cm (2–6in). The Japanese call these bonsai Shôhin. Some of them are very young plants, while others are very old. These bonsai are fascinating, but they are more difficult to grow and demand more attention than other styles, simply because they are so small. These little trees are produced by being placed in very small pots and by regularly trimming their branches. They are also repotted more frequently than the other bonsai. The pot, which is quite small, contains only a small amount of compost, and for this reason the tree is less hardy than other types. In addition, because there is so little compost it dries out quickly, but it is important not to overwater the bonsai in case the roots rot through standing in waterlogged soil. It is also important to position them carefully, because this kind of bonsai is very vulnerable to sun, wind and frost.

Nevertheless, partly because of the difficulties associated with growing them, these plants are very popular with collectors. They are also popular with amateur growers, who do not have much space.

Classic bonsai are those plants that range in size from 15 to 60cm (6–24in) in height, and you need to use both hands to carry them. The category is sometimes divided into two: those bonsai that are between 15 and 30cm (6–12in) high, known as Katate-mochi or Komono, and those that are between 30 and 60cm (12–24in) high, known as Chûmono. More often, however, these bonsai are included in a single group. They can be from five to several hundred years old.

The great bonsai are those that range from 60cm to 1.2m (2–4ft) or more, and they generally have to be carried by two people – that is, they take four hands. The bonsai are known as Ômono, and they often reach very great ages. In the olden days in Japan, such a bonsai would be given a place of honour at the entrance to an aristocratic house as a sign of welcome or, more simply, as an indication of wealth. Nevertheless, it is possible to find some of more tender years, including those that are no more than 15 years old.

The size of these bonsai is calculated vertically from the tip of the tree to the base of the trunk; the height does not include the container.

It is difficult to assign cascade or semi-cascade bonsai to a particular class because they are upright to begin with and then fall back down again, and the semi-cascade kind are often almost horizontal. The height of these plants is generally found by measuring them from their highest point – that is, from the top of the bend that is formed by the trunk before plunging down again.

Apart from the necessity for careful watering and the need to take great care in choosing the ideal location for a mini-bonsai, it is fair to say that the three kinds of bonsai are developed and cared for in much the same way, and that the techniques involved for each type are, in general, the same: pruning, repotting, wiring and watering, and maintaining the appropriate temperature, ventilation and feeding regime.

When it comes to the dimensions of your bonsai, no one size is any better than another. Everything depends on the judgement of the individual growers, and on whether they like their miniature plants to be more or less small and on how much space they have at their disposal. What matters is that the overall shape must always be that of a well-proportioned and harmoniously formed tree.

# SYMBOLS

The bonsai symbolizes eternity. It negates time and represents the harmony that can exist between nature and humans and between earth and heaven. The story is often told how an old sage used to explain his smooth and youthful features by his devotion to bonsai: when he contemplated his work, he could not grow old, because 'while flowers may fade in winter, in his home they were always in bloom'.

In Japan certain plants, linked by common associations, are placed in a container together to provide New Year's gifts for friends. This is an ancient tradition, which is still practised. These plants cannot be expected to last, but they have a special meaning and bring great happiness to those who receive them. Nowadays, they are given both at the New Year and at Christmas. The plants are collectively called *Shô-chiku-bai*, meaning pine, bamboo and Japanese apricot, which, respectively, stand for happiness, long life

From left to right: *Acer palmatum* 'Deshôjô': 15 years old; 30cm (12in) high; Tachiki style. *Pinus parviflora* var. *pentaphylla* (Japanese white pine): 300 years old; 1m (3ft) high; Tachiki style. *Ulmus parvifolia* (syn. *U. chinensis*; Chinese elm): 10 years old; 12cm (5in) high; Nejikan style. Photographed in late spring.

and virtue. Ideally, the apricot tree should be in flower when it is given as a present, and this is because the New Year used to be in early spring.

Today, for an apricot tree that is being given as a present to be in flower on New Year's Day in the northern hemisphere, it is necessary to force its growth for, when it is grown naturally, it flowers in late winter or early spring. To get an apricot tree to flower you must place it in a warm room for a fortnight and spray it once or twice a day with water at room temperature and this will cause it to blossom.

To these three species may be added ferns or shrubs with red berries, which symbolize wealth. Sometimes small flowering plants are also be added, and these will also have been forced into bloom for the occasion – *Nandina domestica* (heavenly bamboo or sacred bamboo, as it is sometimes known), for example, is often included because it is in harmony with the three types of tree. Some people also add an orchid to enliven the whole.

For the people of Thailand bonsai lost its original meaning and became a form of evocation. The treatise on the tree, *Klong*

*tamra mai dat*, which was written by a poet in the nineteenth century, speaks of the metaphor of the tree. The forms of the tree become magic and are reduced to signs (see below) that evoke human attitudes or characters.

In Vietnam, on the other hand, trees became the bearers of man's earthly misfortunes. Thus it was that there was a tree symbolizing a tortoise, a sacred animal that supports the earth on its shell.

**Thai signs**
**(according to the *K'long tamra mai dat*)**

*dancing*

*physical strength*

*cunning*

*Japanese tree*

*the grotesque*

*suppleness*

*the mischief-maker*

*the athlete*

*the forest*

*the fanfare*

*the obsequious person*

*the screen*

11

## STYLES

In every bonsai you will find the shape of the triangle, which may be seen as representing god, earth and humankind. A bonsai joins heaven and earth, becoming a physical allegory that leads humans along the path of spiritual worth. The angle of the triangle varies from tree to tree, and this is the essence of style in these dwarf trees.

The style is defined by the number of degrees in the angle formed by a vertical line traced from the top to the bottom of the trunk.

Bonsai may, therefore, be classified according to their style as defined by the silhouette of the tree. There are four main styles, and all other styles stem from these. They may also be classified according to the number of plants in a single container.

**Group 1** Trees with a single trunk. There are four main styles.

Chokkan: this is the formal, upright style in which the tree grows straight up towards the sky.

Shakan: the trunk bends and may, in fact, be so bent that it forms a semi-cascade.

Kengai: the cascade style, in which the stem plunges downwards.

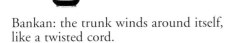

Bankan: the trunk winds around itself, like a twisted cord.

Several styles are derived from the four.

Tachiki: an informal, upright style.

Han-Kengai: a semi-cascade.

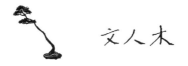

Bunjingi or Literati: a style in which the tree rises obliquely, with a trunk that is bare except at the top.

Hôkidachi: the tree is in the shape of a broom.

Sabamiki: the trunk is split and torn and is bare in places.

Sharimiki: the trunk is stripped of its bark, just as if the tree were dead.

Fukinagashi: in this windswept style the tree resembles those that grow along seashores and that are beaten into shape by strong winds, with their branches on one side of the trunk only.

Neagari: the roots are exposed.

Neku: the tree has aerial roots.

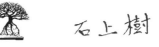

Sekijôju: the root-over-rock style, in which the roots grip the rock before penetrating the earth.

Ishitsuki: the tree is planted on a rock.

Nejikan: the trunk is partially twisted.

Takozukuri: the 'octopus' style.

**Group 2** Multiple trunks from a single root. There are five main styles.

Sôkan: a double trunk.

Kabudachi: several trunks develop from a single root.

Kôrabuki: several trunks develop from a single rootstock and look like the shell of a tortoise.

Ikadabuki: the horizontal trunk forms a raft of stems.

Netsunagari: a sinuous style formed when several trunks grow from a single, curved root.

**Group 3** Multiple trunks and group plantings. Apart from trees planted in pairs, bonsai are always planted in odd numbers.

Sôju: twin trunks.

Sambon-Yose: triple trunks.

Gohon-Yose: five trunks.

Nanahon-Yose: seven trunks.

Kyûhon-Yose: nine trunks.

**Group 4** These are not bonsai in the strict sense of the word.

Yose-Ue: multiple trunks (more than nine).

Yomayori or Yomayose: a natural-looking group.

Tsukami-Yose: multiple trunks emerging from the same point in a clustered group style.

Bonkei: landscapes.

Kusamomo or Shitakusa: planting of grasses and bulbs.

Planting of seasonal grasses and shrubs.

# HOW TO CHOOSE A BONSAI

Every type of plant can be grown in a container, but it is true to say that not all container-grown plants will make beautiful bonsai. When you are choosing a plant that will grow into a fine bonsai it is important, therefore, to bear the following points in mind. No matter how much attention you lavish on the plant, it will never develop into a good bonsai if you choose the wrong plant in the first place.

## GENERAL GUIDELINES

### ROOTS

It is important to distinguish between the underground roots (which are in the soil or contained within the pot) and the roots that you can see developing at the base of the trunk and any aerial roots, which develop on some species.

The underground roots are those that keep the plant anchored in the compost or soil. It is important that the plant has a well-developed root system, with firm, healthy roots that will transport nutrients to the above-ground part of the plant. The fleshy taproot or main root should have sent out lateral roots, a network of fibrous roots and a mass of numerous hair roots. If you take the plant out of the container you should see the creamy colour that characterizes healthy roots, and the compost should be held by the roots in the shape of the container. Reject plants whose roots have grown through the bottom of the container and whose roots appear to be circling around the container. Such plants are pot bound and will rarely make the transition to another size of container or to the open garden. A plant that slides out of the container very easily may be an indication that it has just been potted up and has not yet settled. Do not buy such a plant.

The roots of a tree that are visible around the base of the trunk on the surface of the soil are an integral part of a bonsai's appearance, and it is difficult, if not impossible, to create these roots subsequently. They should look strong and healthy and be evenly distributed around the tree. Reject plants that have roots emerging at an angle from the growing medium. This could be a sign that the plant is pot bound.

Aerial roots are those that develop above ground level, and they are perhaps most frequently seen on plants such as *Hedera* (ivy), when they are adventitious, and on epiphytes, when they develop from the rooting axis. Aerial roots absorb moisture direct from the atmosphere, and in the case of epiphytes they are frequently green and capable of photosynthesis. Buttress or prop roots, which are forms of aerial root, help to support the stem or trunk; climbing or adhesive aerial roots help to elevate the plant.

### COLLAR

The base of the trunk, where it enters the soil, is known as the collar or collet, a word used also to describe the point where a branch emerges from the trunk. Look for a plant that has collar that is in proportion to the height of the trunk and to the canopy of the branches and leaves. It should be smooth and gently curved.

Although a container-grown plant may have a few weeds on the surface, do not buy plants that have liverwort or algae on the surface of the soil, a sure sign that the plant has been in its container for too long. Reject, too, plants that look as if they are too small for their pot. Some of the less reputable outlets may have potted up small plants into larger pots so that they can charge more for them.

### TRUNK

The first point to consider is whether the trunk is in proportion to the overall plant. This is partly a matter of experience with bonsai, of course, for when plants grow in the garden or in the wild, they are subject to the vagaries of nature far more than a container-grown plant, which is pruned and fed and watered by the gardener. Looking at illustrations of bonsai in books will help, but even better is to look at bonsai in collections and at exhibitions. You will quickly develop an eye for a well-proportioned tree.

Choose a plant with a trunk that rises in a smooth taper towards the crown – that is, the top of the trunk should be narrower than the base. If the plant has been grown for too long with a support, the trunk is often the same diameter from the top to the bottom, and when this happens the tree is often unable to support itself without the stake. A tree will produce what is known as reaction wood on load-bearing areas, such as exist at the base of the trunk at soil level. Thus, the greater diameter at the base of a trunk is a sign that the stresses within the trunk are distributed in the lower portion of the trunk, and this will help avoid breaking or cracking.

Make sure the bark is not scarred. Some trees become bark bound – that is, the bark becomes so hard that it cannot expand in the normal way and 'strangles' the tree. One of the most usual causes is lack of moisture, and the usual solution is to split the bark vertically, which sometimes happens naturally but is sometimes done by the gardener. Although this may not cause long-term damage, the resulting scar is unsightly.

### BRANCHES

The branches should emerge smoothly from the upper part of the trunk. They should be appropriately formed according to the species and be well-proportioned and regularly spaced. You can determine the overall health of the plant by looking at the current season's growth and comparing it with the previous season's. The spacing between nodes should be equal, indicating that a plant has grown on steadily and not suffered checks.

Like the trunk, the branches should be in proportion to the overall size of the tree, both in terms of their length and their diameter. The side branches, too, should be regularly and evenly distributed along the branches. Branches should not cross each other within the crown, nor should too many branches or side branches emerge from the same point.

### FOLIAGE

The state of the leaves is probably the first indication of a plant's health. Do not buy any plant that has withered, scorched or distorted leaves. Instead, look for green leaves (unless the plant if variegated, of

*Part of the collection of bonsai at Châtenau-Malabry, France, where about 7000 bonsai are on permanent display.*

course) that are an appropriate colour for the species and for the time of year. Remember that evergreens shed some leaves all year round, so fallen leaves may not be a sign that anything is amiss. Yellowing leaves can be an indication of pest infestation, disease or mineral deficiency, and withered leaves may be the result of lack of water or disease.

## FLOWERS AND FRUIT
The flowers and fruit are the most attractive features of some trees. The ornamental cherries and apples (*Prunus* and *Malus* spp.) are one of the most glorious sights of spring, but subtler pleasures can be found in the flowers of species, such as *Betula* (birch) and *Corylus* (hazel), that take the form of catkins, while conifers bear interesting and sometimes colourful cones.

When trees are miniaturized through being grown as bonsai, the flowers and fruit are also usually reduced in size (wisteria is a notable exception to the rule), and when you are buying a bonsai check that the flowers are fruit are, indeed, in proportion to the branches and foliage. Do not buy plants on which the flowers are too large. In general, however, it is best to avoid buying plants that are in flower, because the flowers are likely to drop when the plant is moved into its new environment and you will have to wait until the next season to enjoy the blooms.

## PESTS
The chief enemy of bonsai are insect pests, which not only damage a plant's leaves and root system but can also transmit diseases. Before you buy a plant, inspect the foliage very carefully, especially the underside, for any sign of pests. If possible, remove the plant from its container so that you can look at the compost and roots. Although there are many chemical treatments available, pests eventually become resistant to chemicals. It is always far better to avoid infestation in the first place, and pests are often introduced to a greenhouse on a new plant and quickly spread to existing plants.

The main pests to which the individual species are susceptible are outlined in the second part of the book, together with suggested remedies.

## DISEASES
Plants are most susceptible to diseases when they have not been properly tended, and the appearance of a disease may be associated with the presence of insects pests (see above). One way of avoiding diseases is to make sure that your plants are healthy, so observe the watering and feeding suggestions included for all the species. The other important factor is to maintain high standards of hygiene. Clear away fallen leaves and faded flowers and quickly remove and burn any dead or damaged branches.

## SPECIAL STYLES

### A SINGLE PLANT
When you are buying just one plant the first thing is to make sure that the roots do not cross each other and that they are well spread out around the trunk. Lift the rootball out of the container to make sure that the rooting is satisfactory, that the root hairs are clean and dense, and that they are not flabby.

Next, examine the trunk. Check that its curves look natural, that there is nothing wrong with the way it rises from the soil, that its bark resembles that of the full-sized trees of the same species and that it looks healthy. Now, check the arrangement of the branches. Make sure that they do not cross each other. They should be firm and solid and positioned elegantly round the trunk.

The leaves should be small, plentiful and the right colour for the season of the year. If you are choosing a deciduous tree it is best to do so in the winter, when the absence of leaves makes it possible to see the silhouette clearly and to note its good and bad points. If the tree is bearing fruit or is in blossom, look carefully at the fruit and the flowers to make sure that there is nothing wrong with them and that they are reduced in size; even if the scale is not exact, they should be small. This, however, does not hold good for wisteria, because it is not possible to produce small blossoms on this plant. There is no fundamental genetic difference between the bonsai and the full-sized tree.

When you have looked at all these details, note the general appearance of the tree from the topmost branches down to the collar. Look carefully at the crown in relation to the foot of the tree and in relation to the whole. Look to see if there is any moss at the foot of the tree, which might mean that the potting was done some time ago. Lift the moss to check the state of the soil. If there is no moss this might mean that it has only recently been potted.

### A GROUP OF PLANTS
Examine each tree individually (as you would a single tree) and then look at the group as a whole. The general appearance should be aesthetically satisfying and natural.

Think of the perspective: the trees should lean in the same direction, and the curves should be parallel and complimentary. Compare the diameter and the height of different trunks. They should be varied and well balanced, for example. The branches of one tree should not get in the way of or cross the branches of the tree next to it.

### A TREE ON A ROCK OR A LANDSCAPE
Pay special attention to the rock and to the roots; you will be able to tell that they are placed well if they sweep gracefully down the side of the rock and are in harmony with the shape of the tree. The base of the plant should be wedged firmly into the rock. Check the layout of the miniature plantations of grasses or bushes; these should be at different levels, according to how dense and tall they are. The colours of the plants and their fruits or their blossoms should match well.

Finally, make sure that the container is big enough, and that it has got a hole at the bottom to allow excess water to drain away. See that the drainage holes are not blocked up, and that the container and the tree go well together.

# PROPAGATING BONSAI

Because bonsai are trees of sacred origin, the work of propagating and looking after them involves a rigorous ritual with its own inflexible rules. The first bonsai were trees taken from their natural environment, which had, because of poor growing conditions, developed as small specimens. These days it is illegal to remove such plants from forests or mountainsides. Nevertheless, it is possible to raise your own bonsai in various ways.

*Juniperus rigida (temple juniper): 120 years old; 55cm (22in) high; Yamayori style. Photographed in late spring.*

## SEEDS AND SEEDLINGS

This method requires much patience and care, but it produces particularly fine trees, and almost all bonsai may be obtained from seeds. There are no special bonsai seeds: they can be taken from other bonsai or from ënormalí trees. Seeds can be bought from a dealer or harvested direct from trees. They are collected in autumn: all kinds of fruit, acorns, berries, nuts, such as beech masts, include seeds that may be harvested and planted to give, after anything from five to seven years, beautiful miniature trees in the desired form. Note that generally only species come true to type from seed. Cultivars should be propagated by another method, such as layering, grafting or cuttings.

The conditions for germination differ for every species from the moment of harvesting. Some seeds should be planted straight away, for they germinate immediately after being collected. Others should be preserved in a cool, dry environment before being planted. Still other seeds will germinate in the autumn or the winter but, so that they retain their ability to germinate, should be buried for a few days in damp sand. Many of seeds have a period of dormancy to protect them from germinating at the wrong time for the new plants to succeed. Stratification is the process by which dormancy, especially in seeds of trees that are native to temperate countries, is broken. It involves placing the seeds in damp sand or in perlite or vermiculite and either standing them outside so that they are stratified naturally by exposure to cold winter temperatures or, more reliably, by placing the seeds in a refrigerator. The length of time required for stratification varies according to species, but in general deciduous trees should be left in the refrigerator for at least six weeks. Some seeds can quite simply be preserved in the vegetable compartment of the refrigerator for anything from a day to a month; after this they should be soaked for 24 hours in warm water. A seed with a hard shell may need to be scarified (have the surface scored or abraded) to assist the process of germination.

There are two particularly favourable times to sow these seeds: either in the spring, or at the end of the summer and in the autumn. More detailed information about the appropriate treatment and sowing times for individual species is included in the second part of this book. Note that seeds of different species should not be sown together because their

### Stratification

Label with the name of the species and the date when it was planted

Sand

Seed

Layer of crocks

Drainage hole

### Sowing

Label the container with the date of sowing

Cover the container with paper to shade the seeds

Seeds (well spaced)

Layer of fibre or moss

Layer of compost

## Sowing seeds

1 You will need a sieve to make sure that the compost in which the seeds are sown is fine enough.

2 Fill a terracotta flowerpot with the mixture of sieved compost.

3 The seeds, which have been stratified, are laid on the soil mixture.

4 The thickness of the layer of compost covering the seeds will depend on the size of the seeds.

5 If, as here, the seeds are fairly large, they will need a good covering of compost. Use a trowel to tamp down the compost gently.

1

2

3

4

5

6

7

8

6 If the seeds are protected by a shell, as these ginkgo seeds are, you will have to break them open with pliers.

7 Once the shell has been broken, carefully remove the seed from its protective envelope.

8 The seeds can now be sown. Because they germinate easily, they do not need to be stratified.

9 Place a circle of paper on the surface of the soil.

10 The paper disc prevents the earth from being disturbed when watering takes place.

9

10

requirements with regard to timing, watering, heat and light and eventually potting up may be different.

To sow seed, take a small seed tray or pan with holes in the bottom so that excess water can drain away. Fill it with compost, which should be a standard seed compost or a mixture of equal parts peat and sharp sand. The tray should be three-quarters full only; do not pile the compost so high air and water cannot circulate. Sift the compost into the seed tray, and then sow the seeds, spacing them evenly over the surface. Cover them with a fine layer of the sifted compost, then water abundantly with a fine sprinkler. Cover the tray with a sheet of glass and place it in the shade and protect it from frost.

As soon as the first shoots appear (which will vary according to species: some germinate surprisingly quickly, some take months) half-open the glass to allow the air to circulate. Remove it completely as soon as the first leaves appear. In spring, when the stem has thickened, plant each seedling in its own container and gradually introduce the plantlets to direct sun. After about two years you will be able to begin shaping this young plant into a bonsai by trimming the branches (in spring and in summer) and the roots (in spring). After a further three to five years the tree obtained from the seeds you sowed will have achieved the desired form and will have an elegant silhouette with no unsightly cuts or swelling on the trunk and with well-proportioned and well-positioned branches.

## PROPAGATION FROM NURSERY SEEDLINGS

It is also possible to gain good results from plants that have been bought as nursery seedlings. These will be between two and three years old and may have interestingly shaped trunk or crowns. Choose plants that are not too tall and that have a good distribution of branches. Trees that are not suitable for sale or ornamental gardens make good bonsai.

When you get your plants home, take them from their pots and trim the roots to two-thirds of their original size. Then pot them up into a fairly large container. The best time to do this in spring. Then treat the new plant as you would a specimen that has just been repotted. What are important here are the trunk and roots. Make sure that the roots spread out from the trunk like a fan and do not cross over each other. Right from the start it is important to cut back the branches growing low on the trunk, bearing in mind as you do so that you are creating the silhouette of the tree as it will finally be. The outline that you achieve at this stage will almost immediately dictate the style of the tree.

The ultimate size of the tree is also determined at this point because you should remove the growing tip. The wood will take some time to harden, although the degree of hardness will depend on the species. When the wood has hardened, it should be bound or wired so that the tree's lines of growth are fixed. This process may take up to six years. It is only after this time the tree will have assumed the shape you have selected for it and may now truly be called a bonsai.

### Taking cuttings of an indoor bonsai

*1 You will need peat, sand, flowerpots, hormone rooting compound and, of course, some recently taken cuttings.*

*2 The growing medium is a mixture of compost and sand. Shake the compost and sand together in a bag.*

*3 Fill the flowerpots with compost and sand and water thoroughly before inserting the cuttings.*

*4 The cuttings should be about 10cm (4in) long. This cutting is from a* Ficus.

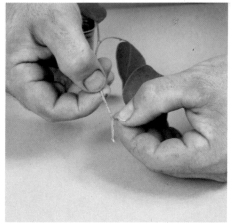

*5 Remove the leaves from the base of the cutting, which will be inserted into the compost.*

*6 Remove part of the leaves from the top of the cutting to reduce evaporation. Use sharp scissors to minimize damage.*

# CUTTINGS

This method requires less time and patience than propagating by seed, and it will give plants that resemble the parent plant.

The technique involves taking sections of stems of plants that have no roots and have been cut from the parent plant and planting them either directly into the earth or submerging them in water before planting. The method can be extended to bonsai: when the branches are pruned, it is possible to obtain cuttings about 10cm (4in) long. Hormone rooting compound, in powder or liquid form, is available, and this is used to speed up the process of rooting. If you use this (and not all gardeners feel it is either useful or necessary) remember to replace your stock every year.

When it comes to taking a cutting, the branch of the parent plant must be cut just above the point where a leaf is about to develop. The growing tip of the cutting is also trimmed back. The stem that is retained should have from six to eight leaves on it and be about 10cm (4in) in length. It should be inserted to a depth of 3cm (1¼in) in a flowerpot containing a mixture of sand and peat. The cutting should be watered thoroughly and then placed inside a polythene bag. Make sure the polythene does not touch the cutting. In order for the cutting to develop roots, it requires light but must be kept away from the sun and protected from frost. To keep the soil humid enough, it should be misted regularly.

When new shoots appear on the stem, roots are developing and the cutting has taken. Now is the time to remove the polythene bag and allow the new plant to get used to sunlight, although it must be protected from direct summer sun. Apply a little fertilizer in spring and protect the cutting carefully from frost the next winter. After one or two years the cutting should be shaped to make it into a bonsai. Be careful that you do not cause the cutting and the young roots to rot by overwatering. You must control the amount of water it receives, and this is where the difficulty lies.

Propagating by cuttings is possible throughout the whole year with certain species, but cuttings taken in the spring and early summer take better and much more quickly than those taken at the end of the summer or in autumn because the sap flows much more freely, and there is more of it when the plant starts to form leaves again.

**Cuttings of deciduous plants**

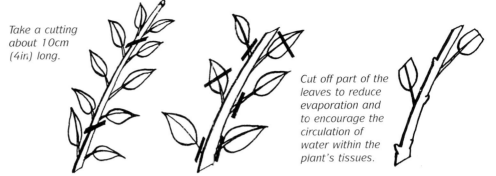

Take a cutting about 10cm (4in) long.

Cut off part of the leaves to reduce evaporation and to encourage the circulation of water within the plant's tissues.

Place the cuttings in a propagator.

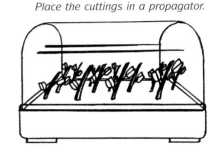

Insert the cuttings into the compost to a depth that equals about one-third of the total length of the cutting.

**Cuttings of coniferous plants**

1 Prepare the cutting (this is a cedar) by removing the needles from the bottom.

2 If used, dip the bottom of the cutting into hormone rooting compost.

3 Use a pencil or dibber to make a hole in the compost and insert the cutting.

4 Firm the compost around the cutting and water thoroughly.

19

# LAYERING

Layering is a method of vegetative propagation. New plants are obtained from side branches that grow from the parent plant. The selected portion of the branch or stem is partially covered with earth and roots eventually develop on it. The link between the two plants is then severed, and the new plant becomes completely independent. By an extension of meaning, the word 'layer' is used to describe this new plant. There are two main methods, simple and air layering.

## SIMPLE LAYERING

This process is particularly appropriate for trees with flexible or hanging branches. The branch selected for layering should be bent over towards the base of the tree, and the part which is about to be buried should be stripped of leaves or needles, either by using clippers to cut the leaves from the stem or by pinching them off between your finger and thumb. Make a cut, about 5cm (2in) long, in the lower part of the section to encourage roots to form. Use a U-shaped piece of wire to hold the layer in place and cover it with soil. Alternatively, hold the layer in place in a container containing an appropriate soil mix.

Make sure that the earth is kept moist by watering it as soon as it starts to dry out. The number of times the plant has to be watered and the amount of water used will, of course, depend on the region and the climate. When new roots have developed, it is possible to separate the branch from the original tree, severing the two with a clean cut. Then replant the branch (now a new plant) in the type of soil that is appropriate for the individual species (see the recommendations in the second part of this book). From this point, the new plant should be treated as a tree that has just been repotted, and the specific requirements of that particular tree should always be borne in mind.

## AIR LAYERING

This is the most suitable method for trees with fairly upright branches. It has the great advantage that the new plant may be shaped while it is still attached to the parent tree. This process normally takes place in mid-spring. Do not choose a branch that is too thick, because it will not develop roots easily; instead, choose a branch about 5cm (2in) in diameter.

Air layering is achieved by making a vertical cut, about 5cm (2in) long, in the branch. To prevent the wound from healing too quickly, use a small piece of wood, a pebble or a small ball of moss to hold the cut open. Wrap a mass of peat and damp sphagnum moss around the wound and hold this within a plastic bag, pierced with holes but tightly sealed at top and bottom. After three to five months, the roots will have developed sufficiently to enable you to remove the plastic bag and cut the layer through cleanly with a small pair of secateurs or loppers, depending on the thickness of the layer and the hardness of its wood. It must be potted up immediately in an appropriate soil mix for the species. Treat the new plant as you would a bonsai that has just been repotted.

### Simple layering

**Method 1** *Make a cut in the shoot at the point at which the roots should form. Hold the shoot down with a U-shaped length of wire so that it remains in contact with the ground. Place a stake in to the ground and tie the free end of the shoot to it to support it. Mound additional soil or compost over the layered section.*

**Method 2** *Make a cut at the point you want the roots to form. Bend down the branch from the parent plant and cover it with soil, leaving the free end exposed to the air. Keep the layer in place by placing a large stone over the soil and supporting the free end with additional rocks and stones. Do not remove the stones until roots have formed.*

### Air layering

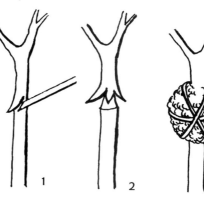

1     2     3     4     5

*1 Use a sharp grafting knife to make cuts in the stem of the parent plant.*
*2 Peel back the bark from the cuts.*
*3 If used, apply some hormone rooting powder to the exposed stem. Cover with damp moss.*
*4 Cover the moss completely with polythene with holes pierced in it. Seal the top and bottom of the polythene sleeve tightly.*
*5 Once the roots have formed, sever the layer and pot up.*

*The parent plant seen at step 4.*

# GRAFTING

Grafting consists of implanting one plant (known as the rootstock) with a segment of another plant (the scion). Eventually, the scion will replace, either completely or partially, the above-ground part of the rootstock, while allowing the new tree to retain its own characteristics.

The best time for grafting is when the sap is rising – that is, in spring. In the majority of cases, the scion and rootstock must belong to the same species. In Japan, however, *Pinus parviflora* (white pine) is often grafted onto *Pinus thunbergii* (syn. *P. thunbergiana*; black pine) to obtain more rapid growth.

The method has both advantages and disadvantages. The results, for example, are rarely all one could wish for, and often swellings occur at the point where the graft has been made on the trunk. Nevertheless, professional nurserymen use this method almost exclusively for propagating fruit trees. It also makes it possible for flowers of different colours to be produced by the same plant. In particular, *Prunus* is capable of producing white, pink and red flowers at the same time.

Grafting is often used to save bonsai whose roots have been damaged. It is also the method that must be used for plants that cannot be reproduced in any other way. Another advantage of grafting is that the grown-on scion retains all the original features of its original parent; variations may occur in plants raised from seed.

Grafting compound can be used to protect those parts of the tree that have become exposed against bad weather and the attacks of parasites and disease. The graft must then be wired and the way this is done will depend on shape. The wiring should be both flexible and yet not too loose, so that the graft does not slip or damage the bark. Both parts must be kept securely together. It may be necessary to provide a support for trees that have been grafted to protect them from the wind.

There are many different techniques to use, and the methods outlined here are those that are most widely used and those that differ significantly from each other. There are many techniques of grafting that vary only slightly from each other, such as in the way in which the cut is made. The most frequently practised and those described here are: wedge grafting, lateral grafting, inarching (approach grafting), root grafting, shield grafting and crown grafting.

## WEDGE GRAFTING

This method of grafting, which is also known as cleft grafting, makes it possible to implant new branches in the tree, and it is suitable for use only with slender branches. In spring make a vertical slit, 3–5cm (1¼–2in) long, in the rootstock and slip a branch of the scion that has been cut to a point about 5cm (2in) long. The scion must be taken either from the same tree or from a tree of the same species as the rootstock. When the scion is firmly in place it should be bound with raffia and smeared with grafting wax or covered with plastic tape.

## LATERAL GRAFTING

Evergreen trees are often propagated by this method. In summer make a notch

**Wedge grafting**

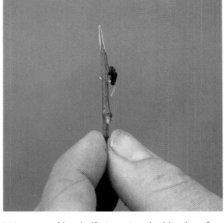

*1 Use a grafting knife to cut a double chamfer (wedge) in the lower tip of the scion.*

*2 Sterilize the blade of your grafting knife in a flame and make a vertical cleft in the rootstock.*

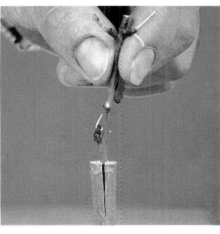

*3 Insert the scion into the cleft in the rootstock, but do not push it in too far.*

*4 Bind the scion and rootstock firmly together with raffia.*

*5 Smear the graft with grafting compound to protect the wound.*

about 5cm (2in) long in the lower part of the trunk of the rootstock, shape the branch (scion) to obtain a chamfered edge and slip it into the notch so that, later on, the earth will hide the point where the graft has been made. The scion will start growing in the following spring. The rootstock should then be cut obliquely, above the scion, to separate the two.

**Lateral grafting**

*1 Make a vertical slit in the rootstock and push the chamfered end of the scion into the slit.*

*2 Bind up the graft and smear it with grafting compound.*

*3 Pot up the rootstock and wait for new shoots to develop.*

*4 Sever the rootstock above the graft.*

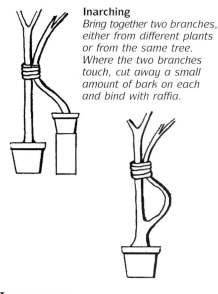

**Inarching**

*Bring together two branches, either from different plants or from the same tree. Where the two branches touch, cut away a small amount of bark on each and bind with raffia.*

## INARCHING

Sometimes known as approach grafting, inarching copies nature's practice directly, and it is, therefore, the oldest and simplest method of grafting. The technique makes it possible to unite two trees in order later to replace branches that are missing or to provide protection for plants that are difficult to obtain using other methods. The scion and stock may even come from the same tree.

Inarching should be done at the end of spring in order to match nature's own cycle. Peel the bark of the scion and that of the stock back for about 3cm (1½in). Bring them into contact, placing one over the other. Next cover the joint with grafting wax and wrap it round with raffia; alternatively, cover with plastic tape. The scion will have taken by the end of the autumn, but it should be left attached to the stock until the two are completely united. Now separate the scion and the stock by making a cut as near as possible to the stock to avoid too large a swelling developing at that point. Every time you make an incision as part of the grafting technique, smear the branch with a healing compound to allow the cut to heal up more quickly and to ensure that pests and other forms of blight do not gain a hold.

## ROOT GRAFTING

This type of grafting should be carried out in spring, and it is necessary to use it for trees with damaged roots. It helps cuttings that are growing to take off if you graft them onto the roots of another species, and it reduces the rate of growth of a tree in which the trunk has become too long in relation to the branches.

Choose roots with well-developed and healthy root hairs. Proceed exactly as you would for wedge grafting, but replacing the branch with the roots. Wire and add wound-healing compound. When the graft has taken (the roots are developing), trim the upper part of the rootstock.

Sometimes you can use the inlaying method. In this case, the graft is made on the root and there is no need to cut off anything. But these are, in general, techniques used by professional growers.

## SHIELD GRAFTING

This is one of the most frequently used methods. The technique makes it possible to unite a male and female tree in order to obtain a composite tree that will bear fruit.

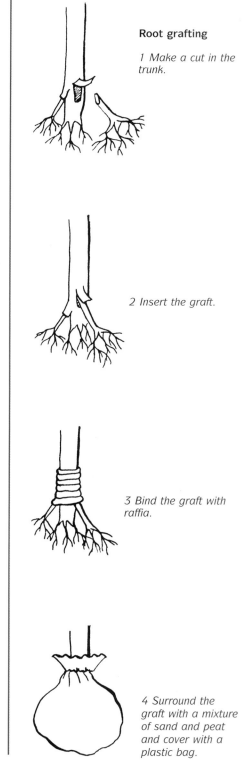

**Root grafting**

*1 Make a cut in the trunk.*

*2 Insert the graft.*

*3 Bind the graft with raffia.*

*4 Surround the graft with a mixture of sand and peat and cover with a plastic bag.*

The grafting should take place when the buds are swollen and the sap is rising. When the stock has been thoroughly moistened by spraying, it should have a T-shape cut into it. Next, implant a bud taken from a branch of the scion. Smear with grafting wax and bind the scion with raffia; alternatively, cover with plastic tape. Be careful that the bud does not dry out during this operation. When the leaf stalk falls (generally the following spring), you will know that the scion has taken.

## CROWN GRAFTING

This technique is used only with large trees, and it is the method used to obtain bonsai with multiple trunks and to improve the appearance of old trees. This should be done in the spring. The diameter of the scion should be smaller than that of the stock. Make an incision in the trunk of the stock 3–4cm (1½in) long and insert in the scion. It is possible for several scions to be inserted in the stock. Place grafting wax on the join and then bind the wound with raffia; alternatively, cover the graft with clear plastic tape.

**Shield grafting**

*1 Make a T-shaped cut in the trunk.*

*2 Peel back the bark.*

Graft

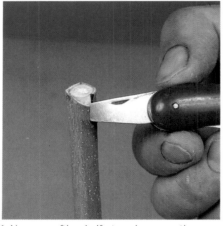

*3 Insert the graft into the cut.*

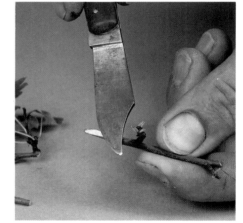

*4 Bind the graft with raffia.*

**Crown grafting**

*1 Use a grafting knife to prise open the vertical cuts made in the bark.*

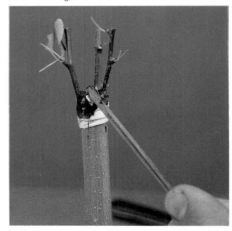

*2 The grafts should be cut with a single chamfer so they come into contact with the cambium layer of the rootstock.*

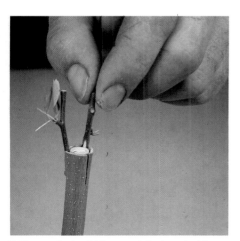

*3 The graft should be carefully inserted into the vertical cuts made in the bark.*

*4 Bind the grafts securely in place with raffia.*

*5 Smear the graft with grafting wax, which will help the healing process.*

# LOOKING AFTER YOUR BONSAI

Once you have got your bonsai, you must think carefully about the best place to put it so that the tree can flourish. You must also choose a container that will show it off well and find out which tools you will need to keep it in trim and what you have to do to look after it all year round.

## POSITIONING

The first thing is to decide whether you have an outdoor or an indoor bonsai. This question, of course, has to be considered in the context of where you live. *Pinus parviflora* (Japanese white pine), for example, might be treated as an outdoor bonsai in a Mediterranean climate but would regarded as an indoor bonsai in the coldest parts of Europe. When the environment, temperature, amount of sunshine and all the atmospheric conditions of your region differ very widely from those of the natural environment of the tree, you must try to recreate the conditions that the plant would encounter in the wild – or at least those aspects that affect the way the tree grows. This requires extreme care: human's contribution goes hand in hand with the natural elements.

The indoor bonsai come from tropical or subtropical regions where they would be growing outside, but they are capable of adapting to conditions in European homes. In 1979 the authors of this book were responsible for introducing indoor bonsai into France. Since then, they have been increasingly successful. They make it possible for many people who have no garden, terrace, balcony or even windowsills, to have their own bonsai.

Outdoor and indoor bonsai pose different problems. Outdoor bonsai should be placed high up on shelves or on elevated stands. If they are stood at ground level they run the risk of being attacked from parasites or even being knocked over and damaged by a household pet. In addition, bonsai roots will not penetrate into the ground and, if you are going to look after them properly, it is easier to have them at eye level.

Indoor bonsai should be placed in the light, in a room heated to a normal temperature. The warmer it is, the more often you will have to water the plant. Choose a container that will show the bonsai off to the best advantage and that will harmonize with the colour tones in the rest of the room. It must also fit in with the rest of the décor and give the room an atmosphere of serenity.

You should get ready in advance the tools you will need for the upkeep and development of the bonsai, which will continue to grow and flourish throughout the whole year. You will need a table, a pedestal table or some other piece of furniture that will enhance the appearance of your plant. To prevent the bonsai from leaving any marks on the surface of the furniture, place a tray, a saucer (without water) or a piece of cloth on it. If you have several bonsai, they can be arranged on a set of shelves intended for just this purpose. Make sure that the shelves are not positioned so close to each other that the top of one tree touches the shelf above and that it has enough space to contain it and to allow air to circulate freely around it.

On no account must you allow a household pet to spoil indoor bonsai. Never expose them to draughts, because they can easily be harmed, and remember that they do not like being moved round continually. In fact, they need a certain time to adapt to a new location. When a bonsai is first moved to a new position, it begins by producing a few yellow leaves, which it then sheds, but after a fortnight it will settle down and get used to its new place. Do not forget that the corners of rooms, even near a window, are dark. Try to place the tree in as much light as possible.

Avoid extremes of temperature: bonsai like a constant temperature. Never leave them near a source of heat that is too strong – close to a radiator, for example – where they will soon dry out. Indoor bonsai can be adapted to suit all kinds of environments, but if, in addition, you have quite a lot of greenery in the room, make sure that you do not place the bonsai in the middle of the other plants or they will not stand out. And if you have a plant infested by pests or suffering from blight, the bonsai will be affected.

# GENERAL CARE

## SUNSHINE

Outdoor bonsai, which are species that are hardy in the area in which you garden, have the same requirements as trees growing in their natural state: some species prefer to be grown in partial shade, others in full sunlight. Indoor bonsai need more or less light according to the species. All that is required to reduce the amount of light in a room is some ordinary net curtains. In any case, all tender species dislike direct sunlight and you must be careful not to put them too near sources of heat, for example, on a mantelpiece above an open fire.

## TEMPERATURE

Treat as outdoor bonsai those species that grow naturally in your own garden without additional winter protection. In some areas, *Citrus* spp. (oranges, lemons and so on) are delicate and need to be protected in winter, even if they are outside in summer, while other species are hardier and are capable of surviving extremes of weather.

Outdoor bonsai are well adapted to the seasonal cycles experienced in northern Europe. You may be tempted to bring the more delicate trees inside during the winter if they are threatened by frost, but whatever you do you must not leave bonsai indoors for more than three days at a time in winter. If you do, the artificial heat will cause the sap to rise, and after three days indoors, deciduous trees start to bud and leaves will appear. Obviously, this artificial spring will be fatal for the tree, because it will exhaust all its reserves and it will not be long before it dies. As a rule, the greater the difference between the outside and the inside temperature, the more dangerous it is to bring the tree inside.

In summer, too, you should not keep an outdoor bonsai inside the house too long. One week is the maximum time and even then you must spray the tree every day and make sure that it stands in good light. If you do bring a bonsai indoors, you must not put it in front of an open window or take it outside at night. Of course, when it is inside, the tree no longer experiences the temperature fluctuations that occur between day and night and neither is there any difference in the amount of moisture in the air; as a result, it will soon start wilting. As far as possible you must respect the natural daily and seasonal cycles of the tree if you want it to remain healthy.

In winter, however, when the temperature goes below freezing, the roots of the bonsai, which are protected only by the small amount of soil in the pot, are at risk from frost. For this reason, when the temperature is below -5°C (23°F), the container should be wrapped round with horticultural fleece, paper, wool or straw,

right up to the base of the trunk, or you might use dead leaves to keep the roots warm and protect them from frost. You could also protect the tree by placing it in an upright, three-sided case – like a niche – if possible sheltered from icy winds. Alternatively, you could dig a hole in the earth and place the tree and its container in it so that only the base of the trunk and top-growth are visible. Another solution is to bury the tree with its pot. Simpler than any of these is to bring the bonsai into a cold room, even one that is not very bright, during the periods of most intense cold. But in this case, you must make sure that the compost is damp and you should water the tree lightly as the need arises and mist the foliage occasionally.

For indoor bonsai the problem is quite different. They can survive high temperatures but are unhappy if the room gets any colder than about 12°C (54°F). In areas that have reliably warm summers, some species may be put outside, provided that they are misted and watered regularly.

## VENTILATION

Outdoor bonsai that have become used to the extremes of your climate are better equipped to deal with the ill-effects of wind. Nevertheless, for certain species it is preferable to find a sheltered location, especially in winter, if you want the tree to grow well. This will avoid both the dangers of dehydration and the sudden onslaught of cold caused by gusts of wind. For indoor bonsai, draughts should be rigorously avoided.

## CONTAINER

A ceramic container is not only something useful, it also has an aesthetic value that complements and enhances the beauty of the tree. The material will, traditionally, be terracotta or stoneware. Remember that, if the sides are to be porous, the inside must

not be glazed. On the other hand, glazes can be used on the outside with colours such as whitish-beige, chestnut brown, willow green and cobalt blue (which is very popular) and, occasionally, black.

Your choice of colour for the container and any decoration will depend on the kind of tree that has been selected. Some pots are plain. Chinese pots are often ornamented with painted or sculpted patterns; if you can find a container that somehow reflects a link between the tree and the designs the result is all the more attractive. If the opposite occurs, the design may destroy the elegance of both tree and pot.

Like all flowerpots, the container you choose must have one or more holes in the bottom, depending on its size, so that any excess water can drain away. The container's shape must, of course, be in harmony with the shape of the tree, and it must suit the taste of the owner. Some species look best in deep containers, although it does not matter if they are oval, rectangular or round. Other styles of tree, however, require particular shapes of container. A tree whose branches sweep down to the ground should be in a deep pot, generally round, square or hexagonal, whereas a plant shaped more like a broom should be in a very shallow, oval pot, and a forest group should generally be potted in a container whose breadth is equal to two-thirds of the height of the biggest of the trees. As a rule, the breadth of the

*A display of indoor bonsai, photographed in late autumn. Bottom row, from left to right: Serissa foetida (syn. Serissa japonica): 6 years old; Podocarpus macrophyllus var. maki (shrubby podocarp): 7 years old. Far right: Ficus microcarpa (syn. F. retusa; curtain fig): 10 years old. Top row, left to right: Ophiopogon planiscapus; Bambusa multiplex (syn. B. glaucescens).*

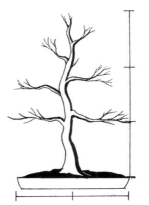

### Choosing a container

*If the tree is broader than it is tall, the length of the container should be slightly more than two-thirds the breadth of the tree at its widest point. It must never be equal to the breadth or the height of the tree.*

*As a rule, the length of the container must be slightly more than two-thirds of the height of the tree.*

*The depth of the container should be equal to the diameter of the trunk, unless the tree is in a cascade style or unless there are multiple trunks.*

*Left: some of these containers were obtained by Rémy Samson in Japan and China; others were made by French potters.*

*The breadth of the container should be a little less than the breadth of the tree at its widest point.*

container should be equal to the average breadth of the branches of the tree; however, it can sometimes be bigger.

When it comes to size, the container should show the tree off to its best advantage and be to the same scale. It is important that the laws of proportion be rigorously observed. A container that is too big will not allow the roots to absorb all the moisture in the soil, and this will mean that they are in danger of rotting, but a container that is too small will cause the roots to become stunted and, in addition, the tree will be receiving too little nourishment.

### REGULAR MAINTENANCE

If you want to keep your bonsai looking healthy and attractive, you will have to keep them tidy and clean. Regularly remove dead leaves and do the same with conifer needles that have turned yellow. Using a small brush and your fingers, brush the earth and remove weeds.

Cut out dead branches with clippers. If you wish, apply a wound-healing compound in and around the area of the cut or the places where the incisions have been made. Sprinkling the foliage with water is another part of the tidying-up process; this is not just done for appearance, but it helps to keep the tree healthy, preventing the build up of pests

and diseases and also helping to keep the tree and its foliage are free from dust and pollution.

### GROWTH

Bonsai are living trees, and they continue to get bigger, which is why it is necessary to prune them just as most of the trees and shrubs you grow in the garden need regular pruning to maintain a fine shape and to remove dead and damaged branches. Generally, conifers grow more slowly than deciduous trees, and some deciduous shrubs and trees grow rapidly and need continual attention to keep them looking their best as bonsai. The rate of growth varies from tree to tree, and this factor is included in the descriptions of the individual species in the second part of this book.

### REPOTTING

If a bonsai is not repotted regularly, the quality of the compost deteriorates, both in terms of it structure and the amount of nutrient it contains.

As they develop, the roots will begin to fill the container, and as they grow they exert pressure on the soil, compressing it and reducing the friability necessary to maintain the moisture-retaining and oxygenating qualities for the root system to function properly. Regular watering,

winter frosts, the continual pressure caused by the increasing size of the roots, the reduction in the porosity of the root hairs as they age, organic waste combine to impoverish the soil and reduce its aerating properties. The pores of the root hairs become clogged up, and the roots themselves prevent water from draining freely through the compost. These processes, in turn, contribute to the deterioration of the roots, which become increasingly less able to transfer nutrients to the plants.

Not only can the roots do their work less efficiently over time, the nutrients within the soil also become depleted. If the proportion of elements in the compost is inadequate the compost becomes acidic. Carbon dioxide is turned into carbonic acid, calcium dissolves in water and becomes calcium bicarbonate. Regular watering washes essential nutrients through the soil, hastening the process of making the compost less valuable to the plant and of making it more acidic.

Being dwarf trees, bonsai grow only slowly and to a limited extent, but they do, nevertheless, steadily increase in size, so you will find that the advice for the individual species in the second part of this book recommends that each time you repot the plant it should usually be placed in a larger pot. (The advice to pot on into a larger container each time is contrary to normal practice in Britain, where this is done only during the early trimming period and until the desired basic size of the bonsai is reached. Thereafter, the plant is returned to the same container for the rest of its life, each time it is repotted, unless unusual circumstance intervene.)

The best time to repot is in spring when the plant is beginning to grow new leaves. This should be after a period of from three to five years for conifers; from two to three years for deciduous trees; from one to two years for fruit trees; and from two years onwards for indoor bonsai.

How often you repot depends upon the age of the plant: the older a bonsai is the less it needs to be repotted. The time to repot has come when you feel that the roots are forming ridges and attempting to extend beyond the span of the branches. As we have noted, a container that confines the tree too much will no longer provide it with sufficient nourishment and consequently it will die. When you are repotting you will have a good opportunity to clean up the roots by trimming the rootlets.

Make sure that the compost is dry, then take the tree out of the pot and allow the soil to crumble away by gently shaking the rootball; this will help to make the roots supple again so that they can continue to grow. The next container you use should be just a little bigger than the old one. Use a piece of plastic netting to cover the hole or holes in the bottom so that excess water can drain away but the compost cannot. Add a layer of fairly large stones across the bottom, then mix compost with some smaller stones and add a further layer cross the base of the container. Before replacing the tree in the container, you should have trimmed anything from one- to two-thirds of the root hairs. Use clippers to do this and take care that you do not damage the main root or roots.

When you are repotting a bonsai, take the opportunity to examine it carefully for any signs of infestation by insects or of disease. Check the compost to make sure there are no insect eggs or larvae – vine weevil larvae are an increasing problem and thrive in containers, where they eat plant roots. Also cut off any dead or damaged roots, and gently wash the roots to remove the old soil. This will also help you see the condition of the root system more carefully and will give you an opportunity to dust them with fungicide or insecticide if other plants in your collection are affected by pests and diseases. (Note that some trees are slow to re-establish after potting up and some old soil should be left on the roots; see advice for individual plants.)

When you put the tree back in its container you can, if you wish to provide it with support; use a length of copper wire.

If you do this, the wire will run from underneath the container, through one of the holes in the base and emerge inside the pot. Next you should fill up the container with soil, mixed with some grit, making sure that it goes well down between the roots. Spread fine earth on top, heaping it up slightly to allow the air and the water to circulate. The compost on the surface should go through a very fine sieve and be well watered, but with a very fine rose on the watering-can. After repotting, the tree will be delicate for about six weeks. Protect it from direct sunlight and, if necessary, from any night frosts by covering it.

## SOIL

In the garden and in the wild, trees are fairly tolerant plants, growing in a wide range of soil types and habitats. Nevertheless, every species has its own particular requirements, and *Pinus* (pine) will not grow well in the same type of compost as *Acer* (maples), while *Malus* (apple) will not thrive in the same type of soil as *Ficus* (fig). It is essential, therefore, to provide the appropriate compost for each plant, and only by providing the correct proportions of the various elements that go to make up soil will you enable your bonsai to thrive. This is especially important when a plant is grown in a container and when the roots are confined within a small area and cannot quest for nutrients from further afield.

It is important that the compost in which plants are grown is both moisture retentive and free draining. So that the roots can take in nutrients from the compost, they need both water and air, and a soil mix that becomes waterlogged because water cannot drain freely away will cause the roots, and then the plant itself, to die. When you add compost to a container, the aim should be as noted above, to have a layer of larger pieces, combined with stones, in the bottom, with subsequent layers gradually decreasing in size towards the top. The topmost layer should be of extremely fine compost, which has been sieved to remove all large pieces. It is important that the compost is of the same type throughout a container and that when you make up your own mixture it is thoroughly mixed before being added to the pot.

Soil contains macro- and micro-nutrients. The macro-nutrients, which plants absorb through their roots, are nitrogen, phosphorus, potassium, calcium, magnesium and sulphur. (Carbon, oxygen and hydrogen are also macro-nutrients, but they are obtained from water and air.) The micro-nutrients are iron, manganese, zinc, boron, molybdenum, copper and chlorine. All these nutrients must be available to plants if they are to thrive.

Soil is usually described in terms of the pH scale, which runs from 1 to 14. The mineral content of soil determines whether it is alkaline or acid. Acid soils – those with a pH of around 6.5 and below – contain little or no lime; this type of soil suits plants such as azaleas, rhododendrons and camellias. Soil that contains lime is described as alkaline, and this has a pH of 7 or more. Soil-testing kits are widely available in garden centres and larger do-it-yourself stores, and it takes only a short time to carry out tests on samples of soil. When you are mixing your own compost from a range of ingredients, you should consider testing the mix from time to time, especially if you intend to grow calcifuges, which are especially susceptible to the wrong type of soil.

Although several different types of compost are available from garden centres and nurseries, mixing individual combinations of ingredients for different plant types will ensure that you give your bonsai the perfect conditions in which they can grow. Precise details about the type of soil appropriate for each species are given in the second part of the book, but in general conifers require equal parts leaf mould, loam, sharp sand; deciduous trees need equal parts loam and sharp sand; and fruit trees and flowering trees need a mixture made of equal proportions of loam and compost. For trees requiring leaf mould the proportions should be two parts leaf mould, to one part loam and one part peat. Indoor bonsai need a mixture of equal parts compost, leaf mould, sharp sand and loam.

Clay is a component of soil that is heavy and that drains poorly or slowly. Although clay soils are often rich in nutrients and trace elements, they tend to compact easily, which means that roots cannot operate efficiently. Red clay contains iron; black clay contains carbon. In the garden, clay soils are slow to warm up in spring, and they may, if they get too dry, bake hard in summer.

Akadama is a special type of compost that is prepared in Japan for growing bonsai. It contains granules of clay, and this means that it drains freely, giving good oxygenation to the root system. It has a pH of between 6.5 and 6.9, which makes it slightly acid to neutral. It is also less likely than clay soil to become compacted and retains these characteristics over a long period. Kanuma is another special Japanese growing medium, also derived from clay but with a low pH, making it very acid. It is ideal for azaleas and rhododendrons. Kyriu, also from Japan, contains a combination of clay and gravel, and it is especially suitable for conifers.

Sand can be added to clay soil to open up the texture. Buy special horticultural sand, and do not use builder's sand nor sand from the seashore. Alternatively, add very fine grit, although you must make sure that you do not use limestone chippings for acid-loving plants. Grit is available in different grades, and can be used with different types of clay soil to improve the drainage of the soil.

Humus is the brown or blackish substance that is produced by the slow

**Pruning branches**
*The branches outlined in dotted lines should be removed. The remaining branches are sometimes shortened.*

**Pruning roots**
*The roots should be cut back to about two-thirds of their original length.*

rotting down of organic material. The bacteria that create humus multiply, breaking down the complex components in the organic matters into the simple chemicals that plants are able to absorb as food through their root systems. The best source is the garden compost heap. Peat, which is often added to the growing medium, is also partially decomposed organic material, but it is derived from mosses or sedges in boggy areas. Moss peat is generally more acid that sedge peat; neither type of peat contains nutrients in sufficient quantity for most plants. Because of the destruction of the environment from which peat is taken, many gardeners prefer to use alternatives such as coir (coconut fibre) and bark. Leaf mould is a useful soil improver. It is made from decomposed leaves, and it is the material that is found on forest floors, where deciduous trees shed their leaves each year. Never remove leaf mould from the wild. If you do not have a garden in which you can make your own, use an alternative organic material to add nutrients to your potting compost.

## PRUNING

Pruning a bonsai consists of cutting back young shoots, leaves and branches, and it is an activity that lies at the heart of the art of bonsai. It is careful pruning that gives a tree its shape and that maintains that shape over the life of a tree. It is an activity that has to be repeated frequently and regularly. Pruning not only serves to strengthen a plant, but also to limit its growth, and it encourages sap to flow more freely. There are several different kinds of pruning.

Pinching out involves the removal of the new shoots as they begin to sprout. It is mainly carried out on conifers and on some slow-growing deciduous trees.

Leaf pruning should be carried out in summer if the tree is healthy. It should be done every two or three years, but never in

the same year that a tree has been repotted. It is a way of artificially creating a second spring, and the leaves that will be produced in this way will clothe the tree with all the finery and splendour of autumn. Cut all the leaves with a sharp pair of scissors, and protect the tree from too much wind and sun. It is also possible to cut off half the leaves of trees that have big leaves to encourage these leaves to become smaller. Finally, it is possible to cut off some of the leaves on a bonsai whose foliage is too dense in order to allow air to circulate more freely around the remaining leaves to breathe and to prevent the centre of the tree from becoming congested.

Pruning the branches is necessary because sap has a natural tendency to rise, and this allows the lower branches to receive a greater quantity of sap. Pruning in this way allows the sap to flow through all the branches and prevents the tree from growing too tall. As a result, you will get a fine set of branches. This type of pruning can be carried out any time between spring and autumn. Using a good pair of clippers, cut back the branches, starting at a point above a leaf joint, leaving two or three leaves on each branch.

Structural pruning is the method used to give deciduous trees a perfect silhouette and prevents them having branches that are too big the following spring. If branches develop that are thought to be undesirable or unattractive in appearance, structural pruning should be carried out in winter on deciduous trees. This is the time when the structure of the tree becomes clear, and you can identify a tree's good and bad points. If a particular branch spoils the overall appearance of the tree, cut it back to the level of the trunk, using a good saw, and apply a wound-sealing compound to the stump. On the other hand, if the leaves have not been cut back in summer, you will have to carry out some pruning in winter in order to restore tree's shape before the wood is too hard. To carry out this pruning, cut the branches that have become too long. It is a good idea to buy a deciduous bonsai in winter, for its good and bad points will then be more obvious.

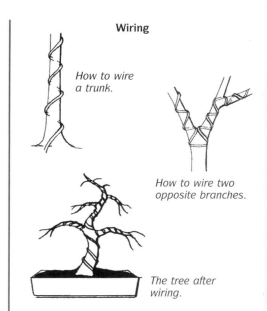

**Wiring**

*How to wire a trunk.*

*How to wire two opposite branches.*

*The tree after wiring.*

## WIRING

A bonsai may be regarded as a sculpture, in which the overall shape is achieved not only through pruning but also by wiring, a technique that is indispensable for giving a particular style to a bonsai.

Wiring consists in winding a copper or brass wire around the trunk and the branches to persuade them to grow in a particular direction or way. The main aim is to shape the tree. In addition, it slows down growth by making it more difficult for sap to rise. You should wind wire around the trunk and the branches from the bottom upwards, working in the form of a spiral and in the direction of growth. Take care not to wind it too tight; if you do, the sap will not be able to flow at all, and the tree would then not receive any nourishment. Make sure that you do not squash any thorns or leaves between the tree and the copper wire. Once the wire is wound round the branch, bend it gently so that it goes in the direction you have chosen. To make a bend more firm, you can wedge a piece of wood between the trunk and the branch as a support, or stretch a length of string between the container and the branch, taking care that

**Creating a shape without wiring**

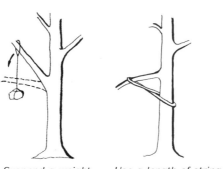

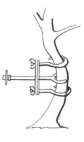

*Suspend a weight to shape a branch.*

*Use a length of string to exert pressure on a branch.*

*Use separate pieces of string, secured to the pot or to each other.*

*A clamp can be used to shape a trunk.*

you do not break the branch by tightening the string too much. However, it is necessary for the string to be taut and not sagging if it is to do any good.

To increase the curvature of the trunk or the main branches you could use a clamp, but if you do you should be careful. Protect the bark with some moss or a piece of rag. Place the clamp where you want the curve to be and gently fix it in place by steadily tightening it. Be careful that you do not crack the wood, but at the same time it should be tight enough to be effective. This can be done at the same time as wiring. It is also essential that the wire does not become embedded in the bark. Pull it out with pliers, being careful not to damage the tree. If the bark is damaged, coat it with a wound-sealing compound.

Conifers should be wired in winter and the wire should be left in place for a period of eight to ten months. Deciduous trees are wired in spring and the wire is left on for between four and six months. Fruit trees

*If a bonsai is standing outdoors in heavy rain, tip the pot so that the soil does not get washed away.*

should be wired in early to midsummer and the wire left for three or four months. Indoor bonsai should be wired when the young shoots have had the benefit of the late summer sun. Remove the wire after about a month, because the bark is not strong. Start the whole operation again two months later if the shape you are aiming for has not been obtained because the bark is delicate.

## WATERING

Water is vital to the well-being of all plants, but the quantity you give to a bonsai must be carefully gauged, and trees should never be given too much or too little. A bonsai will, however, recover more easily from having too little water than too much. If a plant is given too much water, the roots will eventually rot; the sap will not be able to circulate and carry nutrients to each part of the tree. When this happens, the leaves dry up and then fall. Before long the tree will die.

The amount of water you give should be varied according to the climate and the volume of the container (the smaller it is the more often you must water the plant). You should also take into account the state of health of the tree, for if it is not very healthy it will absorb less water because it

has fewer leaves. You should also make allowance for the sun and the wind. In the period between watering make sure that the earth is dry but not too dry. If a bonsai has been receiving too little water, give it a small amount, but then wait about half an hour before giving it some more, this time in greater quantity. Never leave a saucer filled with water underneath the container because this will cause the roots to rot.

In winter you only need water the plant once a day, in the morning, to allow the bonsai to absorb the moisture by nightfall. If you want to get rid of excess water, this should be done by tipping the pot. Never water when the weather is frosty. If the tree is receiving rainwater (which is best), make sure that the earth round the roots does not become soaked. If that should happen, pour the excess water out by tipping the pot. If you get a frost followed by a thaw, take special care that the earth does not get waterlogged. If it is so not in summer that you have to water twice a day, you should not do this in direct sunlight. Because water provides plants with necessary macro-nutrients, never give demineralized water to your bonsai.

Indoor bonsai need different treatment from those kept outdoors. You should only water indoor bonsai once or twice a week, according to how hot it is, the brightness of the room and also the size of the pot. The more heat and light there are, and the bigger the container is, the more you will have to water. When you have just pruned a tree or repotted it, reduce the supply of water. In summer and in winter you should water more frequently than in spring and in autumn.

Although watering might appear to be a straightforward operation, it is actually quite complicated and difficult. It is the most important part of looking after your bonsai because water constitutes such a large part of the tissues of every plant. Watering should be done with a watering can with a fine rose to simulate a shower of rain. Do not stand the containers in bowls of water because this will simply wash the nutrients from the compost and leave the growing medium compacted. It is important that air can circulate through the compost, which cannot happen when the soil is waterlogged.

A lack of water will slow down a plant's growth and may even stop it from flowering. If, for whatever reason, you forget to water your plants and it has been so long since the last watering that they have dried out, fill a glass with water and pour it over the compost. Wait for about 10 minutes, then repeat the process. This time wait for 15 minutes, until the compost is soaked. Allow excess water to drain away before replacing the bonsai in its usual position. After a period of underwatering, do not overwater, but gradually build up the amount of water that you give to your

plants. If you overcompensate by giving extra water all at once, you will risk 'drowning' the roots, which will be unable to function and the plant will die.

The best time for watering is early in the day, and one reason is that it is better for the plants if they are showered with cold water while the air around them is still cold. If you use tapwater, allow it to stand for a while before using it. In spring and autumn, therefore, water in the morning. In summer, however, water late in the day, when the sun is no longer going to scorch tender leaves with droplets on them. It is important that the surface of the compost is wetted by the droplets of water. Unless you are careful, the water will simply fall on the foliage and run off the plant, sometimes onto the ground around the plant.

## MISTING

Misting is an essential part of watering but it is by no means the same thing and should not be used instead of watering. Misting a bonsai will refresh the tree, provide it with a humid atmosphere and help to wash away particles of dust on the surface of the leaves. While you are misting the leaves, it is a good idea to water the surrounding compost, because as the water evaporates it will create a humid atmosphere round the tree.

Outdoor bonsai should be misted in summer. How often you do this will depend on where you live and the prevailing weather in your garden. Indoor bonsai will not be harmed by daily misting. Most of these trees are used to high levels of humidity in the air, and misting restores the level of humidity which is necessary for them to grow well. Never mist flowers, however, for they will fade.

You can use a simple hand-held mister. These are not expensive and are available in garden centres, supermarkets and do-it-yourself stores. If you have only a few plants them are all you need. If you have several plants and if they are arranged in tiers and not easy to reach, you may prefer to use a spray attachment for a hose. These attachments are operated by a trigger, and some are adjustable so that you can change from a jet of water to a fine mist. Mid-way between the small mister and the hose attachment is the portable sprayer, similar to a knapsack, which has a lever to pump the water through a short hose. These systems have the advantage that they can be easily operated some distance from a tap.

## FEEDING

Applying fertilizer to a plant has purposes: it is a source of nutrients, and it acts as a tonic. The fertilizer replaces the chemicals that the bonsai has absorbed from the compost. You should use an organic fertilizer – bonemeal, dried blood, fishmeal, hoof and horn – which will break down slowly so that the tree is not harmed. The fertilizer may be in the form of powdered pellets or a liquid. Fertilizer in the form of pellets or powder may be kept in place with the help of a little plastic basket, which can be turned upside down and inserted in the earth. Alternatively, slow-release fertilizers can be mixed in with the compost before the tree is planted. These pellets provide sufficient nutrients for a single growing season. Liquid mineral fertilizer may be applied in diluted form when you are watering the plant if you think it needs a boost. It does not matter whether you give the fertilizer in the form of powder or as pellets.

In general, fertilizer should be applied to bonsai at the beginning of spring and the end of autumn, but not in midsummer. There are three things that you must not do: never give fertilizer during the winter; never give any fertilizer to unhealthy trees; and never give fertilizer to trees that have just been repotted. Because no fertilizer is given in the winter, you should increase the last dose given in the autumn.

Fertilizer tends to turn moss yellow, and you should, therefore, rub the yellow moss away before applying the fertilizer. The less soil you have, the more frequently you must apply fertilizer, but remember that too much fertilizer is worse than too little.

For outdoor bonsai, apply fertilizer at the following times: for conifers from mid-spring until mid-autumn; for deciduous trees from the beginning of spring (after the buds have opened) until mid- to late autumn; for fruit trees from just before the fruit appears until mid- to late autumn.

Indoor bonsai have different requirements, and these are outlined in the descriptions of the individual species in the second part of the book.

Fertilizer should be applied in the following quantities. If you use powdered fertilizer sprinkle one or two teaspoons on the soil where the bonsai is growing, once a month for outdoor bonsai, once a fortnight for indoor bonsai. You should place solid pellet of fertilizer (two in the case of large pots) on the compost, a fair distance away from the trunk, and allow it to sink in as the plant is watered. Alternatively, the pellets may be placed either in the open air or in a clear plastic container. Liquid fertilizer can be diluted in the watering can. Another possibility is to place the bottle of fertilizer in the soil and leave the contents to drip out slowly.

### ADDING MOSS

When a bonsai is grown outdoors in the conditions that it would encounter if it were growing in the wild, a carpet of moss will naturally form on the soil around it. It is possible to replicate the conditions that will encourage the formation of moss.

A covering of moss on the surface of

Juniperus chinensis *(Chinese juniper): 70 years old; Sekijôju style. The roots can be clearly seen as they grip the rock and 'pour' down, like a waterfall, before spreading out attractively over the soil.*

the compost plays an important part in conserving moisture, but it is important that it does not grow so vigorously that it smothers the plant. Do not use the thick moss that grows in woodlands because that will prevent evaporation from the surface of the compost and harm the plant. In addition, if you add moss that subsequently dies, there is a danger that fungal problems may develop.

The type of moss that you need to encourage to grow over a bonsai is the type of delicate, rather thin moss that is found growing on old walls, steps and stones. Spread it out on newspaper and leave it to dry. Roughen the surface of the soil, and then sprinkle the dried moss over the surface. Carefully and gently water the soil, and the moss will, little by little, grow.

If you prefer to achieve a more rapid covering of moss, you can take a small piece of moss already growing on another plant. It is important to roughen the surface of the soil and to make sure that the point to which you move the moss contains the same type of compost as the original container. Continue to mist the moss until it becomes established and spreads across the surface of the compost, which it will do eventually.

Take care that moss does not begin to grow up the trunk of the tree. Brush the trunk regularly, especially around the collar, so that moss does not take hold. It is an ideal hiding place for pests and a starting place for diseases if it is allowed to become established on trunks and branches.

It is often difficult to get moss to grow over the compost of an indoor bonsai. The atmosphere is often must drier than outdoors, and this discourages moss from becoming established and, even if it does begin to grow, it is often patchy and poorly developed. It is important to provide a good balance of light, heat and humidity to encourage the moss to grow. Often, if an indoor bonsai is stood outside in summer, moss will grow of its own accord, but it may die back once the plant is taken back indoors for winter.

## SPECIAL TECHNIQUES

Some artificial techniques are used to make bonsai more closely resemble plants that are grown in unusual or difficult conditions in the wild or that have been adversely affected by the weather. For example, trees are sometimes struck by lightning, while others are exposed to strong winds, which contort their branches. These techniques, especially those known as jin and shari, are designed to make bonsai look old, and they give them unusual and distinctive silhouettes. They are used especially for bonsai that are included in landscape and group arrangements, when the aim is to recreate a rocky or woodland countryside, and although the techniques involve artifice, their aim is to recreate a scene that would be found in the natural world.

### JIN

This technique is a means of giving an artificial appearance of age to the large branch of a mature bonsai. Strip back the bark of the branch, using a knife, then rub it with very fine sandpaper. Trim the end of the branch and apply a proprietary product that will clean the wood, bleaching it and protecting it at the same time. By treating the tip of the tree, using this jin method, the tree will be made to look smaller. The technique can also be used to reduce the size of trees.

## SHARI

This technique is similar to jin, but it can be applied to older bonsai. Simply peel back a single strip of bark and not a whole branch. Choose a strip on the trunk or on one of the major branches, then continue as for jin. You should also make sure that the product you are using to clean the wood does not penetrate beneath the bark. These two techniques may only be used with very fine, mature trees. Apply the proprietary cleaning fluid every two or three years to bleach the branch again and protect it against pests.

## PLANTING ON ROCKS

There are two styles of planting on rocks: bonsai rooted in a rock and root over rock.

For a bonsai rooted in a rock, choose a stone that is in proportion to the tree, which should be a small one. The same piece of rock can quite easily support several trees of different sizes and different species. You should select a porous stone that has several cavities in it. The bonsai can be placed firmly in these, once you have chosen which part will be the back and which the front.

The tree must be attached to the rock, preferably with a copper wire. Fill the hollow with a suitable mixture of soil, press it down firmly on top and keep everything in place by securing it with a small piece of fabric, which should remain on the tree for a year. This should all be done in the spring. Your planting can be completed by adding grass and ferns. Protect it from the wind, direct sunlight and cold, just as you would a bonsai that has been repotted. Once the bonsai has taken root in the rock, you must not try to remove the support. Repotting is out of the question. But from time to time you will have to renew the surface layer of soil. The plants can dry out quickly, so you must water them using a fine rose on the watering can. Bonsai grown in this way are particularly susceptible to frost, which is capable of detaching the roots from their support.

For a root over rock bonsai you should choose a fine piece of rock to support the tree and keep it in place. Some of the roots will penetrate the rock. You should plant the roots in the soil mixture suitable for the species, having first spread out the roots symmetrically around and over the rock. Keep everything in place with the help of a piece of fabric wound round the tree, which should be slipped right down to the roots. The fabric will keep the soil and the roots tight against the stone. Cover the compost with damp sphagnum moss, because this will help keep the roots fresh and this will assist their growth. Protect the

bonsai from the wind and sun, as you would a bonsai which has just been repotted. Wait two months before giving it any fertilizer.

Choose a fairly flat container to wedge the rock into and into which you will then bed the roots. The repotting and the soil mixture will depend on the species. These plantings should be created in the spring.

## FORESTS

Forests occupy a special place in the affections of bonsai enthusiasts. They can be created with young plants or with trees of different ages, but there must always be an odd number of trees. The style may vary, but all the bonsai should be of the same species. Forests should be planted in the spring. Choose a long, shallow container and healthy trees, whose roots and branches should be trimmed. Plant the larger trees at the back, the medium sized at the side and the smallest in front to create perspective.

The longest branches should be turned outwards; be careful that the trees do not get in each other's light. Vary the spacing between the trees to create the illusion of unplanned growth. It is very important to place the main tree first. It may be attached to the container with wire, as can the others. The roots of each tree should be wrapped round with a ball of moist earth. When all the trees are in place, heap up the soil mixture. As you are gently building up this mass of earth, you must be careful to leave sufficient space for the air and the water to circulate. Water well. Treat your forest as if it were a newly potted bonsai.

## TOOLS AND EQUIPMENT

There is a specific tool for each activity. Nevertheless, it is not absolutely necessary to have one of each unless you are growing several species of tree and you are carrying out all the tasks yourself. Otherwise, a good pair of narrow clippers will be quite sufficient for pruning branches, leaves or roots without harming the tree. You must also have some healing compound to heal any cuts or abrasions that the tree has suffered, although recent research has shown that most trees heal well without additional treatment provided cuts are made cleanly.

Always clean tools thoroughly after you have used them, if possible with alcohol, and then you should put them away tidily. If you do this you will prevent the spread of parasites and disease.

*Pruning saw, trowel, rakes (with tweezers and spatula) and a variety of brushes.*

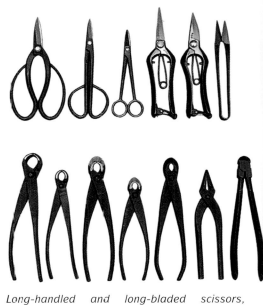

*Long-handled and long-bladed scissors, secateurs, loppers and wire clippers.*

*Watering can, measuring cups (for fertilizers), sieves, turntable, hose extension and copper wire.*

# PESTS AND DISEASES

Bonsai may fall victim to the same pests and diseases that attack normal trees. To prevent or cure such attacks, your bonsai should be checked at regular intervals. Hygiene is very important. Use only clean tools and containers, and when you are looking after your plants – repotting, pruning, wiring and so on – take care that you do not damage them.

Pests and diseases can attack the roots, the trunk, the branches or the leaves, and it is, therefore, important to prevent an attack from spreading. Diseases are less often encountered with bonsai, however, because the roots, branches and leaves are frequently pruned and inspected. Some pests – scale insects, aphids and spider mites, for instance – reappear regularly and will have to be dealt with each time.

A wide range of proprietary fungicides and pesticides is available to amateur gardeners. Some are multipurpose, others are formulated to treat a specific condition only. Before buying a product, make sure that you know exactly what pest or disease you have got to deal with.

Before treating an infected tree, you must water it thoroughly, either the preceding day or several hours beforehand. If the bonsai is thirsty, fungicides and insecticides will be less effective. It is a good idea to protect the soil with a sheet of plastic when you are spraying with chemicals or sprinkling a solution over a bonsai. The chemicals in these products are often harmful to humans, and you should, therefore, wash your hands after use and make sure that the leaves do not get near to your face. When you are using insecticides and fungicides use a different sprayer or watering can for the chemicals from the equipment you use for everyday

watering and misting. Even the slightest taint of a chemical can harm a plant for which it is not intended.

If a plant is wounded when you are pruning, apply a wound-sealing compound. It is important to encourage a callus to form over the wound to minimize the chances of unsightly scars forming on the trunk. An open wound is often the point at which pests and diseases first attack a plant. Remember to clear away dead leaves, which can harbour pests, and to cut out and burn any infected branches.

If you look after your bonsai properly – especially by re-creating the conditions occurring in its natural habitat – there is no reason they should fall victim to disease. If the leaves turn yellow, then wither and fall, do not immediately think about pests and diseases but check first to see if you are the cause of the problem. Giving a plant too much water often causes the leaves to turn yellow, wither and drop because in waterlogged soil the roots stagnate and rot, the sap no longer circulates and the tree dies through lack of nourishment. Lack of light causes etiolation – that is, the tree loses its compact shape and grows long stems with small pale leaves. Too much strong or direct sunshine, on the other hand, will scorch the leaves. The amount of light the tree receives must be carefully controlled;

likewise the amount of sunshine, which provides warmth, reduces growth and helps the sap to circulate properly. There must be a correct balance between the amount of water given to the soil and the amount lost through transpiration. So, before focusing your attention on pests and diseases, it is important to check that the tree is being properly cared for.

Below are descriptions of the main pests and diseases that can attack bonsai and suggestions on how to treat them. At

*Glasshouse red spider mite on* Acer buergerianum.

the end of the each plant description is a summary of the main pests and diseases.

## PESTS

**Glasshouse red spider mites**
*Symptoms* Glasshouse red spider mites (*Tetranychus urticae*) are found on the underside of the leaves and pierce the foliage. The leaves usually develop a yellow mottled appearance and may turn silver-grey if the attack is severe. There is a danger that the tree may wither.
*Treatment* The foliage should be well sprayed, particularly the underside, as soon as the first symptoms appear. Use a variety of products, such as heptenophos and

*Red spider mite on* bougainvillea.

permethrin and pirimiphos-methyl, so that the mites do not develop tolerance to any chemical. Introduce the predatory mite *Phytoseiulus persimilis* as biological control.

**Red spider mite**
*Symptoms* The needles of conifers become discoloured. They turn yellow, reddish-brown, then brown and eventually drop. A

matted webbing is produced between the branches, which hinders photosynthesis. Eggs are laid at the base of the needles and in cracks in the bark.

Eggs overwinter on the branches of deciduous trees and red patches may develop on the bark. In spring, holes appear in the leaves. The mites are found mainly on the underside of the leaves, where small discoloured blotches may appear. The leaves turn silver-grey and later, if the attack is severe, brown. They eventually drop. The spiders weaken the tree by sucking at the sap.

*Treatment* When the air is warm and dry you should leave the conifers well alone. Cut away and destroy the infested branches. At the end of winter, when the new growth appears, spray with tar oil (handle with caution) to destroy the eggs. In spring and summer (if necessary) spray with systemic acaricides. Remember that the mites thrive in hot, dry conditions but do not like humidity. It is important to mist the foliage thoroughly. In summer, the tree should be generously watered.

## Caterpillars

Caterpillars are the larvae of butterflies or moths. They sometimes weaken a tree by feeding on the tissue, and they may sometimes cause fatal damage. They can be divided into several groups.

### Bombyx moth, Owlet moth
*Symptoms* Both groups of moth (which are from the superfamilies Bombycoidea and Noctuoidea) produce silken threads between the needles or the leaves. A spongy looking nest appears in the foliage, which is why they are often known as 'spongy caterpillars'. They eat away at the needles or leaves.
*Treatment* As soon as symptoms appear, spray with contact insecticides. In the greenhouse, introduce the bacterial disease *Bacillus thuringiensis*.

### Goat moth, Leopard moth
*Symptoms* The goat moth (*Cossus cossus*) and the leopard moth (*Zeuzera pyrina*) are nocturnal moths that are regarded as pests because they eat away at the bark of the trunk and branches, perforating it and then tunnelling upwards. A small heap of sawdust accumulates at the mouth of the tunnel. The caterpillars are red or yellow.
*Treatment* Cut away the infested parts. Insert a length of iron wire into the

*Leaf-rollers on lilac leaves.*

tunnels. This can be wrapped round with cottonwool soaked in carbon disulphide. Block up the hole with wood-sealant.

### Leaf-rollers
*Symptoms* Leaf-rollers nibble away at young shoots, flowers, buds and leaves. Silken threads wrap around the leaves and roll them into a cigar shape. The damage is done at night. The caterpillars can sometimes be seen.
*Treatment* In spring, spray with parathion-based insecticides.

### Leaf miners
*Symptoms* The caterpillars of a species of moth make tunnels in the leaf tissue and holes in the leaves. The cavities are surrounded by black specks. Photosynthesis is reduced.
*Treatment* Spray regularly with heptenophos and permethrin or malathion, following the manufacturer's instructions.

### Geometer moths
*Symptoms* The name geometer is applied to this group of moths because the caterpillars appear to 'measure' twigs by stretching out to full length then drawing up their bodies to form a loop. They are also known as loopers. They eat foliage and buds. The caterpillars produce silken threads by which they can climb from the foliage down to the ground.
*Treatment* At the end of winter apply a tar oil wash to destroy the eggs. In spring, use lindane or parathion-based synthetic insecticides.

### Tortix moths
*Symptoms* The caterpillars bind leaves together with silky threads or leaves are folded back on themselves. Brown patches appear on the leaves.
*Treatment* Pick off and destroy affected leaves. Spray with pirimiphos-methyl or permethrin.

## Scale insects
There are two types of scale insect, hard-

*Scale insects on a quince.*

shelled and soft. Hard-shelled scale insects are sedentary insects, which colonize leaves, fruit and branches. They are protected by grey-brown or dark brown waxy shells, and they measure about 3mm (⅛in). Soft scale insects are protected by a shell that forms part of the insect. They are round and convex in shape.
*Symptoms* Clusters of brown, yellow or white waxy shells appear on the leaves, the trunk and the branches. Inside each shell is a scale insect. The trunk becomes distorted, the branches die, and the leaves (or needles) turn yellow and drop. The tree withers, and photosynthesis is reduced. These are a particular problem for plants grown in greenhouses.
*Treatment* Clean the stem and leaves with a sponge soaked in water and alcohol. Cut away and destroy the infested branches. Spray with pirimiphos-methyl, meptenophos and permethrin or malathion at regular intervals. However, scale insects are not easy to get rid of, as they are protected by their shells. Be careful not to damage the leaves. Isolate the tree so that other bonsai or other plants are not affected. Beware when treating fragile varieties: treatment applied in too large doses could be fatal. A parasitic wasp, *Metaphycus helvolus*, can be used in greenhouses.

## Mealy bugs
*Symptoms* These tiny, sap-eating pink insects are found in patches on leaves. They are covered with tufts of white

*Mealy bugs on white poplar.*

woolly or mealy wax. Photosynthesis is reduced and growth slows down. The bugs are active and look like blobs of cottonwool. The leaves turn yellow and drop.
*Treatment* As soon as the first symptoms appear, spray with a systemic insecticide such as heptenophos and permethrin. For biological control, introduce *Cryptolaemus montrouzieri*, a beetle that eats mealy bugs, to the greenhouse.

## Aphids
*Symptoms* Greenfly, blackfly and gall aphids lay eggs that hibernate on the bark. In mid-spring, larvae appear on the tips of the shoots. The aphids, visible to the naked eye, colonize the tender young shoots and suck at the sap. If conifers are affected, the

*Greenfly on beech.*

needles shrivel: they become distorted and silver blotches appear on them. They wither and eventually drop. The aphids excrete honeydew, which leads to the growth of sooty mould. Growth slows down and cankers appear. If the tree is infested with gall aphids, galls develop on the shoots. The blackfly is a carrier of virus diseases. Although green and blackfly are the most often seen, aphids may also be pink, red or yellow.

*Treatment* When watering the tree, aim a strong jet of water at the foliage to wash away the aphids. Try to catch an

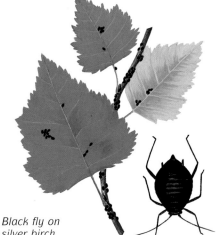

*Black fly on silver birch.*

infestation in the early stages and remove the insects by hand. Once the infestation takes hold, spray plants thoroughly with a systemic insecticide such as heptenophos or dimethoate. Alternatively, use a non-systemic insecticide such as malathion, pirimiphos-methyl, pyrethrum, fenitrothion or derris. Pirimicarb will leave most other beneficial insects unharmed. Wash with an insecticidal soap. Outdoors, try to encourage predators, such as ladybirds, bluetits and hoverflies, into the garden to control aphid numbers, and introduce lacewing larvae as a biological control. In the greenhouse introduce Aphidoletes or Aphidius. Remember that if you introduce a biological control into the greenhouse to tackle one pest, you will not be able to use a chemical control against other pests.

### Woolly aphids
*Symptoms* Tufts of white, waxy wool, produced by aphids, can be seen on trunks, branches and twigs in spring. Galls

*Woolly aphids on a crab apple.*

are also sometimes seen, and when these split, infections enter the plant.

*Treatment* Remove the galls and disinfect the wounds with a copper-based solution. In winter, spray with tar oil wash. When the pest is seen spray with malathion, dimethoate, heptenophos or pirimicarb. This is a difficult pest to control.

### Bark beetles
These members of the Scolytidae family are cylindrical beetles, black or brown, and from 1 to 5mm (½–¼in) long. They live in the wood or under the bark of trees, where they make tunnels. They do a great deal of damage. Conifers are the main victims.

*Symptoms* The eggs are laid in longitudinal tunnels between the bark and the cambium layer. The larvae extend the tunnels at right angles to the parent gallery. Fungus develops in the tunnels. The emerging adult make holes in the bark, which may fall off. The circulation of sap is disrupted, and branches die. *Scolytus*

*Bark beetles bore holes in the bark and galleries in the underlying wood.*

*scolytus* is the species that is believed to be responsible for spreading Dutch elm disease.

*Treatment* Remove and destroy the affected branches. Enrich the soil with phosphorus and potassium. Halfway through spring spray the trunk and branches with parathion and lindane-based insecticides to destroy the adults on the bark and, if necessary, spray again in midsummer. To destroy the larvae, spray at the end of winter with just a thin film of oleoparathion.

### Eelworms
There are several types of eelworm (nematode), and the harmful kind inhibit growth by attacking a plant's root system. They multiply extremely fast.

*Symptoms* Cyst eelworms cause rot and over-development of rootlets. Root-knot eelworms (*Meloidogyne* spp.) attack many garden plants and those grown in a greenhouse. They cause galls on the roots, leading to stunted growth. The leaves turn yellow and the plant may die. Ectoparasitic eelworms arrest growth. There is a gradual

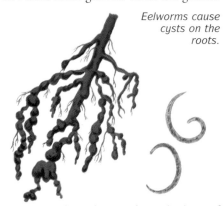

*Eelworms cause cysts on the roots.*

yellowing of the foliage, from the base of the tree to the top. These eelworms may be carriers of viral diseases. Root-lesion eelworms build nests which cause canker in the roots, thereby destroying them. The foliage turns yellow. Fungus may develop.

*Treatment* There is no reliable chemical treatment available to amateur gardeners. Remove and burn all affected plants, and remove and destroy yellowing leaves. Because nematodes are usually found in poorly drained soils, make sure that the growing medium never becomes waterlogged.

Ants are not pests, but they do indicate the presence of aphids, which excrete a sticky substance called honeydew that attracts ants. It is, however, best to get rid of ants by washing the growing medium before planting. Earthworms are not harmful, either, but they should be removed from the compost because they make tunnels in the soil.

## DISEASES

### Powdery mildew
This fungal disease affects trees and shrubs as well as many annuals, perennials and indoor plants.

*Symptoms* Whitish, powdery patches (mycelium) appear on the upper parts of the tree (leaves, stem, flowerbuds). The patches grow larger and the powder thickens. The leaves become distorted. Small black granules may appear on the leaves, which wither. The tree weakens. The fungus thrives in warm, dry conditions.

*Powdery mildew on the leaves of an English oak and a willow.*

*Treatment* Cut away and burn affected branches. Remove dead leaves. Spray with a fungicide, such as benomyl, dinocap or triforine. Water the plant thoroughly and apply a mulch of garden compost. Avoid nitrogenous fertilizers. If the tree had mildew the year before, preventive treatment must be carried out in spring, before the buds open. Sulphur (applied as a dust) is particularly useful for this purpose.

### Honey fungus

This serious condition is caused by caused by fungal mycelium. It can develop if the tree is wounded during pruning or if it is pierced by insects.
*Symptoms* The roots turn brown and

*Honey fungus on an Acer*     *The infected roots.*

wither. White patches (mycelium) and black threads (rhizomorphs) can be seen under the bark. Shoots are stunted, the leaves (or needles) drop, the branches die and the tree withers. In the autumn yellow-capped fungi with brown scales and white gills appear at the base. Patches spread over the tree.
*Treatment* As soon as the first symptoms appear, remove and destroy dead and dying plants. Sterilize the soil with Armillatox. However, this disease is hard to eradicate and the tree may die.

### Root rot

*Symptoms* Rot and canker develop on the roots and collar of the tree. As a result, the root system may be reduced in size. The

rot is brown and spongy. The foliage changes colour, becoming brown and dry. Conifer needles drop. The tree may then wither very quickly.
*Treatment* Do not let the container stand in water and if necessary improve the drainage of the container. Avoid damaging the collar of the tree. If necessary disinfect the soil. Burn badly infected plants. There are no suitable chemical controls available to amateurs.

*Root rot on a cypress.*

### Rust

This is a fungal disease affecting both foliage and stems.
*Symptoms* In late spring long yellow patches appear on the bark of young shoots. Blisters develop and then burst, releasing an orange substance. Resin flows from the wounds. The branch grows in an S-shape. The shoot may wither and growth is thereby disrupted. The leaves become

*Rust on pine and on a magnolia leaf.*

covered with yellow or brown patches and then wither.

Red patches appear on conifer needles: red patches develop on the needles. In the second year, in mid- to late spring white vesicles on the needles burst open, releasing an orange powder, and then heal. In the third year new vesicles develop and the needles eventually drop.
*Treatment* Cut away and burn affected parts and clean the wounds. Spray with special antirust fungicide such as myclobutanil or mancozeb. This may be repeated 10 to 15 days later. Follow the

manufacturer's instructions and take care that you do not apply too large doses because the chemicals can damage the tree.

### Leaf spot

*Symptoms* Round, oval or (sometimes) triangular spots appear on the leaves. They may be white, turning brown, or they may be grey, with black circles developing on the lesions. Parts of the foliage wither and the leaves fall prematurely.
*Treatment* Remove and destroy diseased leaves. Spray plants with a copper-based fungicide (such as Bordeaux mixture) or benomyl. Avoid moistening the leaves too much and do not mist and water in direct sunlight.

### *Verticillium* wilt

This disease is caused by a fungus that penetrates damaged areas and attacks the roots and collar of the tree.
*Symptoms* Leaves wilt at the base of the tree. They turn yellow and shrivel up. The tree weakens. The sap cannot adequately feed the upper parts of the tree.
*Treatment* Avoid using too much nitrogenous fertilizer. Remove weeds. Attend carefully to any damaged parts of the tree. Destroy dead leaves. Disinfect the soil and spray the trunk and neck of the tree with mineral-based fungicides.

If you are unsure about the symptoms or the cause of any problem, seek professional advice. On the whole, however, bonsai are rarely troubled by serious outbreaks of pests and diseases. Gardeners who observe high standards of hygene and who keep both their plants and their tools and equipment clean and tidy are unlikely to experience anything worse than the occasional infestation of aphids.

*Verticillium wilt on the leaves of a lime*

# TREES SUITABLE FOR TRAINING AS BONSAI

# JAPANESE MAPLE

Aceraceae. Deciduous. The Japanese maple is native to Japan, and it is particularly attractive because of the variety of colours provided by the foliage throughout the year. Even in winter, when there are no leaves, it is still beautiful because of the way the branches are held. Its leaves are opposite and finely cut. The fruit is a double key, made up of two seeds held in a membranous wing. The foliage is generally green, but it can be variegated in shades of green and white or green and pink. Some forms have purple-pink or purple foliage in spring, and in autumn the leaves turn every shade of yellow, orange, red and brown. In summer the foliage tends to turn green. There are so many varieties and cultivars that they cannot all be named here.

## SPECIES

*Acer palmatum* 'Asahi-zuru' When they are young, the variegated leaves are green and white or green and pinkish-white.

*Acer palmatum* 'Aureum' The five-lobed leaves of this upright tree turn yellow in autumn but are always edged with pink.

*Acer palmatum* 'Deshôjô' In spring the leaves are blood red, but they turn green in late spring until autumn, when the tree displays brilliant autumn colours.

*Acer palmatum* var. *dissectum* Atropurpureum Group The deep reddish-purple, finely divided leaves look like lace.

*Acer palmatum* 'Rubrum' This form has dark reddish-purple, palmate leaves, which open from red buds. It takes its autumn tints early, when the foliage turns red. It is rich in sugar, which explains why the leaf colour is more intense the more sun there is.

*Acer palmatum* 'Seigen' This is similar to *A. p.* 'Deshôjô', but the leaves are pinkish-red.

*Acer palmatum* 'Tamahime' The small, light green leaves deepen in colour a few weeks after they have unfurled.

## PROPAGATION

**Seed** Collect the seeds when the fruit has fallen. Clean them and spread them out to dry. Only seeds with a green embryo are of any use. Separate the seeds from the wings and store them in a dry place. Before planting them in early spring, lay them between layers of sharp sand for three days. Plant in a cold frame, protecting the young shoots from frost. Keep the new shoots dry in summer. When they are two years old, replant them in spring.

**Simple layering** Choose a young branch and strip leaves from the part to be buried. Lay it lengthways in a depression in the soil in early spring. Make notches in the stem to encourage roots to form. Cover with soil, which must be kept slightly damp. This method is slow (you have to wait for two years) and does not always work.

**Air layering** In mid-spring use a sharp, clean knife to make a notch in the bark of the trunk or branch to be layered. Sprinkle hormone rooting powder in the slit and wedge it open with a ball of moss or a piece of gravel. Wrap the cut with damp sphagnum moss and cover this with a plastic bag. Make this covering airtight and then cover the plastic with a piece of hessian or sacking or with aluminium foil to protect it from direct sunlight and to stop it getting overheated. New roots will appear by the following spring. Cut through the layer, pot carefully and place in the shade.

**Cuttings** Take cuttings in early summer from either a full-sized or a bonsai tree.

Shakan

Kengai

Tachiki

Han-Kengai

Sekijôju

Sôkan

Kabudachi

Ikadabuki

Netsunagari

Sôju

Sambon-Yose

Gohon-Yose

Nanahon-Yose

Kyûhon-Yose

Yose-Ue

Yamayori

Tsukami-Yose

Bonkei

STYLES

Strip off a thin layer of bark and cut off the tip. Insert the cutting in a mixture of two parts peat to one part sand, dipping the cutting in hormone rooting compound before inserting the slip. Make sure the compost can drain freely to prevent water stagnating. This method gives good results.

**Grafting** Always choose a rootstock that belongs to the same group as the variety to be grafted to avoid incompatibility (the varieties and cultivars actually belong to a number of different groups). See pages 21–3 for more information.
*Side veneer grafting* This is the most usual method and is usually carried out in late winter or summer.
*Shield budding onto woody branches* This can be done from early summer. Do not select a rootstock that has grown too large or the bark will have covered the growth buds. Graft onto wood produced that year. If a first graft fails, you can try again in late summer.
*Veneer grafting* In late summer choose a rootstock that is pencil thick. The scions are woody, one-year-old side branches. Paint with a sealing compound. Keep in moist conditions in a greenhouse. The graft should have knitted within four weeks. Open to the air. Wait another year before the top of the rootstock can be cut off.
*Whip-and-tongue grafting* This method is most often used with fruit trees and should be done in early spring. Sloping cuts are made in both the rootstock and scion, which are slotted together so that the cambium layers of both rootstock and scion are in contact.

## CARE

**Sunlight** Grow *A. palmatum* in sun or partial shade. Do not grow in direct sun, which can scorch the tips of the leaves, although it can tolerate greater exposure to the sun as long as the base of the roots is kept moist.

**Temperature** Protect from frosts below -3°C (27°F). *A. palmatum* will not thrive in dry heat.

Acer palmatum 'Deshôjô' (Japanese maple): 15 years old; 20cm (8in) high; Shakan style. Photographed in mid-spring. From mid-spring to early summer the leaves are blood red. In summer they tend to become green before turning a shimmering, fiery orange in autumn.

**Ventilation** Protect from cold, drying winds. Good ventilation around the tree helps to prevent powdery mildew from developing in summer.

**Container** Plant an *A. palmatum* bonsai in a flat, elongated bowl to allow the roots to spread and benefit from summer warmth. Oval containers are most usual, although they are sometimes rectangular, and brown, willow green, light blue and beige are the most appropriate colours. Good drainage is essential.

**Regular maintenance** After the leaves have fallen, remove dead leaves from the soil or from the tree. At the onset of winter, remove any dead branches.

# Acer palmatum

### Leaf pruning a Japanese maple

**1** *The leaves of this* Acer palmatum *(Japanese maple) should be completely pinched out.*

**2** *Use leaf clippers or scissors to remove most of the foliage.*

**3** *Special leaf clippers, are the best tools for leaf pruning an acer.*

**4** *Completely remove all the foliage with clippers.*

**5** *After a few weeks masses of new leaves will appear and these will be smaller than the previous ones.*

**Growth** Japanese maples are slow-growing plants.

**Repotting** Repot about every third year in spring; every second year for young specimens. Prune the roots to half their length, if necessary washing them in water. Be careful to remove dead or damaged rootlets and old roots.

**Soil** Use a mixture of two parts loam to one part sharp sand. *A. palmatum* will not develop fully in soil that is too alkaline; it prefers dry, even stony, well-compacted, chalky soil.

**Pruning**
*Pinching back* Prune terminal branches to leave only two nodes, and laterals to just one node. Wait for the shoots to grow and pinch them out again. Pinching out the new shoots before they become too long makes it possible to shape the tree gently without leaving scars.
*Leaf pruning* Cutting off the leaves allows you to achieve a tree with thick, bushy, small foliage, tapering at the tips. Do not strip a tree of its leaves in the same year as it is repotted nor if it is weakly. Leaf stripping should be done in early summer;

Acer palmatum (Japanese maple):
15–50 years old; 80cm (32in) high;
Gohon-Yose style. Photographed in
early summer.

leaf cutting is done during the growing period, usually every second year.

*Pruning branches* During the growing period prune the branches so that only one or two pairs of leaves are left on each side branch. When a branch is growing too fast, prune it, and remove the buds and leaves from the part that is left.

*Structural pruning* This is done in winter when the tree is bare. Study its outline, then use secateurs to make a concave cut flush with the trunk to remove any branches that are crossing, any that are growing vertically near the trunk or any that are parallel to the trunk. Leave only every second branch. Good structural pruning leads to better branch growth in spring.

**Wiring** *Acer palmatum* is generally shaped by pruning, but it is sometimes necessary to use wire. When you wire, protect the bark with raffia because it is fragile and will be damaged by copper wire. Wire the tree when it is in full leaf and remove the wire after six months.

**Watering** Water sparingly. *A. palmatum* can be allowed to become dry between waterings but needs constant humidity on the surface of the roots. Be careful, however, because excessive water will cause the roots to rot.

**Misting** The foliage needs a damp atmosphere, so it should be misted frequently, especially if it is exposed to a drying wind or to direct sun.

**Feeding** In spring and autumn apply a slow-release, organic fertilizer. Wait for two months after repotting and do not feed a weakened tree.

## PESTS AND DISEASES

### PESTS

#### Gall mites
*Symptoms* Red or light green pimples or spikes appear on the upper surface of the foliage, while the undersides are felted with beige, grey or brown. A thick down causes the leaves to crinkle and become distorted. Galls (abnormal growths) can be seen on the leaves.
*Treatment* Remove and burn affected leaves. There is no effective chemical treatment, but spray with a parathion- or lindane-based insecticide or, if the attack is severe, with lime sulphur.

**Bark beetles** See page 34.

**Goat and leopard moths** See page 33.

**Geometer moth** See page 33.

**Bombyx and owlet moths** See page 33.

#### Leafhoppers
*Symptoms* Pale, coarse spots are visible on the upper surface of leaves, which become discoloured, stem growth slows and the leaves may drop off. The green insects (or their cast-off skins) may be seen on the undersides of leaves. Leafhoppers do not, in themselves, cause serious damage to plants, but they can spread viral diseases.
*Treatment* Cut out affected branches. Spray with permethrin, malathion, pirimiphos-methyl, dimethoate or pyrethrum.

**Scale insects** See page 33.

**Aphids** See page 33.

### DISEASES
**Powdery mildew** See page 34.

#### Canker
*Symptoms* Where there are scars or clefts between branches sores develop, deepening, cracking and swelling and causing the branch to die. Golden-coloured gum oozes from the affected area. Adjacent branches form excrescences as a defence mechanism. When the canker encircles stems or branches, die-back occurs.
*Treatment* Cut out and burn diseased branches, applying wound-sealant paint to the cuts. Spray with a copper-based fungicide in late summer to early autumn. Badly affected trees should be completely destroyed.

#### Coral spot
*Symptoms* This disease is caused by a fungus (*Nectria cinnabarina*). Branches and laterals suddenly die back. Dead bark is covered with orange-pink spots, and if the fungus enters living tissues, the plant may die completely.
*Treatment* Cut out and burn diseased material. Sterilize your tools. Dab a copper-based fungicide on the wounds and check that the compost is not waterlogged.

#### Witches' brooms
*Symptoms* This fungal disease causes a mass of stems and shoots to appear from a single point.
*Treatment* Cut out diseased branches at least 15cm (6in) below the affected point.

#### Tar spot
*Symptoms* This is a fungal disease causing yellow patches on the upper surface of the leaves. The patches turn black or reddish-brown.
*Treatment* Remove and burn affected leaves. Add nitrogen to the fertilizer. Guard against the disease by spraying with a copper-based fungicide or bupirimate and triforine. Spray again when the buds are opening.

#### Die-back
*Symptoms* Shoots and young branches wither, usually from the tips. Cankers form on branches.
*Treatment* Cut out and burn diseased or dead branches.

#### Cercospora
*Symptoms* This fungal disease causes brown patches to appear on the shoots of young trees, and the trees gradually wilt.
*Treatment* Spray with a copper-based fungicide or zineb.

**Verticillium wilt** See page 35.

**Leaf spot** (fungal) See page 35.

#### Anthracnose
*Symptoms* In spring or during wet, mild summers leaves curl and become discoloured before falling. Die-back may follow severe attacks.
*Treatment* Cut out infected shoots and burn. Burn affected leaves. Spray with a copper-based fungicide.

**Honey fungus** See page 35.

**Leaf pruning**
*Leaves that have grown
too large must be removed.*

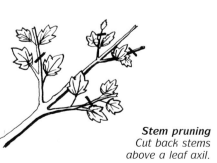

**Stem pruning**
*Cut back stems
above a leaf axil.*

# Trident maple, Three-toothed maple

Aceraceae. Deciduous. Native to the cool temperate areas of China, Korea and Japan, *Acer buergerianum* (syn. *A. trifidum*) can grow to a height of 12m (40ft). The tree's straight, light beige trunk loses its bark in patches as it grows old. The three-lobed leaves are glossy green in spring and summer, and yellow-orange, even red, in autumn. The fruit is a winged key.

## Propagation

**Seed** Collect the seeds, clean them, dry them and sow them at the end of autumn. They can also be stored between layers of sharp sand (stratified) and kept in a cool place. Plant in a warm place. Protect the young shoots from frost. Replant seedlings in spring of their second year.

**Cuttings** Take cuttings in early summer. Strip off a thin layer of bark and dip in hormone rooting compound before planting in a mixture of two parts peat and one part sand. Pinch out the tip. Make sure that the compost is free-draining because waterlogged roots can be fatal. *A. trifidum* roots easily.

**Air layering** In mid-spring use a clean, sharp knife to make a cut through the bark in the part to be layered. Sprinkle the area with hormone rooting powder and wedge the slit open with a twist of moss or a pebble. Pack moist sphagnum moss around the layer and wrap polythene around the whole area, making airtight seals at each end. New roots should appear the following spring. Carefully cut through the layer and pot it up. The new tree will remain delicate for a year.

**Simple layering** This method is slower and does not give as good results as air layering. Follow the procedure outlined on page 20.

## Care

**Sunlight** Although this acer tolerates full sun, in areas with strong sunshine it should be placed in partial shade in summer.

### SPECIES

*Acer monspessulanum* (Montpellier maple) This species is naturalized in countries that border the Mediterranean, but it is native to Iran and west Asia. It is variable, but usually grows to 12m (40ft). It grows quite quickly and has a rather bushy habit, with a rounded crown. The three-lobed leaves are to 20cm (8in) across; they are dark, glossy green above and light green below. Greenish-yellow, honey-scented flowers, which are borne in pendent racemes, are followed by the red-winged fruit. The bark is dark grey with brown stripes. There are several forms and naturally occurring varieties, which differ largely in the size of their leaves.

**Temperature** *A. buergerianum* must be protected from frost, but it can withstand high temperatures.

**Ventilation** This will withstand winds, and it does need to have plenty of air circulating around it. In Japan, where it is planted along roads as an ornamental tree, it withstands pollution well.

**Container** Use a fairly deep pot unless the acer is planted over stone or in a group. The pot can be rectangular or oval, and earthy colours are usually chosen.

**Regular maintenance** Make sure that all leaves fall at the end of the autumn. Clear away dead leaves and wood to prevent any attack by parasites or diseases. Brush the trunk gently.

Chokkan
Shakan
Kengai
Bankan
Tachiki
Han-Kengai
Bunjingi
Neagari
Sekijôju
Ishitsuki
Sôkan
Kabudachi
Korabuki
Ikadabuki
Netsunagari
Sôju
Sambon-Yose
Gohon-Yose
Nanahon-Yose
Kyûhon-Yose
Yose-Ue
Yamayori
Tsukami-Yose
Bonkei

**STYLES**

by a third of their length to maintain the tree's shape.

*Structural pruning* Cut back the branches in late winter, well before the growing season, to improve the branch structure. Remove any branches that mar the tree's appearance.

**Wiring** The shape of *A. buergerianum* is largely produced by pruning, but it may be necessary to wire the tree to perfect some styles. Wiring is carried out from early to late summer to avoid breaking the branches, and the bark must be protected with raffia.

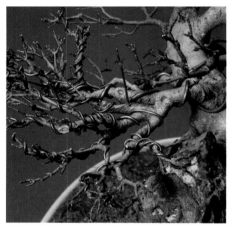

*It is possible to see the wiring quite clearly on this* Acer buergerianum, *which was photographed in winter.*

**Watering** Water freely from spring until autumn, but less frequently and less copiously in winter.

**Misting** Mist the leaves in spring and summer, but never in full sun. Misting will help to rid the foliage of possible parasites.

**Feeding** Feed from early spring to late autumn (but not in mid- and late summer) with a slow-release, organic fertilizer. Wait six weeks after repotting, and do not feed a tree that is in poor condition.

## PESTS AND DISEASES

*Acer buergerianum* is susceptible to the same pests and diseases as *A. palmatum* (see page 41).

**Growth** Young trees grow quickly, but as they mature acers grow more slowly.

**Repotting** Every second or third year repot into a larger container. Cut away between one-half and two-thirds of the root hairs and take care to remove all damaged or dead roots.

**Soil** Use a mixture of two parts loam to one part sharp sand. Any dry, stony, chalky soil is suitable, but avoid using excessively alkaline compost.

**Pruning**
*Pinching back* Pinch back the terminal shoots, leaving only two nodes on each

*Acer buergerianum (syn.* A. trifidum; *trident maple, three-toothed maple): 18 years old; 40cm (16in) high; Yose-Ue and Sekijôju styles. Photographed in late spring. It is difficult to say which style dominates in this planting of acers. A group of acers (Yose-Ue) has been planted on a rock so that the roots are displayed on the rock (Sekijôju)*

side branch. When new shoots appear, repeat the process.

*Leaf pruning* From spring to autumn prune the leaves, which will otherwise become too large. *A. buergerianum* is seldom stripped of its leaves.

*Pruning branches* Prune the side branches hard, generally reducing them

# AMPELOPSIS

Vitaceae. Deciduous. This is a genus containing 25 species, which are native to woodlands in North America and to eastern Asia. They are ornamental climbers with bark that does not peel away. The leaves have three, occasionally five, lobes, and they are bright green, glossier on the underside, and can be variegated with cream. The yellowish-green flowers are borne in cymes. Fruit forms in early to mid-autumn, but it is not edible.

## PROPAGATION

**Seed** Pick the fruit when it is ripe. Remove the seeds, wash, dry and stratify them. Plant in spring under glass or in a greenhouse.

**Cuttings** In spring, after bud burst but before the new leaves have hardened, take a cutting, cut off the tip and plant it in a warm, well-lit place.

**Simple layering** In mid- or late spring in a greenhouse or in a light, warm room.

## CARE

**Sunlight** Ampelopsis requires a lot of light, particularly the variegated forms.

**Temperature** These plants are not reliably hardy. They do best in a conservatory and in winter need temperatures that do not fall below about 12°C (54°F).

**Ventilation** Ampelopsis cannot tolerate draughts, but it must be in a well-ventilated position.

**Container** Choose a pot of medium depth. Glazed containers are appropriate.

**Regular maintenance** Keep the foliage free of dust, which blocks the pores. When the leaves fall, remove all the dead and withered leaves. Cut away any suckers and shoots that arise from the base of the trunk.

**Growth** Ampelopsis grows slowly but steadily. Stems are reluctant to divide.

**Repotting** Every second year in mid-spring prune the roots by a half and pot up into a larger container if necessary.

### SPECIES

*Ampelopsis brevipedunculata* This is a vigorous climber, with jointed stems. The bright green, three-lobed leaves are glossy on the undersides. The grape-like fruits appear in autumn and are at first purplish-pink but later turn bright blue.

**Soil** Use a mixture of equal parts leaf mould, ericaceous compost, loam and sharp sand. The soil must be cool.

**Pruning**
*Pruning branches* When the tree is in leaf allow side branches to grow to three to five growth buds, then cut back, leaving only one or two buds. Repeat throughout the growing season. At the final autumn pruning, leave the side branches a little longer.
*Leaf pruning* You can strip a perfectly healthy tree of its leaves in late spring or early summer so that it will produce denser foliage with smaller leaves.
*Structural pruning* In midwinter, when the tree is bare, prune out untidy or damaged stems that are superfluous to the overall shape.

**Wiring** It is seldom necessary to use wire, but when it is, wire from spring to summer. Start coiling the wire when the new shoots have hardened.

**Watering** Water requirements vary according to light and heat. Give more water in summer. Cut down on watering when the leaves have fallen.

**Misting** Mist the leaves and trunk daily. Do not mist when the tree is in sunlight.

Shakan

Kengai

Bankan

Tachiki

Fukinagashi

Neagari

Han-Kengai

Sekijôju

Ishitsuki

Nejikan

Takozukuri

Sôkan

Kabudachi

STYLES

*Ampelopsis brevipedunculata 'Elegans': 10 years old; 15cm (6in) high; Neagari style. Photographed in mid-autumn. The variegation in the foliage disappears with successive prunings.*

**Feeding** In spring and autumn apply a slow-release, organic fertilizer. Do not feed a plant that is sickly or has been recently repotted.

# PESTS AND DISEASES

## PESTS
**Scale insects** See page 33.

**Aphids** See page 33.

## DISEASES
**Downy mildew**
*Symptoms* The fungus causes yellow patches on the upperside of the leaves, and a white fur covers the underside. The leaves drop off.
*Treatment* Cut out and burn diseased leaves. Spray with a copper-based fungicide.

**Black rot**
*Symptoms* This is a fungal disease causing brownish-red patches on the leaves. Black specks appear on the patches.
*Treatment* Cut out and burn diseased leaves. Spray with a copper-based fungicide.

# ARALIA

Araliaceae. Deciduous or evergreen. The species of this genus are found in Asia, Malaysia and North, Central and South America, and many have been re-classified and are now found under *Schefflera* (see pages 170–71) and other genera. Aralias are grown for their large, often divided leaves. The white or greenish-white flowers are often followed by round black fruits.

## PROPAGATION

**Seed** Sow seed in autumn in a dark, warm room. Keep the soil moist. This method is tricky and the results are uncertain.

**Root cuttings** The best way to propagate aralias is from a root cutting. Cut off roots that are about 10cm (4in) long. Plant these in autumn in a mixture of equal parts sand and humus in an unheated greenhouse. Leave in a seed box for a year, then replant the following spring.

**Tip cuttings** Tip cuttings should be taken in a heated greenhouse where high levels of humidity can be maintained.

**Air layering** Air layering can be done in spring in a warm room. It is important that the layer is not allowed to dry out.

## CARE

**Sunlight** As long as they have relatively good light, aralias have no special needs. Do not place them in direct sun.

**Temperature** The winter temperature should not fall below 16°C (61°F). Aralias like humid heat.

**Ventilation** Keep aralias out of draughts, but it is important that air can circulate freely around the plants.

**Container** Choose a flat dish or one of medium depth; it can be glazed or unglazed.

**Regular maintenance** Remove any of the branches that have turned yellow and any shoots that are growing out from the trunk.

**Growth** Growth is slow; it takes four or five years for the trunk to develop.

**Repotting** Every second year in mid-spring you should prune the roots by

---

### SPECIES

*Aralia* 'Blacky' This is a new form. It is a shrub of upright habit with quite a large trunk. Thick, dark green leaves, with fairly smooth edges, are scroll shaped and corrugated.
*Dizygotheca castor* (syn. *Aralia castor*) A species that is similar to *Schefflera elegantissima* but has smaller leaves.
*Polyscias fruticosa* (ming aralia) An erect shrub or small tree, to 8m (26ft), with woody branches and whitish bark.
*Schefflera elegantissima* (syn. *Aralia elegantissima, Dizygotheca elegantissima*) A shrub with linear, toothed leaves that are dark green marbled with white and slightly drooping. The branches are straight and erect.

---

between one-third and one-half and repot into a larger, well-drained container.

**Soil** Use a mixture of equal parts leaf mould, ericaceous compost, sharp sand and loam. The soil must be fertile, light and cool.

**Pruning**
*Pruning side branches* Keep cutting the branches back to two pairs of leaves as soon as they have four or five. Leave them a little longer at the final autumn pruning.
*Leaf pruning* Use scissors to cut off any leaves that are too large.
*Pruning branches* To get a good spread of branches, you can cut back all the branches at the start of the growing season. Put the bonsai in a greenhouse or in a plastic bag to encourage buds to form.

**Wiring** This is seldom necessary with aralias. It can be done throughout the year, but it is easier to wire in warm conditions, when the wood of the branches is more flexible.

**Watering** Water freely. Keep the compost damp. Good drainage is essential so that water does not stagnate around the roots.

---

Shakan

Tachiki

Han-Kengai

Neagari

Sekijôju

Nejikan

Ishitsuki

Sabamiki

Sôkan

Takozukuri

Korabuki

Ikadabuki

Kabudachi

Netsunagari

Sambon-Yose

Sôju

Yose-Ue

Tsukami-Yose

Plantations saisonnières

Bonkei

Dizygotheca castor *(syn.* Aralia castor*):*
*8 years old; 25cm (10in) high; Tachiki*
*style. Photographed in early summer.*

## PESTS AND DISEASES

### PESTS

**Eelworms and root-knot eelworms** See page 34.

**Tarsonemid mites**
*Symptoms* The tiny mites, which are especially prevalent in warm countries, feed on concealed parts of the plant, causing the foliage to discolour and become distorted. The leaves fail to develop, and the plant fails to thrive.
*Treatment* Although dusting with powdered sulphur may help, there is no effective chemical control. Good hygiene is the best protection.

**Glasshouse red spider mites** See page 32.

**Soft scale insects** See page 33.

### DISEASES
**Verticillium wilt** See page 35.

**Root rot** See page 35.

**Alternariose**
*Symptoms* This is a fungal disease, causing oily patches on the leaves, and these are sometimes ringed with red. The branches become discoloured near the nodes, and the upper part of the branch may wither. Black specks form on the diseased parts.
*Treatment* Cut out diseased branches. Spray with maneb-based fungicide.

**Bacterial canker**
*Symptoms* Small brown spots appear on the leaves in spring, and uneven holes form. Golden-coloured gum oozes from lesions on infected shoots.
*Treatment* Cut out and burn the diseased branches. Spray with Bordeaux mixture.

**Misting** Mist the foliage daily with rainwater to maintain a high level of moisture in the atmosphere, which is essential for aralias to thrive.

**Feeding** In spring and autumn apply a slow-release, organic fertilizer. If the tree is in good condition, give it one application of liquid fertilizer in winter.

# ARAUCARIA

Araucariaceae. Evergreen conifer. Native to the southern hemisphere, these are big, geometrical trees, which can grow to 70m (230ft). They have straight trunks, with branches in regular tiers. The cones are their characteristic feature. The needle-shaped, tapering leaves curve upwards.

## PROPAGATION

**Seed** Sow ripe seed in mid- or late spring in small seed boxes in seed compost in a warm place. Germination is slow. Keep the soil moist. Plant out the seedlings after about two years.

**Cuttings** Take cuttings from terminal shoots, never from laterals. Cut the growing tip off a branch and plant it in sandy compost. At first, leave it in a cold frame, then move to a warm place to allow the new roots to develop.

## CARE

**Sunlight** Keep out from full sun. Araucarias prefer a shady, but well-lit position.

**Temperature** *Araucaria heterophylla* likes heat all year round. In winter the temperature must not be allowed to fall below 17°C (63°F).

Araucaria heterophylla *(syn.* A. excelsa; *Norfolk Island pine): 10 years old; 25cm (10in) high; Sôju style. Photographed in early to midsummer. The branches can be cut back as long as you take care that the tips do not turn brown.*

### SPECIES

*Araucaria heterophylla* (syn. *A excelsa*; Norfolk Island pine) This evergreen is native to Norfolk Island in the Pacific Ocean. It has a pyramid-shaped crown and overlapping, needle-shaped, green leaves.

**Ventilation** This araucaria dislikes draughts. However, it should be kept in a well-ventilated room.

**Container** Use a fairly flat or medium-deep container. Glazed pots are sometimes used, but decorated ones are rarely seen.

**Regular maintenance** Remove any yellowing twigs, helping them to drop, and place the leafy part of the tree under the shower to remove any dust that has settled on the needles.

**Growth** Slow but steady.

**Repotting** Every second year in spring prune the roots by a half and repot into a larger container.

**Soil** Use a mixture of equal parts ericaceous compost, leaf mould, loam and sharp sand. Araucarias do best in deep, dry, sandy soil that is free draining.

**Pruning**
*Pinching back* Pinch the young shoots between your thumb and index finger in mid- to late spring to shorten them.
*Pruning branches* If necessary, at the start of the growing season reshape the outline of the tree by carefully pruning the branches.
*Leaf pruning* Do not leaf prune araucarias. The leaves are so small that this would be futile.

**Wiring** Although araucarias can be wired at any time of year, avoid wiring when the shoots are soft. Do not leave wire on the tree for more than four months.

Chokkan
Tachiki
Shakan
Han-Kengai
Fukinagashi
Bunjingi
Sekijôju
Ishitsuki
Sabamiki
Sôkan
Kabudachi
Korabuki
Ikadabuki
Sôju
Sambon-Yose
Gohon-Yose
Nanahon-Yose
Kyûhon-Yose
Yose-Ue
Tsukami-Yose
Bonkei
Plantations saisonnières

STYLES

Araucaria heterophylla *(syn. A. excelsa; Norfolk Island pine): 50 years old; 35cm (14in) high; Han-Kengai style. Photographed in mid-autumn. This outstanding specimen was photographed in Taiwan at an exhibition organized by a society of bonsai enthusiasts.*

**Watering** Water regularly, allowing the soil to dry out well between waterings. Araucarias prefer dry soil, and the compost must drain freely.

**Misting** Mist daily to provide the humid conditions in which araucarias thrive.

**Feeding** Feed with a slow-release, organic fertilizer in spring and autumn.

## PESTS AND DISEASES

### PESTS
**Glasshouse red spider mites** See page 32.

**Red spider mites** See page 32.

**Scale insects** See page 33.

**Mealy bugs** See page 33.

### DISEASES
**Honey fungus** See page 35.

**Chlorosis**
*Symptoms* The needles turn yellow along the edges or near the ribs. New needles are discoloured.
*Treatment* Apply nitrogen, iron, magnesium and zinc to the soil. Do not give too much calcium, sodium or water. Keep out of draughts and protect from cold. Keep away from noxious gases. Place in the light. Mist the foliage

# BAMBOO

Gramineae. Evergreen. This is a large genus of more than 100 species, which are native to woodlands of the temperate zones of Asia, Africa and Central and South America. The bamboo is a giant grass, with some species growing to a height of over 30m (100ft). These are long-lived plants – some species can live for 100 years. The culms (canes), which are woody and often hollow, are nodose and grow in bunches, while the sheaths are evergreen and auriculate.

Some bamboos bear flowers at irregular intervals, sometimes as long as 100 years apart, and the flowering stems die after flowering. The Incas of Central America knew how to use bamboo, and in Asia, of course, it is valued not only for the dried canes but also as food. It symbolizes wisdom and, like cedar, has the value of bending without breaking. Buddhists use it to help them achieve inner peace. In China bamboo is a symbol of honesty, of eternal youth (from its evergreen foliage) and of healthy old age (from the erect stems). In Vietnam it is regarded as mankind's brother.

## PROPAGATION

**Division** Select a rhizome (a multiple one if you want a mass of stems) that is growing horizontally, with closely spaced growing points. Dig up a rhizome that is already growing well. Leave a healthy shoot on it, with root hairs growing from the nodes. The shoot left on the rhizome should be two years old. It will be removed a year later, when new shoots have appeared. Plant the rhizome in mid-spring, before new shoots have sprouted, plant in a deep pot and keep the soil moist. Prune away half of each sheath from the new growth.

## CARE

**Sunlight** The bamboo needs a lot of light, but should not be in direct sun.

**Temperature** These plants need humid heat throughout the year. In winter the temperature should not fall below 19°C (66°F).

**Ventilation** Keep out of draughts, but position the plants where air can circulate freely around them.

**Container** Select a fairly deep pot. Some pots are decorated with bamboo leaves,

### SPECIES

***Bambusa multiplex*** (syn. *B. glaucescens*; hedge bamboo) This half-hardy species, native to China, has fine stems with small, elongated, mid-green leaves. In the wild it grows to 15m (50ft).

***Bambusa ventricosa*** (Buddha's belly bamboo) The common name is derived from the swollen internodes that appear on the canes. This tender plant, native to south China, will grow to 25m (80ft) or more in the wild and 2.4m (8ft) or more in a normal container. The internodes swell in poor conditions.

and one of these would be ideal. A brown or reddish-brown, unglazed pot is to be preferred. A group of stems should be planted in a flat bowl.

**Regular maintenance** Bamboos produce yellow leaves, and these should be removed. Remove shoots growing from the trunk.

**Growth** Fast growing in spring. A stem will develop within months or even weeks.

Chokkan

Tachiki

Sôkan

Kabudachi

Ishitsuki

Korabuki

Kyûhon-Yose

Sambon-Yose

Tsukami-Yose

Gohon-Yose

Sôju

Nanahon-Yose

Yose-Ue

Yamayori

Plantations saisonnières

Bonkei

Kusamono

*Bambusa ventriccsa (Buddha's belly bamboo): 35cm (14in) high; Tachiki style. Photographed in late autumn. The age of the bonsai is immaterial because the main trunk forms in a single year, and its height and diameter do not change thereafter.*

**Pruning** If you want a single-stemmed bamboo, remove all new growth every spring. Prune with an upward-sloping cut. At the point where each node emerges, prune the sheath by a half. When the shape has been established, use your hands to pull emerging shoots out of their sheaths before they develop to keep the bonsai compact.

**Wiring** Bamboos can be wired to form the initial shape, but when plants are established they do not need further wiring.

**Watering** Water copiously and often, and make sure that water, and make sure that water penetrates right down to the roots. Do not allow the soil to become waterlogged, however, and make sure that the container can drain freely. Keep the surface of the compost moist.

**Misting** Mist the foliage daily. Bamboos like a humid atmosphere.

**Feeding** In spring and autumn apply a slow-release, organic fertilizer.

## PESTS AND DISEASES

### PESTS
**Aphids** See page 33.
**Mealy bugs** See page 33.

### DISEASES
**Melancolium culm** (bamboo smut)
*Symptoms* Canes that have been badly tended turn black at the base, and the discoloration climbs up between the internodes.
*Treatment* Cut out the damaged canes and rhizomes until you reach sound material. Disinfect the wound with sulphur.

Note: There is a danger that a bamboo will produce a great many yellow, drooping leaves if the soil around the roots becomes waterlogged. It is essential that the growing medium is well drained. Good drainage, frequent watering and good levels of light should prevent discoloration of the leaves.

**Repotting** Between late spring and early autumn every second or third year repot into new compost, spreading the roots right through the pot. Make sure that you use the whole surface area of the container.

**Soil** Use a mixture of two parts loam, one part leaf mould and one part sharp sand. Bamboos prefer deep, slightly damp soil.

# BARBERRY

Berberidaceae. Deciduous or evergreen. This is a large genus, which includes about 450 species of shrubs. They are native to Europe, North Africa, America and central and eastern Asia and have a range of sizes and habits. The evergreen shrubs have green leaves, but the deciduous species have green or purple leaves and bright autumn colours. The leaves are generally oval or broadly obovate, and they may be smooth or have spiny edges. The stems are spiny, and the leaves are borne in the spine axils. The flowers are yellow to orange-red, and the berries that follow the flowers in autumn are in a variety of colours.

## PROPAGATION

**Seed** Clean the seeds after harvesting and stratify them. Sow in spring. Germination is rapid, and shoots will appear quickly. Pot up straight away.

**Cuttings** Take softwood cuttings in early summer. Evergreen species are grown from hardwood cuttings taken in late summer or early autumn so that they do not rot. Remove the thorns and cut off leaves, but leave the growth buds on the cutting. Evergreen species take longer to form roots. Wait until the following spring before repotting.

**Air layering** In spring (see page 20).

**Young nursery stock** See page 18.

## CARE

**Sunlight** Deciduous species like sun and need good light if the leaves are to achieve their vivid colours. Evergreen species prefer partial shade.

**Temperature** The species mentioned above are hardy; some species, however – *B. hypokerina*, for example – need protection from prolonged winter cold.

**Ventilation** Berberis have no special requirements.

**Container** In the wild these plants grow in fairly shallow soil, so it is not necessary to choose a very deep pot. However, do not choose a container that is too shallow or the overall proportions of the plant will look wrong. Try to choose a colour that will harmonize with the tones of the foliage and flowers.

**Regular maintenance** Remove the dead leaves from the tree and surface of the compost. Remove some fruit if there is heavy crop and remove berries as soon as they shrivel.

**Growth** The rate of growth varies according to species. *B. verruculosa* grows

---

### SPECIES

*Berberis darwinii* A vigorous evergreen shrub, native to Chile and Argentina, this bear racemes of golden-yellow flowers in spring. The flowers are followed by blue-black fruits.

*Berberis thunbergii* Native to Japan, this deciduous shrub has a compact habit. The smooth leaves are green, but cultivars have red or purple leaves. The red- and orange-tinged yellow flowers are followed by glossy red berries.

*Berberis verruculosa* This compact, evergreen shrub is native to China. The arching stems are covered with warts and thorns. The leaves are compact and shiny. The golden-yellow flowers are followed by blackish-purple fruits.

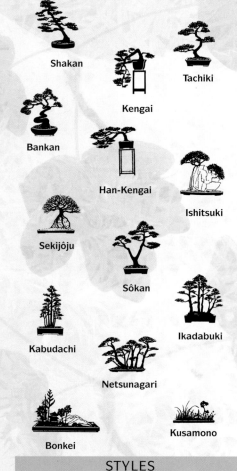

Shakan

Tachiki

Kengai

Bankan

Han-Kengai

Ishitsuki

Sekijôju

Sôkan

Kabudachi

Ikadabuki

Netsunagari

Bonkei

Kusamono

STYLES

more slowly than the fast-growing *B. thunbergii* and the vigorous *B. darwinii*.

**Repotting** In early spring every year or every second year repot into a larger container. Prune the roots by between one-third and one-half.

**Soil** Use a mixture of equal parts loam and leaf mould. Berberis will grow in any soil, even if it is dry and shallow, but does not like wet compost.

**Pruning**
*Pruning sub-branches* Pruning is done after flowering. Berberis bear flowers on one-year-old shoots coming off two-year-old wood. If you prune too early, it will not flower.
*Pruning branches* Cut back branches that have grown a lot. Keep shortening new shoots until early autumn.

**Wiring** This can be done at any time of the year, but do not leave copper wire in position for more than a few months.

**Watering** Water more freely in warm weather. Allow the compost to dry out well between waterings. Berberis dislike damp conditions.

**Misting** In summer mist the foliage lightly to increase the humidity around the plant. Do not mist when the plants are in flower.

**Feeding** Do not feed until flowering has finished for the year; flowers appear in spring and continue intermittently until late autumn. Apply a slow-release, organic fertilizer. Do not feed non-flowering plants in mid- or late summer nor for six to eight weeks after repotting. Do not feed a weak tree.

Berberis thunbergii f. atropurpurea: 10 years old; 20cm (8in) high. Photographed in early summer.

## PESTS AND DISEASES

### PESTS
**Sawflies**
*Symptoms* Leaves are eaten by yellow-spotted white grubs, and black insects may be seen.
*Treatment* Pick off and kill the larvae and spray with a lindane-based insecticide.

**Aphids** See page 33.

### DISEASES
**Powdery mildew** See page 34.

**Verticillium wilt** See page 35.

# BIRCH

Betulaceae. Deciduous. Native to the temperate and cold areas of the northern hemisphere, there are about 60 species of trees and shrubs in the genus and they are found in a wide range of habitats. They are elegant and graceful plants, and some species have attractively peeling bark. The toothed leaves are usually oval or triangular, and the catkins are light yellowish-brown, the male catkins being longer than the female ones. The leaves assume attractive shades of golden-brown in autumn.

## PROPAGATION

**Seed** Collect seeds between late summer and late autumn. They are ripe when the cones are yellow, but they do not all ripen at the same time. Spread the seeds out, and dry them by turning them over and over. Once they are dry, keep them in a bag in a cool, airy place. Sow in early to mid-spring on moist soil, covering the ground with twigs to protect the seeds. Keep the compost damp. Germination gets under way in four weeks. Water the seedlings, which appear within eight weeks, as necessary. Remove the twigs and make sure

Shakan

Tachiki

Sôkan

Kabudachi

Ikadabuki

Netsunagari

Sambon-Yose

Sôju

Gohon-Yose

Nanahon-Yose

Kyûhon-Yose

Yose-Ue

Yamayori

Tsukami-Yose

that the bed does not dry out. Pot up the following spring.

**Grafting** This is rarely used because the graft union can be seen for a long time. It is useful only when a new variety is being propagated or when you can obtain a bonsai by no other means. See pages 21–3 for more information.
*Inarching* In early summer, using old wood (see page 22).
*Shield budding* In late summer or early autumn using two shields, or late spring to early summer when the stock is in growth.

**Young nursery stock** See page 18.

# CARE

**Sunlight** Birches like to be in a sunny position; they need a lot of light.

**Temperature** Birches do best in warm, dry places, but all species are fully hardy.

**Ventilation** Birches will tolerate quite strong winds, but they do best in open, but sheltered positions.

**Container** Choose a shallow or flat container, preferably reddish-brown or blue.

**Regular maintenance** Remove any dead material. Take care that moss does not grow up the trunk. Remove any shoots coming out of the trunk.

**Growth** Birches are fast growing.

**Repotting** Repot into a larger container every second year. Prune the roots by between one-half and two-thirds. Leave some of the old earth on the roots when repotting to help the tree to re-establish.

**Soil** Use a mixture of two parts loam, one part sharp sand and one part leaf mould. Birches like light, cool, friable earth, but they will tolerate soil that is acid, poor, sandy or stony.

**Pruning**
*Pruning shoots* From early spring to late autumn throughout the growing season. After each side branch has produced three to five nodes, use scissors to cut back to one or two.

*Betula pendula (syn. B. verrucosa; silver birch): 25 years old; 40cm (16in) high; Neijikan style. Photographed in late spring. It is important to allow the branches to develop fully before pruning the foliage.*

*Pruning branches* During the growing season, when the birch starts to lose its basic shape, prune the branches hard back. Cut above the point where a leaf breaks.
*Structural pruning* This is done only early on, when the tree is being created. It should subsequently be avoided because birches do not like being pruned.

**Wiring** The shape is mainly produced by cutting back new shoots. When it is essential to wire to achieve certain styles, protect the bark with raffia. Wire in spring and summer.

**Watering** Birches need light but frequent watering. *Betula pubescens*, *B. mandsburica* var. *japonica* and *B. tauschii* need more water than *B. pendula*.

**Misting** Birches prefer a fairly dry atmosphere and do not need to be misted except in very hot weather.

**Feeding** From spring to autumn (except in early to midsummer) apply a slow-release, organic fertilizer. Do not feed for two months after repotting nor if the tree is in poor condition.

## SPECIES

***Betula pendula*** (syn. *B. verrucosa*; silver birch) The old specific name arises from the white warts on the branches. The diamond-shaped, toothed leaves are mid-green, turning bright yellow in autumn. Catkins appear in early spring. The bark is golden-brown when it is young, later becoming silvery white, and it peels off in thin layers.
***Betula pubescens*** (downy birch) This birch, which is native across central Europe to Siberia, will tolerate poor, acid soil. It is grown for its peeling bark and yellowish-brown catkins.

# PESTS AND DISEASES

## PESTS
**Birch leaf mining sawflies**
*Symptoms* Leaves and shoots are gnawed and eggs can be seen in the veins. The leaves are curled into a cigar shape.
*Treatment* Pick off and burn the rolled-up leaves. Spray with liquid derris or fenitrothion.

**Bark beetles** See page 34.

**Wasp moth**
*Symptoms* The damage is similar to that done by tortrix moths. The bark on the trunk and branches is gnawed and holes can be seen. Galleries run from the holes, and piles of sawdust can be seen under the holes. Caterpillars are sometimes seen.
*Treatment* Push a wire through the galleries to kill the caterpillars.

**Geometer moth** See page 33.

**Bombyx moth** See page 33.

## DISEASES
**Powdery mildew** See page 34.

**Leaf blight**
*Symptoms* White swellings appear on the leaves, which tear and shrivel.

*Treatment* Burn dead leaves. Spray with a copper- or thiram-based wash in spring and autumn.

**Witches' brooms**
*Symptoms* This fungal disease causes a mass of stems and shoots to appear from a single point.
*Treatment* Cut out diseased branches at least 15cm (6in) below the affected point.

**Leaf spot** See page 35.

**Canker**
*Symptoms* Sores develop if there are scars or clefts between branches, and these deepen, crack and swell, causing the branch to die. Golden-coloured gum oozes from the affected area. Adjacent branches form excrescences as a defence mechanism. When the canker encircles stems or branches, die-back occurs.
*Treatment* Cut out and burn diseased branches, applying wound paint to the cuts. Spray with a copper-based fungicide in late summer to early autumn. Badly affected trees should be burned completely.

**Honey fungus** See page 35.

# BOUGAINVILLEA

Nyctaginaceae. Evergreen or deciduous. This genus of 14 tender species of trees, shrubs and thorny climbers is native to South America. The alternate leaves are ovate to elliptic. The insignificant flowers, are surrounded by large, showy bracts, producing the typical 'flowers' for which these plants are grown.

## PROPAGATION

**Cuttings** Take softwood cuttings in spring. Lightly strip off the bark and insert the cutting in a mixture of equal parts loam and peat. Make sure the container is well crocked. Remove the tip. Place in a warm, light position. In winter put in a cold greenhouse or in a light, unheated room. Repot the following spring.

**Air layering** Use an older shrub for this (see page 20).

## CARE

**Sunlight** Grow bougainvilleas in full sun and good light.

**Temperature** These plants likes warmth, and although they can be grown outdoors in warm areas, they should be grown in a conservatory in frost-prone gardens. Plants that are stood outdoors in summer need a winter temperature of 12–16°C (54–61°F) if they are to flower the following year.

**Ventilation** Keep out of draughts, although plants grown outdoors can withstand a warm wind.

**Container** Choose a fairly deep dish, to which plenty of crocks can be added to improve the drainage. It is a good idea to cover the bottom with a layer of crocks and to add a layer of gravel above this. You can use a glazed, decorated pot, but choose a colour that will complement the colour of the flowers.

**Regular maintenance** Remove flowers as soon as they wither.

**Growth** Fast to begin with, but growth will slow down somewhat when the plant is grown in a pot.

**Repotting** Every second year in mid- to late spring prune the roots to half their length and repot into a larger container.

### SPECIES

***Bougainvillea glabra*** (paper flower) A species from Brazil, this evergreen climber has elliptic, mid- to dark green leaves. It is the parent plant of many cultivars. 'Golden Glow' has warm, pink-tinged yellow bracts, 'Mrs Butt' has deep red bracts, and 'Alexandra' has magenta bracts.

***Bougainvillea*** 'Pixie' (syn. *B.* 'Mini-Thai') This semi-evergreen cultivar originated in Taiwan. It is a shrubby bush, with light grey bark on young stems. It bears masses of violet-coloured flowers.

***Bougainvillea spectabilis*** This evergreen or semi-evergreen species, which is native to Brazil, will grow to 12m (40ft). The stems are thorny, and the light green leaves are downy. Pink or purple bracts appear from early spring to early summer. Cultivars have been developed with carmine or brick-red bracts, and there is also a variegated (green-cream) form.

**Soil** Use a mixture of equal parts ericaceous compost, leaf mould, loam and sharp sand. Bougainvilleas like rich, well-drained soil that is not too heavy.

**Pruning**
*Pinching back* Pinch back hard after flowering to keep the bonsai compact and shrubby.
*Pruning sub-branches* After flowering cut all side branches back to two or three growth buds.
*Pruning branches* In winter when there are fewer leaves on the stems prune overlong branches to keep the overall shape. Remove dead or damaged branches in late winter.

Shakan

Kengai

Bankan

Tachiki

Han-Kengai

Sharimiki

Bunjingi

Fukinagashi

Ishitsuki

Neagari

Nejikan

Sabamiki

Hôkidachi

Sôkan

Kabudachi

Sôju

Korabuki

**STYLES**

Bougainvillea spectabilis: *10 years old; 40cm (16in) high; Tachiki style. Photographed in late spring. This plant will continue to flower throughout spring and summer. There is sometimes a second flush of blooms in autumn.*

**Wiring** Wire woody branches, but leave the wire in place for no more than three to five months.

**Watering** Water often and regularly, but not too freely, because bougainvilleas lose their leaves when they are overwatered. In summer water daily. Just before flowering give no water for at least a week to encourage flower buds to form. Limit watering while there are flowers, and begin watering freely again when the flowers are over.

**Misting** Mist the foliage daily, but do not mist when plants are in flower.

**Feeding** After flowering and in autumn apply a slow-release, organic fertilizer about once a fortnight. Alternate liquid fertilizer with solid fertilizer.

## PESTS AND DISEASES

### PESTS
**Greenfly** See page 33.

**Scale insects** See page 33.

### DISEASES
**Chlorosis**
*Symptoms* The existing leaves gradually turn yellow, and new leaves are small and discoloured.
*Treatment* Add iron, nitrogen, magnesium and zinc to the soil. Do not give too much sodium, calcium or water. Keep out of draughts and protect from cold. Keep away from noxious gases. Place in the light. Mist the foliage.

# BOX

Buxaceae. Evergreen. The genus contains about 70 long-lived shrubs and trees, which are found in Europe, Asia, Africa and Central America. Box plants tend to be dense, and they are often grown for their ability to withstand clipping and topiarizing. The small, opposite leaves are smooth and almost round. Insignificant yellowish-green flowers are borne in spring. The species described here are not hardy.

## PROPAGATION

**Cuttings** Take cuttings of semi-ripe wood in late summer to early autumn. Plant in a mixture of equal parts peat and sand in a cold frame or in the open garden. It is also possible to take cuttings in early spring before bud break. Pot up the following spring, when the young plants are well rooted.

## CARE

**Sunlight** Place the species listed above near a window in good light. In warm gardens they can be kept outdoors in summer, when they should stand in partial shade.

**Temperature** These species like warmth, and in winter the temperature should not drop below 12°C (54°F).

**Ventilation** Keep these species out of draughts. If they are kept outside in summer, they should be protected from strong, drying wind.

**Container** Use a deep pot so that the tree is really stable.

**Regular maintenance** Do not hesitate to remove any yellowing leaves by hand.

**Growth** These are slow-growing plants.

**Repotting** Every second year in mid- to late spring prune the roots by a half and repot into a larger container.

**Soil** Use a mixture of equal parts ericaceous compost, leaf mould, loam and sharp sand. The soil should not be too dry, but box plants have no special requirements when it comes to soil type and will tolerate some lime.

---

### SPECIES

*Buxus harlandii* This semi-tender, slow-growing shrub is native to south China and Hong Kong. It grows to about 1.5m (5ft). It has an upright habit, and a greyish trunk. The tiny, bright green leaves are evergreen. (This is not the same plant as the hardy *B. microphylla* var. *japonica*.)
*Buxus sinica* (syn. *B. microphylla* var. *sinica*) This species, native to China, has very hard, light brown wood, and small, round, glossy, leathery leaves.

---

**Pruning**
*Pruning sub-branches* Cut back new growth to two pairs of leaves as soon as shoots have produced five or six throughout the growing season.
*Leaf pruning* The leaves are too small for this even to be attempted.
*Structural pruning* In late spring box can be cut back hard to improve its shape. Take the opportunity to remove all dead or damaged stems.

**Wiring** Box can be wired at any time of year but do not leave the wire in place for more than two months.

**Watering** Water fairly generously, but allow the soil to dry out before giving more water. If the tree is in a cool room in winter, give slightly less water. Give the soil and roots a thorough soaking and then allow to dry out.

**Misting** Mist the foliage daily.

**Feeding** Apply a slow-release, organic fertilizer, in spring and in autumn, alternating liquid and solid forms. In winter, if the temperature is around 22°C (72°F), feed once.

Chokkan

Shakan

Tachiki

Nejikan

Sôkan

Sambon-Yose

Sôju

Buxus harlandii *(box): 12 years old; 15cm (6in) high; Tachiki style. Photographed in early summer. As soon as the soft young shoots start to lengthen, it is important to cut them back regularly.*

## PESTS AND DISEASES

### PESTS
**Blackfly and greenfly** See page 33.

**Red spider mites** See page 32.

### DISEASES
**Honey fungus** See page 35.

**Rust** See page 35.

# CAMELLIA

Theaceae. Evergreen. This genus contains 250 species, found in acid soil throughout northern India and Burma to China and Japan. Most of the best known species and cultivars are hardy, but some are tender. The leaves are usually dark, glossy green, and the lovely flowers, sometimes scented, are white or in shades of pink or red.

## PROPAGATION

**Seed** Immerse the seeds in water and plant only those that sink after they have been left to soak for 24 hours in warm water to soften the outer casing, which should be removed at the point when the seed is to be planted. Sow in a heated greenhouse. Germination is quick.

*Camellia: 15 years old; 35cm (14in) high; Tachiki style. Photographed in midsummer.*

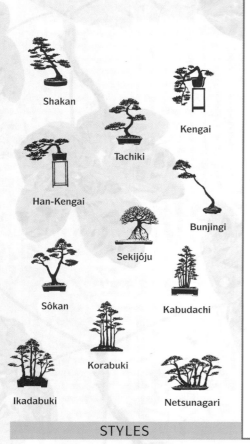

Shakan
Kengai
Tachiki
Han-Kengai
Bunjingi
Sekijóju
Sôkan
Kabudachi
Korabuki
Ikadabuki
Netsunagari

**Cuttings** In mid- or late winter root tip cuttings or stems with three leaves; alternatively, in mid- or late summer take semi-ripe cuttings. Plant in a mixture of one part ericaceous compost and two parts sand. Keep in a warm place. Roots should form within six weeks.

**Air layering** In spring (see page 20).

**Young nursery stock** See page 18.

# CARE

**Sunlight** Camellias need light to produce flowers but do best in partial shade. Avoid sudden changes in the amount of sunlight to which the plants are exposed.

**Temperature** Avoid sudden changes from warm to cold. Most camellias will withstand frosts to -12°C (10°F) provided that they do not last long. Remove snow from the foliage, which could be damaged by frost. Camellias prefer mild weather and need warmth to produce flowers.

**Ventilation** Keep sheltered from the cold wind but make sure that there is a constant supply of fresh air.

**Container** Try to find a container that complements the flower colour. The bowl should be of medium size and depth. Camellias will thrive in a growing medium that conserves warmth and humidity.

**Regular maintenance** Remove withered flowers, especially if they are white because they will turn brown and detract from the tree's appearance. Remove any dead leaves.

**Growth** Camellias are slow growing.

**Repotting** Repot each year in late spring or very early summer when branches have finished growing and buds have formed. Pot up into a container that is only a little larger than the previous one. Prune the roots lightly.

**Soil** Use a mixture of two parts ericaceous compost, one part leaf mould and one part peat. Camellias will only grow in acid soil and do best in moist, well-drained, humus-rich soil, mixed with topsoil, peat and, possibly, a small amount of sharp sand.

**Pruning**
*Pruning sub-branches* Prune with long-handled clippers when the flowers have faded but before new shoots harden.

**Wiring** Camellias can be wired at any time of the year except early spring. Protect brittle branches with raffia or use wire wrapped in paper. Do not leave wire on the tree for more than a month or two.

**Watering** Water well in summer, especially if it is hot and dry. Reduce the amount of water given in early autumn. Allow the branches to droop for lack of water to encourage flowering, but keep plants moist when the flowers are in bud to prevent the buds from dropping off.

**Misting** Mist the leaves in summer, unless the plants are in full sun and when the camellia is in bud. Do not mist the flowers, which would wither.

**Feeding** Camellias react badly to chemical fertilizers. Feed with a slow-release, organic fertilizer. The best fertilizer is a compost of its own leaves.

# PESTS AND DISEASES

## PESTS
### Vine weevils
*Symptoms* These are a very serious pest of all container-grown plants. The first sign may be the total collapse of the plant, but inspection will show that the roots have been eaten by the brown-headed, white larvae. Adult weevils eat the edges of leaves.
*Treatment* At the first sign of attack, remove the plant from the pot. Remove and kill the larvae. Prune the roots and repot in good soil. Spray with contact insecticide from late spring to midsummer. Under glass, use the parasitic nematode *Heterorhabditis megedis*.

### Scale insects See page 33.

## DISEASES
### Sooty mould
*Symptoms* This fungal problem is associated with sap-feeding insects. Dark brown or black fungus is seen on leaves and stems with a sticky deposit.
*Treatment* Wipe the leaves with a damp cloth. Apply a systemic insecticide, such as dimethoate or pirimicarb.

### Leaf blight
*Symptoms* White swellings appear on the leaves, which tear and shrivel.
*Treatment* Burn dead leaves. Spray with a copper- or thiram-based wash in spring and autumn.

### Mosaic virus
*Symptoms* The leaves become patterned with yellow and may eventually fall.

*Treatment* Once infected, plants cannot be cured and should be burned. The infection is transmitted by sap-sucking insects, so control aphids to prevent infection.

### Chlorosis
*Symptoms* The leaves turn yellow or even white and new leaves are discoloured.
*Treatment* Apply nitrogen, iron, magnesium and zinc to the soil. Do not give too much calcium, sodium or water, and do not expose plants to cold, draughts or noxious gases. Place in good light.

### Scorching
*Symptoms* The leaf surface becomes discoloured, and the leaves turn papery or develop holes, eventually withering and dropping.
*Treatment* Do not mist the foliage in sunlight and protect from direct sun, cold and late frosts. Do not apply fertilizer that is very rich in nitrogen, and protect plants from chemicals, pollution and animals. Do not let fertilizer touch the leaves; apply it at some distance from the trunk. Mist the foliage to clean it and water around the foot of the tree in the evening.

### Blossom wilt
*Symptoms* Brown patches appear on the petals and the flowers wither, although they cling to the stems rather than dropping. Nearby leaves may also be affected.
*Treatment* Remove and burn affected flowers. Spray with a copper-based fungicide.

# CARAGANA, PEA TREE

Leguminosaceae/Papilionaceae. Deciduous or semi-evergreen. Native to eastern Europe and central Asia, including southern Russia, Manchuria and the Himalayas, the genus contains about 80 species of spiny shrubs. Most have alternate, pinnate, rather prickly leaves, which often grow in clusters. The flowers are usually yellow, but may be white or pink.

## PROPAGATION

**Seed** Collect the seeds and soak them for 12 hours in lukewarm water before planting, in late spring, in a warm place in the open. Germination gets under way three weeks later and takes at least two months. Pot up the following spring.

**Cuttings** Take cuttings in midsummer and plant them in a mixture of equal parts sand and peat.

**Air layering** From late spring to early summer (see page 20).

## CARE

**Sunlight** Caraganas like a sunny, well-lit position.

**Temperature** The species are fully hardy and can withstand both heat and cold.

**Ventilation** Keep out of draughts but stand plants in a well-ventilated site.

**Container** Choose a medium-deep pot. Glazed containers are suitable, but decorated ones are seldom used.

**Regular maintenance** Remove yellow leaves, which appear regularly.

**Growth** Slow; but you can quickly show off the roots at the base of the trunk to advantage.

**Repotting** Every two years in spring prune the roots by half and repot into a larger container.

**Soil** Use a mixture of equal parts ericaceous compost, leaf mould, loam and

### SPECIES

*Caragana arborescens* (pea tree) Native to northern Russia and China, this hardy species has a narrow, upright habit and bright green, oblong leaves. It can grow to a height of 6m (20ft). Pale yellow flowers appear in late spring and are followed by brown pods.
*Caragana frutex* (Russian pea shrub) Native to southern Russia and Turkestan, this can grow to 3m (10ft). It has dark green, obovate leaves. The bright yellow flowers are produced in the leaf axils.
*Caragana sinica* (syn. *C. chamlagu*) This shrub, which is native to northern China, grows to about 1m (3ft) tall and has spreading branches and prickly stems. The glossy, dark green leaves are semi-evergreen. Pale yellow, red-flushed flowers are borne in early summer.

sharp sand. Caraganas do well in all types of soil, even calcareous, poor, dry soil.

**Pruning**
*Pruning sub-branches* After flowering prune side branches with clippers, leaving only two or three growth buds. During the growing season allow the side branches to grow to five growth buds, then cut back to two. At the end of autumn any late growth should be cut back hard.
*Leaf pruning* This is not worth attempting because the leaves are so small.
*Structural pruning* At the end of winter cut out dead branches and any that detract from the overall shape.

Shakan

Bankan

Kengai

Tachiki

Fukinagashi

Han-Kengai

Neagari

Sekijôju

Ishitsuki

Nejikan

Sôkan

Kabudachi

Sôju

Korabuki

Yose-Ue

**STYLES**

Caragana arborescens (*pea tree*): 10 years old; 20cm (8in) high; Sôkon style. Photographed in early summer.

**Misting** Mist the leaves daily. Even in winter it is important to mist regularly if the plant is kept in a warm room and has kept its leaves. Do not mist a plant that has shed all its leaves.

**Feeding** In spring and autumn feed once a month with a slow-release, organic fertilizer.

## PESTS AND DISEASES

### PESTS
**Greenfly** See page 33.

**Red spider mites** See page 32.

**Mealy bugs** See page 33.

### DISEASES
**Downy mildew**
*Symptoms* The fungi cause yellow blotches on the upperside of the leaves, and a white fur covers the underside. The leaves eventually drop off.
*Treatment* Cut out and burn diseased leaves. Spray with a copper-based fungicide. Improve the circulation of air around plants.

Note: In general, if the leaves turn yellow, wither and fall, it is because of overwatering. If the tree becomes etiolated, it is not getting enough light.

**Wiring** This can be done throughout the year, but try not to wire new shoots until they have hardened. Do not leave wire in place for more than six weeks.

**Watering** Caraganas tolerate drought, and you should allow the soil to dry out between waterings. Give a little more water in summer and in winter.

# CARMONA

Boraginaceae. Evergreen. This genus contains one species, *Carmona retusa*; however, the related genera, *Cordia* and *Ehretia*, contain similar plants, and species once included in *Carmona* have been reallocated among other genera. Cordia, for example, contains about 300 deciduous and evergreen species, including shrubs, trees and climbers, which are native to Central and South America, tropical Africa, the Middle East and Asia. *Cordia alliodora* (cypre, salmwood) is valued for its timber, which is used in tropical America for furniture and house-building. *Ehretia elliptica* is used to make the handles of farming implements in Mexico. *E.dicksonii*, which grows to 10m (33ft), has attractive grey-brown bark and glossy green leaves.

The species, which is native to south Asia, grows to a height of about 10m (33ft). The grey bark has a cracked surface, and the dark green leaves are oval, pilose on the upper surface, and lighter and reticulate underneath. Cymes of scented, white flowers appear in early summer.

## PROPAGATION

**Cuttings** Cuttings taken from small branches are propagated in a greenhouse, preferably in spring.

## CARE

**Sunlight** Carmonas need a light, sunny position. When it is outdoors in summer, place the bonsai in partial shade.

**Temperature** Keep warm. In winter the temperature should not fall below 17°C (63°F). It can be put outside in summer in warm gardens.

**Ventilation** Carmonas must be protected from draughts, but they must be in well-ventilated rooms.

**Container** Choose a fairly deep pot; it can be glazed or unglazed.

**Regular maintenance** Remove any yellow leaves from the tree. Also remove any shoots growing out from the trunk and any suckers.

**Growth** Relatively fast when the tree is young.

### SPECIES

*Carmona retusa* (syn. *Ehretia microphylla*) In some countries the small leaves are used to make a type of tea.

*Ehretia macrophylla* This is a deciduous tree or shrub, native to the Himalayas and China, which will grow to 6m (20ft). The long, oval leaves are toothed and covered in bristles on both surfaces. Panicles of white flowers are borne in summer.

**Repotting** Every second year in mid-spring prune the roots to about half their length and pot up into a slightly larger container.

**Soil** Use a mixture of equal parts ericaceous compost, leaf mould, loam and sharp sand. Carmonas like a fertile soil.

**Pruning**
*Pruning sub-branches* Reduce young laterals to two or three leaves as soon as

Chokkan

Shakan

Bankan

Kengai

Tachiki

Han-Kengai

Bunjingi

Sharimiki

Fukinagashi

Neagari

Sekijôju

Ishitsuki

Nejikan

Sabamiki

Sôkan

Korabuki

Kabudachi

Ikadabuki

Netsunagari

Sôju

Sambon-Yose

Gohon-Yose

Nanahon-Yose

Kyûhon-Yose

Yose-Ue

Bonkei

**STYLES**

Carmona retusa *(syn.* Ehretia *microphylla): 70 years old; 80cm (32in) high; Neijikan style. Photographed in early spring.*

leave wire in position for more than eight weeks at a time.

**Watering** Water freely all year round but allow to dry out between waterings. Give less water after pruning or repotting.

**Misting** Mist the foliage daily.

**Feeding** From early spring to early autumn feed with a slow-release, organic fertilizer. Do not feed from mid- to late summer. Perfectly healthy trees can be given one application of fertilizer in winter.

## PESTS AND DISEASES

### PESTS
**Scale insects** See page 33.

**Mealy bugs** See page 33.

**Aphids** See page 33.

**Glasshouse red spider mites** See page 32.

**Snails**
*Symptoms* Presence of slimy trails and eaten leaves and young shoots.
*Treatment* Do not let the soil get too wet and remove dead and dying leaves. Pick off the snails and scatter methiocarb or metaldehyde pellets on the soil.

### DISEASES
**Chlorosis**
*Symptoms* The leaves gradually turn yellow or white, and new leaves are small and discoloured.
*Treatment* Apply iron, nitrogen, magnesium and zinc to the soil. Do not give too much sodium, calcium or water. Keep out of draughts and protect from cold. Keep away from noxious gases. Place in the light. Mist the foliage.

Note: If the plant's leaves turn yellow and fall, there is too much water in the soil. If it becomes etiolated, it is not getting enough light.

they have produced six or seven. Continue to do this throughout the growing season.
*Pruning branches* This should be done in late winter before growth restarts. Get rid of dead or damaged branches or any that are too long.

**Wiring** Shaping is mainly achieved through the regular pruning of sub-branches. However, carmonas can be wired at any time of year except when the branches have not yet hardened. Do not

# HORNBEAM

Corylaceae. Deciduous. This is a genus of about 35 hardy species, which are native to the temperate areas of the northern hemisphere: Europe, central and eastern Asia and the northern Himalayas, and North America. Hornbeams, which are often used for hedging, have toothed or entire, oval leaves with prominent veins. Flowers take the form of male or female catkins, and in autumn female catkins develop into clusters of winged seeds. In the garden you are most likely to find *Carpinus betula* (common hornbeam), of which there are many attractive cultivars.

## PROPAGATION

**Seed** Collect seeds when they are ripe and sow straightaway. If this is not possible, stratify the seeds and plant them the following late winter or very early spring. Germination will take place in late spring. When you sow dried seeds in late winter, they may take a year to germinate. Protect seedlings from late frosts.

**Cuttings** In spring, when you are pruning, take greenwood cuttings and lightly strip off the bark. Dip in hormone rooting compound, remove the growing tip and plant in a mixture of equal parts sand and peat. Protect from cold.

**Air layering** In spring, using a fairly slender branch (see page 20).

Carpinus laxiflora: *between 7 and 20 years old; 45cm (18in) high; Yose-Ue style. Photographed in midsummer.*

**Grafting** If a hornbeam cannot be propagated by any other method, try side veneer grafting in winter in a greenhouse, using two-year-old wood.

**Young nursery stock** Hornbeams respond well to being cut back hard and to regular pruning (see page 18).

### SPECIES

*Carpinus coreana* This species is native to Korea. It has pendulous branches and brownish young shoots.
*Carpinus japonica* (Japanese hornbeam) This beautiful trees bears elongated, markedly corrugated leaves.
*Carpinus laxiflora* This tree, which is native to Korea and Japan, bears small, glossy, slightly leathery leaves.

Shakan

Han-Kengai

Tachiki

Sekijôju

Nejikan

Sôkan

Kabudachi

Sôju

Sambon-Yose

Gohon-Yose

Nanahon-Yose

Kyûhon-Yose

Yose-Ue

STYLES

*Carpinus betulus var. carpinizza: 40 years old; 60cm (24in) high; Tachiki style. Photographed in early spring. The catkins (inflorescences) appear just before the leaves. The smooth, greyish-white bark is specific to this variety.*

any dead or damaged roots.

**Soil** Use a mixture of two parts loam and one part coarse sand. Hornbeams do best in cool, damp, clayey soil but will tolerate lime and will grow in poor soil.

**Pruning**
*Pruning branches* Use clippers to cut back side branches as soon as four or five pairs of leaves have been produced, leaving one or two pairs on each lateral.
*Structural pruning* At the end of winter prune hard to maintain a neat shape and encourage the production of well-balanced branches. Hornbeams respond well to pruning.

**Wiring** The shape is produced mainly by pruning, but if necessary wire in spring and summer.

**Watering** Water freely, especially from mid-spring to mid-autumn, but there must be good drainage so that the compost does not become waterlogged. The compost should be moist, but not sodden.

**Misting** Mist the foliage in summer to wash dirt and possible insect infestations from the leaves.

**Feeding** Feed in spring and in autumn with a slow-release, organic fertilizer. Do not feed from mid- to late summer. Leave for two months after repotting. Give no fertilizer to a tree that is in poor condition.

## PESTS AND DISEASES

### PESTS
**Red spider mites** See page 32.

**Geometer moth** See page 33.

**Bombyx moth** See page 33.

### DISEASES
**Powdery mildew** See page 34.

**Leaf spot** See page 35.

## CARE

**Sunlight** Young specimens need shade. Hornbeams are naturally woodland trees and do not like full summer sun, although they will tolerate sun during the rest of the year.

**Temperature** Hornbeams are fully hardy trees, and they withstand frost and heat equally well.

**Ventilation** Hornbeams are often used as hedging and withstand wind.

**Container** There are no special requirements. Hornbeams adapt to a flat container when grown in a multi-stemmed style.

**Regular maintenance** Remove dead leaves from the branches and soil in autumn. Do not let moss form on the base of the trunk.

**Growth** These are slow-growing trees.

**Repotting** In early spring every second or third year repot into a larger container. Prune the roots by at least half and remove

# CEDAR

Pinaceae. Evergreen conifer. This a small genus of four species. Cedars are fully hardy, large, long-lived trees, which can grow to 40m (130ft) or more. They are native to the Himalayas and countries of the Mediterranean littoral. The foliage takes the form of needle-like leaves, which are borne in clusters on short side shoots. In autumn upright, egg-shaped cones appear. These have a smooth surface, with wide but thin scales that fit tightly over one another.

## PROPAGATION

**Seed** The seed is gathered in winter from the cones when the lower scales lift. Soak the seeds in water for 48 hours to soften them, then plant in a mixture of peat and loam. Keep the seeds in the cones until they are planted. Seed can also be planted in late spring, after being stratified for about three weeks, when it will germinate more readily. When the seed has germinated, pot up saplings after a year. To get a straight trunk, stake the one-year-old sapling when it is first potted up.

**Simple layering** Layer a low branch in spring. Strip off the needles of the section to be buried and make a shallow cut into the bark to encourage rooting. Bury the branch and keep the earth damp. When the section has developed roots, sever the layer and pot it up. Protect the young plant from extremes of weather as you would a bonsai that has just been repotted.

**Cuttings** Cuttings can be taken in late spring or in autumn. Short hardwood cuttings are taken in autumn and kept in a greenhouse. In a warm place roots will form in winter, and the plantlets can be transplanted the following spring into small pots containing a mixture of peat and loam.

**Grafting** Side veneer grafting can be carried out in early to mid-autumn.

**Young nursery stock** See page 18.

## CARE

**Sunlight** Cedars will tolerate full sun throughout the year, but protect young specimens from extremes of light and shade.

**Temperature** Although full-sized cedars are hardy, plants in containers are sensitive to extreme cold and can die in periods of prolonged frost. It is vital to protect container-grown plants directly it becomes cold, especially in the root area. In gardens that are not prone to prolonged frosts, however, plants can be left outdoors all year round.

**Ventilation** Cedars will tolerate wind, but not draughts. Protect young specimens and trees that have just been repotted from strong winds.

**Container** A medium-deep pot is suitable for young trees, which are slow growing. A mature tree needs a wide, deep container. They look best in glazed or unglazed

### SPECIES

*Cedrus atlantica* (syn. *C. libani* subsp. *atlantica*; Atlas cedar) Native to the Atlas Mountains, this has a pyramidal shape, and the branches often hang down.

*Cedrus brevifolia* (syn. *C. libani* subsp. *brevifolia*; Cyprus cedar) This bears small, dark green needles with silvery grey highlights.

*Cedrus deodora* (deodar, Himalayan cedar) Native to the western Himalayas, this has a broadly pyramidal outline. The bark is brown or black. The branches are rather pendulous and bear sparse, light green, glaucous foliage.

*Cedrus libani* (cedar of Lebanon) Now found mainly in Syria and Turkey, this has spreading, horizontal branches and silvery grey or dark green needles. The stout trunk has very dark grey or brown bark, which is scored by numerous fissures.

Chokkan

Sekijôju

Sôkan

Sabamiki

Kabudachi

Sambon-Yose

Sôju

Gohon-Yose

Kyûhon-Yose

Nanahon-Yose

STYLES

*Cedrus deodora (deodar, Himalayan cedar): 15 years old; 40cm (16cm) high; semi-cascade style (this is similar to the weeping habit that is seen in trees that are grown in the garden). Photographed in late spring or early summer.*

containers that are brown, brick or another neutral colour.

**Regular maintenance** In autumn pick off any yellow needles. Make sure that you prune away and remove any dead or damaged stems from inside the tree so that it develops well. Remove any dead leaves or twigs from the soil's surface.

**Growth** Like most conifers, cedars are slow growing. The majestic habit develops with age.

**Repotting** Repot every three to five years in early to mid-spring. Prune the roots by between one-third and one-half. Keep some of the old soil when you repot. Cedars are hard to re-establish if their roots are uncovered when they are transplanted.

**Soil** Use a mixture of equal parts leaf mould, loam and sharp sand. Cedars tolerate calcareous soil, but will thrive in any soil provided it is not too wet. They do best in humus-rich, moist but well-drained, slightly acid soil.

**Pruning**
*Pinching back* In spring use your fingers to pinch back new shoots hard. Do not cut the needles. In summer remove new shoots.
*Leaf pruning* The needles of conifers are never cut. Remove a third of the foliage on each branch as necessary.
*Pruning branches* In autumn take off the tips of any branches that have grown a lot. In spring prune branches that tend to spread by cutting just above a cluster of needles.

**Wiring** Cedars have to be wired if you want to train them into specific shapes. The outline should be established by pinching back and pruning. Put the wire in position in autumn and remove the copper wires 10–12 months later. If the wire has grown into the bark, do not pull it out but carefully remove any bits that are accessible using pliers. Repeat this process annually until you have achieved the desired shape. Do not allow needles to become trapped between the wire and the bark.

**Watering** Water freely in spring and summer. Give the plant time to absorb all the moisture from the soil before watering again because cedars do not like wet

compost. Water less frequently in autumn. In winter, in very wet weather, prop up the container at an angle so that water does not stand on the surface of the compost.

**Misting** In summer mist the foliage thoroughly. Cedars like humidity around the needles. Misting also helps to clean the trunk and needles of dust and dirt, although cedars are relatively unaffected by pollution.

**Feeding** Feed once a month in spring and autumn with an organic fertilizer. Increase the amount given in autumn to build up the plant for winter. Do not feed a cedar that has just been repotted for two months, and do not feed one that is in poor condition.

## PESTS AND DISEASES

### PESTS
**Bark beetles** See page 34.
**Pine sawfly**
*Symptoms* The caterpillars attach silky nests to the needles in winter. The needles are eaten, leading to defoliation. The branches may be distorted.
*Treatment* Remove the caterpillars and their nests. Burn badly infested branches. Apply a fungicide, such as malathion, pyrethrum, permethrin or fenitrothion.

### DISEASES
**Honey fungus** See page 35.

# NETTLE TREE, HACKBERRY

Ulmaceae. Deciduous or evergreen. This is a genus containing more than 70 species of trees and shrubs, most of which are native to tropical or subtropical zones, but about 15 hardy species are native to the temperate zones of the northern hemisphere.

## PROPAGATION

**Seed** Collect the seeds when they are ripe and stratify for a year. Plant in spring, although germination will be patchy. Keep the soil moist until the seeds have germinated.

**Cuttings** In summer take softwood cuttings and dip in hormone rooting compound. Remove the growing tip before planting.

**Air layering** Strip the bark off the section to be layered. Make a slit in the stem to encourage rooting and keep it partly open. Wrap damp sphagnum moss around the cut. Cover with polythene and make airtight so that it cannot dry out. Sever the stems when roots have formed. Pot up and protect from frost.

## CARE

**Sunlight** Nettle trees do best in sun or partial shade; in cooler areas they will grow in full sun.

**Temperature** *Celtis occidentalis* is fully hardy, but other container-grown plants will need protection form frosts. They like warmth.

**Ventilation** Plants must have good air circulation around them, but they should not be exposed to strong or prolonged winds.

**Container** Nettle trees need deep earth, so choose a fairly deep pot.

**Regular maintenance** Take care to remove all dead leaves in autumn. Remove any moss that forms on the trunk.

**Growth** These are slow-growing plants, achieving 3m (10ft) in 20 years.

**Repotting** In early spring about every three years, repot into a larger container.

Prune the roots by between one-third and one-half and remove any dead, damaged or old roots.

**Soil** Use a mixture of two parts loam and one part coarse sand. These trees thrive in light, rich, cool soil; they do not like heavy, badly drained soil. In cooler areas they will grow in calcareous, dry and stony soil.

**Pruning**
*Pruning shoots* This is done from spring until the end of summer. Wait until new shoots have three or four nodes, then use scissors to cut back to one or two. Take out any shoots that are about to burst into growth.
*Pruning sub-branches* Cut back branches that are too long to achieve a good framework. Prune at the leaf axils and two new shoots will branch out. These should be left with a single pair of leaves.

*Celtis formosanum (hackberry): 90 years old; 60cm (24in) high; Sabamiki style. Photographed in mid-autumn. Fissures in the trunk make the tree look especially old.*

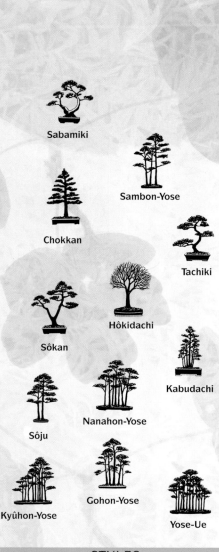

Sabamiki

Sambon-Yose

Chokkan

Tachiki

Hôkidachi

Sôkan

Kabudachi

Nanahon-Yose

Sôju

Kyûhon-Yose

Gohon-Yose

Yose-Ue

STYLES

*Celtis australis* (southern nettle tree). Native to the Mediterranean littoral and southwest Asia, this long-lived, deciduous tree grows to about 20m (65ft). It has a short, grooved trunk and a rounded, bushy crown. The lower branches are horizontal. The long, pointed leaves are asymmetric, oblique and smooth at the base, sometimes dentate, and they are dark green above and grey and downy underneath. Red fruit ripens to purplish-brown in mid-autumn.

*Celtis occidentalis* (hackberry, sugarberry) This is a spreading, deciduous tree, native to North America, which will grow to 15m (50ft). The ovate leaves, which are sharply toothed, are glossy green above and paler below. The yellow or red fruits ripen to purple in autumn.

*Celtis sinensis* (Japanese hackberry) The large, deciduous leaves are oval, shiny and dark green, and there are red-orange decorative, edible fruits. The tree has spreading habit and can grow to about 12m (40ft) or more.

Celtis australis *(southern nettle tree): 20 years old; 18cm (7in) high. This was grown in an unusual combination of two styles, Chokkan and Hôkidachi.*

*Pruning branches* Do this in early or mid-spring, before growth gets under way.

**Wiring** The shape should be developed mainly by pruning shoots, sub-branches and branches, but wiring can be done from spring to autumn. Protect branches with raffia.

**Watering** Water freely in hot weather, allowing the soil to dry out well between waterings. Nettle trees will not do well in wet soil.

**Misting** Sprinkle water on the foliage when you water the tree.

**Feeding** From spring to autumn apply a slow-release, organic fertilizer, in pellet or in liquid form. Do not feed from mid- to late summer or if the tree is weak. A liberal application of fertilizer will harden the branches and make them stronger.

## PESTS AND DISEASES

### PESTS
**Mites** See page 32.

**Bark beetles** See page 34.

**Bombyx moth** See page 33.

**Greenfly and gall-forming aphids** See page 33.

### DISEASES
**Mosaic virus**
*Symptoms* The leaves become mottled and streaked with yellow, and old leaves turn yellow and drop off. The disease's virulence varies according to climate and environment. It is not a common problem.
*Treatment* Destroy all infected plants. There is no chemical cure for mosaic virus, and the only possible way to avoid infection is to apply insecticides that will control the aphids that spread the virus.

**Elm disease**
*Symptoms* Only *Celtis australis* is affected by this viral problem. The leaves turn yellow, veins turn brown, and side branches wither. The leaves fall off and the branches bend. Buds are dry and brittle.
*Treatment* Apply a systemic fungicide.

# FLOWERING QUINCE, JAPANESE QUINCE

Rosaceae. Deciduous. The three species in this genus are native to China and Japan. The shrubs have alternate, toothed leaves, striking spring blossom and yellow, green or purplish fruit. The twisted branches are spiny.

## PROPAGATION

**Seed** Crush the fruit after it has ripened and remove and clean the seeds. Sow them straightaway in a seed bed or stratify them and sow them in early spring. They germinate rapidly.

**Cuttings** Take semi-ripe cuttings in early or midsummer. Dip the cuttings into hormone rooting compound. Roots form fairly slowly.

**Simple layering** From late spring to midsummer layer a section of wood produced in that year. Allow the roots to form before severing the new plant from the parent plant the following spring and then pot up individually.

## CARE

**Sunlight** *Chaenomeles* needs sun and light and should be placed in a south-facing place outdoors. At the height of summer, protect from direct sun.

**Temperature** *Chaenomeles* is fully hardy; *Pseudocydonia* is frost tender. All tolerate hot weather.

**Ventilation** Protect from the wind, but make sure that the plants are well ventilated.

**Container** Choose a container that is fairly shallow to medium deep; the container is often decorated with a pattern reminiscent of the flowers borne on the bonsai.

**Regular maintenance** After they have ripened, pick some of the fruit because it would exhaust the tree if it was all left on.

**Growth** All species will grow more slowly when they are cut back annually.

**Repotting** After flowering every second year in early spring repot into a larger container. *Chaenomeles* can also be repotted in mid-autumn but must be protected from extremes of weather and from frost after repotting. Prune the roots by about half.

**Soil** Use a mixture of two parts loam, one part leaf mould and one part coarse sand. It prefers a light, fertile soil without much lime.

### Pruning

*Sub-branches* After flowering cut new shoots down to two growth buds. Cut out late shoots.
*Branches* In early summer cut back old branches and side branches. In early

---

### SPECIES

***Chaenomeles japonica*** (syn. *C. maulei*; maule's quince) This compact, prickly bush grows to about 1m (3ft). It has a spreading habit. The smooth, green leaves are oval. Brilliant red flowers appear in early spring, and in mid-autumn round, yellow-green, red-tinged fruit appears. It is fragrant but not edible.

***Chaenomeles speciosa*** (syn. *C. lagenaria, Cydonia speciosa, Pyrus japonica*) A twisted prickly shrub, to 2.4m (8ft) tall, with shiny, green, oval leaves, which are toothed and glabrous. It flowers in early spring, bearing dark red, pink and sometimes white blossom. The fruit, which appears in mid-autumn, is yellow, scented and bitter.

***Pseudocydonia sinensis*** (syn. *Chaenomeles sinensis*) This shrub or small tree can reach 6m (20ft) tall. The branches are not prickly, and the grey or white bark flakes off. The dark green leaves are oblong and dentate leaves. They are downy in spring, turning scarlet in autumn. Salmon pink or white flowers are borne in mid- to late spring and are followed by hard, ovoid, dark yellow fruit in mid-autumn.

---

Kengai

Shakan

Bankan

Han-Kengai

Tachiki

Bunjingi

Neagari

Ishitsuki

Sekijôju

Sôkan

Kabudachi

Korabuki

Ikadabuki

Netsunagari

Tsukami-Yose

Yamayori

Bonkei

Plantations saisonnières

**STYLES**

*Chaenomeles speciosa (syn. C. lagenaria):
20 years old; 25cm (10in) tall.
Photographed in mid-spring. The style
cannot be defined because two trees that
bear different flowers have been planted in
the same container.*

**Misting** These plants can withstand summer dryness. Do not wet the flowers or the fruit.

**Feeding** This is not necessary; feed a little in the growing season, but never in mid- or late summer, after repotting or if the tree is sickly.

## PESTS AND DISEASES

### PESTS
**Aphids** See page 32.

### DISEASES
**Brown rot**
*Symptoms* Flowers wither and then the branches bearing them wither and die.
*Treatment* Cut out and burn diseased branches. Spray with a copper-based fungicide at bud break.

**Crown gall**
*Symptoms* A hard or soft gall appears on the collar and upper roots. It takes the form of a white (later brown), cauliflower-shaped excrescence, which looks woody and cracked. Rot sets in, endangering the tree. There may be secondary infections.
*Treatment* Cut out and destroy infected branches. Improve the drainage so that the compost is not waterlogged. Take care not to wound trees during cultivation so that bacteria can enter the plant tissue. Use clean tools.

**Fireblight**
*Symptoms* Flowers and shoots wither and blacken in spring and summer as if they have been burned. The leaves remain on the branch. The whole plant may die.
*Treatment* This is a serious bacterial disease. Cut out and burn all diseased branches. Sterilize tools. Do not use fertilizer containing nitrogen and do not let the soil get too wet.

autumn cut the tree back hard. Be sure to remove all unwanted shoots from the trunk.

**Wiring** This can be done from spring to the end of summer. Leave wire on for about four months, then remove it, taking care not to wound the tree. Repeat every year until the desired shape has been achieved.

**Watering** Water regularly, but allow the compost to dry out slightly before the plant flowers to encourage blossom. Too little water, and the buds will not flower; too much water, and the flowers will wilt.

# CYPRESS, FALSE CYPRESS

Cupressaceae. Evergreen conifer. The seven or eight species in the genus are native to North America, Japan and Taiwan and were introduced into Europe more than 150 years ago. They are long-lived trees, and in the wild they can grow to a height of 60m (200ft), although cultivated specimens are seldom more than 40m (130ft) tall. They have rather flattened, frond-like branches, which distinguish them from *Cupressus* spp. (cypress). They produce small, almost spherical cones with a terminal point at the centre.

## PROPAGATION

**Seed** This is the best method of propagation. In autumn collect the seeds by placing the cones in a warm place. Stratify the seeds and sow them in spring. Before planting, soak the seeds in lukewarm water and, if necessary, make a slit in the outer seed case. Plant in a mixture of equal parts peat and sharp sand. Keep in the shade. It takes a long time for the seeds to sprout – you may have to wait a year – but as soon as shoots appear, pot up the seedlings individually and protect from drying winds and direct sunlight.

**Cuttings** Take a cutting from young wood in mid- or late summer. Keep in a cool place. Plant the rooted cutting the following spring in a small pot and keep in a shaded place. For best results, use lateral shoots. Prune from the first year of cultivating to produce a denser tree. Cuttings taken from the *Chamaecyparis obtusa* are usually successful and produce fine bonsai specimens.

**Simple layering** This can be done in late summer from a young plant. Strip off the needles from a low branch and make several shallow cuts in the section to be layered to encourage roots to form. Bury the branch in compost, holding it in position with a piece of bent wire. Do not remove the needles from the tip of the branch, which should be left sticking out of the ground. It should be possible to sever the branch by early autumn if the soil is friable and moist. If necessary, add leaf mould to the earth to make sure that it is friable.

**Grafting** Veneer grafting is used in summer. It is vital that the roots should not dry out during the process. Bind the scion and rootstock firmly together. Make the graft at a slight slant and make sure that the scion is turned towards the light. It is best to use a cold frame for the graft. Keep the surrounding atmosphere moist. Keep in partial shade and mist if it is hot. As soon as the graft has taken, new shoots will appear.

**Young nursery stock** Select a tree with an interesting trunk and a lot of branches (see page 18).

### SPECIES

*Chamaecyparis lawsoniana* (syn. *Cupressus lawsoniana;* Lawson cypress) Many cultivars have been developed from this species. It is an upright plant, native to North America, which will grow to 40m (130ft). The foliage is bright green, and the horizontal branches droop downwards. The species and its cultivars are characterized by the slightly drooping leading shoots.

*Chamaecyparis obtusa* (syn. *Cupressus obtusa;* Hinoki cypress) This is the species that is most often grown as a bonsai. It is a large, broad tree, native to Japan, which grows to 40m (130ft). The foliage is shiny, dark green and scale like, and the leaves have white marks on the underside. Small orange (male) and brown (female) flowers are borne at shoot tips in spring, and green, later brown, female cones and orange male cones appear in autumn.

Chokkan

Sekijôju

Sôkan

Kabudachi

Ikadabuki

Netsunagari

Sôju

Sambon-Yose

Gohon-Yose

Kyûhon-Yose

Nanahon-Yose

Yose-Ue

Yamayori

Tsukami-Yose

STYLES

# CARE

**Sunlight** False cypresses prefer slightly shaded sites. They do not like full sun, especially in summer, because they quickly become parched.

**Temperature** Both these species, *Chamaecyparis lawsoniana* and *C. obtusa,* are fully hardy and will withstand cold temperatures well. They will also tolerate maritime climates.

**Ventilation** Protect your plants from drying winds, although humid winds will do no harm.

**Container** Choose a deep bowl, which can be round, oval, hexagonal or rectangular, depending on the style in which the tree is trained. Good drainage is essential.

**Regular maintenance** Remove any yellow needles that you see in autumn and cut away any dead or damaged foliage or wood. Keep the soil clean to prevent pests and diseases.

**Growth** Mature false cypresses are majestic trees. They grow slowly and steadily if conditions are right for them.

**Repotting** Every three to five years, in early to mid-spring, prune between one-third and one-half of the root hairs. Repot into a deep, well-drained container.

**Soil** Use a mixture of equal parts leaf mould, loam and coarse sand. False cypresses like cool, light, calcareous soil open to warmth, but they are not fussy about the soil type, provided it is deep.

**Pruning**
*Pinching out* Pinch out shoot tips during the growing season. Repeat two or three times.
*Pruning branches* Prune side branches that are becoming over-developed by removing a tuft of needles (do not cut individual needles). They can usually be pinched out with your fingers, but if you have to cut a larger branch, use clippers and cut at a joint so that the cut cannot be seen. Remove a third of the foliage.
*Structural pruning* At the end of winter cut out any large, unattractive branches. Remove all dead and dying stems and branches.

**Wiring** Wiring is used to shape *Chamaecyparis* into the desired style. Put the wire in place at the end of autumn and do not leave it on the tree for more than 10 months. Do not get needles caught between the bark and the wire. Rewire every year to achieve the shape you are aiming for. If the branches have grown over the wire in places, leave it where it is, but carefully use tweezers to remove any pieces of wire you can get at.

**Watering** Make sure that the roots do not dry out. Keep the earth slightly moist, but never soak it. Water well in summer and check that excess water escapes through drainage holes. Stagnant water will cause the roots to rot and the tree will die. Never water during frosts.

**Misting** *Chamaecyparis* needs a humid atmosphere. Mist frequently in summer, making sure both foliage and bark are moistened. If plants are exposed to wind, mist in autumn and spring, too. The needles will be all the greener, denser and shinier.

**Feeding** If the bonsai is in good condition, feed in spring and autumn. Increase the amount of fertilizer given at the end of autumn to boost the tree before winter. Feed once a month with a slow-release, organic fertilizer. Leave for two months after repotting.

Chamaecyparis obtusa *(syn. Cupressus obtusa; Hinoki cypress): 12–15 years old; 50cm (20in) high; Nanahon-Yose style. Photographed in late spring.*

## PESTS AND DISEASES

### PESTS
**Red spider mites** See page 32.

**Eelworms** See page 34.

**Hard-shelled scale insects** See page 33.

### DISEASES
**Verticillium wilt** See page 35.

**Coryneum canker**
*Symptoms* The needles turn red, and black pustules are seen on the bark with resin running from them.
*Treatment* Cut out and burn infected branches. Disinfect the cut surfaces with a wound-sealing compound. Try not to wound the tree. Enrich the soil with potash. Apply a systemic fungicide and, as a precaution, spray with a copper-based fungicide after spring rains and in autumn.

**Root and stem rot** See page 35.

# COTONEASTER

Rosaceae. Deciduous, evergreen or semi-evergreen. The more than 200 species of shrubs and trees in this genus are native to the temperate mountainous areas of Europe, north Africa and Asia, excluding Japan. The plants can be spreading or creeping, or tall and slender, with erect stems. They have alternate, ovate to lance-shaped leaves, and saucer- or cup-shaped white or pink flowers. Red or black fruit are borne in autumn.

## SPECIES

***Cotoneaster horizontalis*** This deciduous, sometimes semi-evergreen, species, which is native to China, has horizontal, wide-spreading branches that form a herring-bone pattern. It grows to a height of 1m (3ft). The rounded, dark green leaves turn fiery red in autumn. Pinkish-white flowers, which bloom in late spring or early summer, are followed by bright red fruit, which sometimes last all winter long.

***Cotoneaster integerrimus*** This deciduous shrub, native to Europe and western Asia, grows to 1.5m (8ft). It has spreading, brownish-red branches, which sometimes creep along the soil. The deciduous, oval leaves green are glabrous on their upper surface and grey underneath. Pink flowers appear between mid-spring and early summer, and shiny red fruits follow in late summer or early autumn.

***Cotoneaster microphyllus*** An evergreen shrub with wide-spreading branches and growing to about 75cm (30cm). The bright green leaves curl at the edges and are grey on the underside. In late spring it produces white flowers, and in early to mid-autumn there are scarlet berries.

## PROPAGATION

**Seed** Pick the fruit when it is ripe and leave to rot. Crush the berries and stratify them in sand until midwinter. Plant in the open and cover with peat. Germination will take place in mid-spring. Propagation from seed produces saplings that do not ripen as well as those obtained by other methods.

**Cuttings** Take cuttings in midsummer in a greenhouse for evergreen species and from early to midsummer for deciduous species. Roots should form within six weeks. Then pot into a mixture of equal parts garden loam, compost and mixed sand and peat. Cut back branches the following spring when you repot.

**Air layering** When the new buds are swelling remove the bark from the section to be layered. Wrap sphagnum moss around the stripped stem and enclose in polythene, making it airtight. Keep damp. After three to four weeks, roots appear. After two months, sever the branch and pot it up.

**Young nursery stock** See page 18.

## CARE

**Sunlight** Grow in full sun. Cotoneasters like a sunny position but can grow in partial shade. In full shade they become etiolated.

**Temperature** These are fully hardy plants, but protect bonsai from frosts below -3°C (27°F). They will tolerate heat.

**Ventilation** Cotoneasters tolerate wind.

**Container** They are seldom grown in a flat dish because good drainage is essential. The medium-deep pot can be glazed or unglazed.

*Cotoneaster horizontalis: a close-up of the berries, which are popular with birds. Photographed in mid-autumn.*

Tachiki

Shakan

Sekijôju

Kengai

Han-Kengai

Nejikan

Neagari

Ishitsuki

Ikadabuki

Sôkan

Kabudachi

Bonkei

Netsunagari

Kusamono

## STYLES

Cotoneaster horizontalis: 25 years old; 50cm (20in) high; Tachiki and Hokidachi styles. Photographed in mid-autumn.

*Pruning branches* Prune branches in early spring before growth restarts. Prune when you repot to keep the shape compact.
*Structural pruning* Before the growing season begins prune long branches, suckers and any superfluous branches that spoil the outline of the tree.

**Wiring** Wire the trunk and branches before the buds come out. Protect the bark with raffia. Wire new stems.

**Watering** Cotoneasters prefers dry soil so do not overwater. Allow to dry out between waterings, but soak the compost thoroughly each time you do water.

**Misting** Mist the leaves to humidify the surrounding atmosphere. Cotoneasters thrive in a moist atmosphere and are not happy in hot, dry weather.

**Feeding** In spring and autumn apply a slow-release, organic fertilizer. If necessary, add some phosphate. When the plant has berries, it is best to give liquid fertilizer.

**Regular maintenance** Remove dead leaves and withered flowers or fruit. If the tree has a heavy crop of fruit, remove some berries to prevent the plant from becoming exhausted.

**Growth** Cotoneasters grow quite fast in the early years, but more slowly when raised in a pot.

**Repotting** Repot annually in spring before the new shoots break. Prune the roots by a third and repot into a larger container.

**Soil** Use a mixture of two parts loam, one part leaf mould and one part coarse sand. Cotoneasters are not fussy about soil type and do well in fertile, sandy, clayey, humus-rich soil. They are happiest in dry, light soil, which can be sandy and stony.

**Pruning**
*Pruning shoots* In early summer shorten new shoots to two growth buds. In early autumn prune long stems.

## PESTS AND DISEASES

**PESTS**
**Aphids** See page 33.

**Woolly aphids** See page 34.

**Scale insects** See page 33.

## DISEASES
**Leaf blight**
*Symptoms* White swellings appear on the leaves, which tear and shrivel.
*Treatment* Burn dead leaves. Spray with a copper- or thiram-based wash in spring and autumn.

**Fireblight**
*Symptoms* New shoots turn black, and leaves wither, as if burned, but remain on the stems. Seeping cankers may form on the branches.
*Treatment* This is a serious bacterial disease.

Cut out and burn diseased branches and sterilize all tools. Do not use fertilizers containing nitrogen and keep the soil from getting too wet. In spring use a copper-based fungicide, and repeat during the growing season. If the attack is severe, use a combined fungicide.

**Crown gall**
*Symptoms* A hard or soft gall appears on the collar and upper roots. It takes the form of a white (later brown), cauliflower-shaped excrescence, which looks woody and cracked. Rot sets in, endangering the tree. There may be secondary infections.
*Treatment* Cut out and destroy infected branches. Improve the drainage so that compost is not waterlogged. Take care not to wound trees during cultivation so that bacteria can enter the plant tissue. Use clean tools.

# HAWTHORN, ORNAMENTAL THORN

Rosaceae. Deciduous or semi-evergreen. Native mainly to North America, Asia and western Europe, there are about 200 species of hardy trees and shrubs in the genus. They are small, rather thorny plants, with dentate or lobed leaves. White, pink or sometimes red flowers bloom in spring and summer. A few species produce edible red, orange, yellow or black fruit.

## PROPAGATION

**Seed** Pick the fruit before it is ripe and allow it to rot. Stratify between layers of sand and sow in the open the following autumn. Germination takes place in late spring. Some fruit will not germinate in the first year, in which case you have to wait for the second and sometimes a third year.

**Air layering** Do this in spring.

**Shield grafting** Make sure that the stock and the scion are reasonably homogeneous so that the graft will take. This method is seldom used, because it is difficult and leaves an unattractive swelling.

## CARE

**Sunlight** Hawthorns like sun and light, but even so, they should be placed in partial shade at the height of summer.

**Temperature** These plants do not like intense heat, but they are not affected by cold.

**Ventilation** Often used in hedgerows, hawthorns stand up to wind well. They are also good in seaside gardens.

**Container** Choose a medium-deep bowl, which can be glazed or unglazed. The bowls are sometimes decorated so that they harmonize with the hawthorn blossom.

**Regular maintenance** Remove some fruit from overloaded branches so that the tree does not become exhausted. After flowering and fruit formation, remove any withered flowers or berries. Keep the soil clean.

**Growth** Hawthorns grow moderately fast.

**Repotting** Once a year, in early spring or in early autumn, reduce the roots by a good third before repotting.

**Soil** Use a mixture of two parts loam, one part leaf mould and one part coarse sand. Hawthorns are tolerant about the soil they grow in – it can be poor, dry and stony – but avoid calcareous or clayey soil, and damp or light soil.

**Pruning**
*Pinching back* Pinch out the tips of new shoots when the leaves on the new growth are beginning to harden.
*Pruning sub-branches* In early to midsummer cut the branches to keep them short. In early autumn shorten long branches again, pruning them lightly. The main branches may be pruned before flowering or after the fruit has formed.

### SPECIES

*Crataegus cuneata* This deciduous shrub is native to Japan and China. It has dentate leaves. The flowers are pink in spring, then white. The fruit is red or yellow.
*Crataegus laevigata* (syn. *C. oxyacantha*; English hawthorn, quickset hawthorn) This deciduous, thorny tree, with a round, spreading habit, grows to 8m (25ft). It has glossy leaves and whitish flowers, which are sometimes tinged with pink. The round fruits are red. There are several cultivars, of which one of the best is *C. laevigata* 'Paul's Scarlet', which has double red flowers.
*C. laevigata* 'Plena' has double white flowers, and the pretty double flowers of 'Rosea Flore Pleno' are pink.

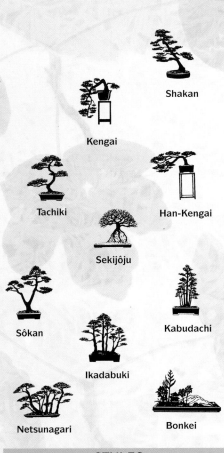

Shakan

Kengai

Tachiki

Han-Kengai

Sekijôju

Sôkan

Kabudachi

Ikadabuki

Netsunagari

Bonkei

**STYLES**

Cotoneaster cuneata: *25 years old; 50cm (25in) high; Neijikan style. Photographed in late spring.*

**Wiring** Wire from spring until autumn, beginning after new shoots have hardened and protecting the bark with raffia.

**Watering** Water copiously and often. Slightly reduce the amount of water given during flowering, but make sure that the blossom does not wither.

**Misting** Avoid wetting the tree when it is in flower. In warm, dry weather mist the foliage thoroughly.

**Feeding** Apply a fertilizer after the growing spurt in spring and in autumn. Reduce the supply of fertilizer when the tree is in flower. It is best to use a liquid fertilizer in autumn. Add potash and phosphate when the tree is bearing fruit.

## PESTS AND DISEASES

### PESTS
**Gall-forming aphids** See page 33.

**Pierid butterfly**
*Symptoms* The caterpillars of cabbage white butterflies eat the leaves, leaving irregularly shaped holes.
*Treatment* Destroy the eggs by squeezing them in the leaf. At the first sign of infestation spray with derris, malathion or permetrhin.

**Ermine moth** See page 33.

### DISEASES
**Powdery mildew** See page 34.

**Leaf blight**
*Symptoms* White swellings appear on the leaves, which tear and shrivel.
*Treatment* Burn dead leaves. Spray with a copper- or thiram-based wash in spring and autumn.

**Scab**
*Symptoms* The fungal diseases causes brownish-green patches on the fruit, and these burst onto the leaves and shoots.
*Treatment* Remove and burn affected leaves in autumn. Spray with a copper-based fungicide.

**Rust** See page 35.

**Fireblight**
*Symptoms* The flowers and young shoots wither and blacken as if burned. The leaves turn orange-brown but cling to the stems. Oozing beige-coloured cankers may appear on infected branches.
*Treatment* This is a serious bacterial disease. Cut out and burn diseased branches and sterilize all tools. Do not use fertilizer with nitrogen in it and make sure the soil is not too wet. Before flowering use a copper-based fungicide. Repeat when growth is under way.

# JAPANESE CEDAR, CRYPTOMERIA

Taxodiaceae. Evergreen conifer. Native to China and Japan, *Cryptomeria japonica* is the only species in the genus, but many cultivars have been developed. In Asia cryptomerias can grow to a height of 60m (200ft), but in European gardens they seldom get above 25m (80ft). They have a generally conical shape, with a straight trunk, brick-coloured bark, which peels off in narrow strips, and hard wood. The tapering, evergreen needles are pointed and bright green-blue, turning russet coloured in winter. Needles tend to be shed readily in dry areas. In autumn cryptomerias produce globular, slightly prickly, scaly cones.

## PROPAGATION

**Seed** Seeds are planted under glass as soon as they have been gathered in a mixture of equal parts sand and peat. They do not germinate reliably, and other methods of propagation are usually more successful.

**Layering** Select a low, flexible branch. Strip off the needles from the section to be buried and make two or three cuts into the branch to encourage rooting. Bury the branch, leaving the tip protruding; the needles should still be on the tip. Keep the soil moist. When you see new growth, the roots have formed. In spring sever the new plantlet and pot up into a mixture of peat and sand. The cultivars in the Elegans Group grow best.

**Grafting** Grafting in early spring is possible in a greenhouse, but this is a method more widely used by professionals.

**Young nursery stock** Select a tree with an interesting trunk and a lot of branches (see page 18).

## CARE

**Sunlight** Place cryptomerias in partial shade. They do not thrive in full summer sun.

**Temperature** Cryptomerias need warmth. The needles turn brown in winter but will revert to their green colour in spring if the tree is protected from winter cold and frosts. Trees may be affected by late spring frost.

**Ventilation** These plants prefer a humid atmosphere and fresh air, but they should be shielded from strong winds (especially young or recently repotted specimens).

**Container** Cryptomerias grow best in deep, moist, cool, well-drained soil. Select a simple, deep bowl that is neutral, brown or willow green in colour, and make sure that the drainage is good.

**Regular maintenance** In dry areas cryptomerias lose more needles. Pick withered needles off the tree and soil. Cut out dead wood. Keep the inside of the tree clean to guard against any problems.

**Growth** Old needles fall after four or five years, and this is how the branches are formed. Cryptomerias are slow growing but in the growing season put out a lot of new shoots.

**Repotting** Every three to five years repot in mid-spring when growth is under way. You should not repot too early in spring.

**Soil** Use a mixture of equal parts leaf mould, loam and sharp sand. Cool, rich, deep, moist but well-drained soil is essential.

**Pruning** Regularly pinch out new growth from the needles from spring to mid-autumn. Remove shoots growing from the trunk or the main branches. Pinching back a cryptomeria is a long, painstaking task,

Chokkan

Sekijôju

Sôju

Sôkan

Kabudachi

Ikadabuki

Netsunagari

Kyûhon-Yose

Sambon-Yose

Gohon-Yose

Nanahon-Yose

Yose-Ue

Bonkei

Kusamono

**STYLES**

*Cryptomeria japonica: 30 years old; 45cm (18in) high; Chokkan style. Photographed in late spring.*

but it is essential to keep the foliage compact. If it is carried out properly, it will not be necessary to prune the side branches. Prune out any side branches that have lost too many of their needles and any branches growing in the wrong place in spring, cutting precisely at a fork so that the cut cannot be seen.

**Wiring** Use string to tie up any branches tending to grow away from the trunk (which would spoil the compact appearance). Wire the tree to train it from

*Pinching out the needles on a cryptomeria.*

the end of spring to summer. Do not carry out any work on these plants in winter.

**Watering** Water frequently from spring to autumn and less often in winter. Do not water if there is a frost. Water should never stagnate, so always make sure before you water that the roots have absorbed all the water from the bottom of the pot. Cryptomerias are thirsty plants.

**Misting** Cryptomerias do not thrive in dry conditions, which cause their needles to fall early. They do best in areas with high humidity, and in dry regions the foliage should be misted frequently and regularly.

**Feeding** Feed healthy cryptomerias with a slow-release, organic fertilizer from spring to autumn with a break in mid- and late summer. Wait for two months after repotting before feeding. Increase the last amount of fertilizer given in late autumn slightly to set the tree up for winter.

## PESTS AND DISEASES

### PESTS
**Red spider mites** See page 32.

**Scale insects** See page 33.

### DISEASES
**Die-back**

*Symptoms* The branches wither and turn brown. The needles drop off. Weak trees kept in poor conditions are especially vulnerable to die-back.

*Treatment* Cut out diseased branches. Spray with copper-based fungicide.

# FERN PALM, SAGO

Cycadaceae. Evergreen. The genus includes about 20 tender species of 'palm-like' gymnosperms, which are native to tropical and subtropical areas from east Africa to Japan. They have stout, cylindrical, rather woody trunks, which may be several metres (yards) high and which end in whorls of pinnate, thick, leathery, shiny green leaves. Cycads are dioecious: male 'flowers' are cone-like and to 80cm (32in); female flowers look like small, modified leaves with marginal globules.

## PROPAGATION

**Seed** Collect seeds from a female cycad when they are ripe and sow in a warm greenhouse. Germination will take about four weeks. Plant out in a mixture of equal parts peat and sand with good bottom heat in a light place.

**Division** In spring separate any suckers thrown up by the parent plant, and plant out separately, keeping warm and dry.

## CARE

**Sunlight** Cycads likes heat and light, and in reliably warm areas they can be placed outside between late spring and early autumn. They can withstand full sun.

**Temperature** These plants need warmth. In winter the temperature should not fall below 17–18°C (63–64°F).

**Ventilation** Keep out of draughts. If it is

### SPECIES

*Cycas revoluta* (Japanese sago palm) This species, which is native to Japan, can grow to 2m (6ft). The dark green, pinnate leaves are long and linear, with spear-shaped, spiky ends, and the trunk is thick.

placed outside in summer, it should be sheltered from the wind.

**Container** Choose a pot of average depth, usually a hexagonal or round one. Blues go well with these plants. Good drainage is essential.

**Regular maintenance** Brush the trunk to make sure that no moss grows on it. Cut off fronds that have turned yellow at the base.

*Cycas revoluta These old specimens were photographed in Taiwan, where they were being grown under an awning.*

**Kabudachi**

**Korabuki**

**Bonkei**

**Tsukami-Yose**

**Plantations saisonnières**

**STYLES**

**Growth** Cycads grow slowly. For small, well-proportioned palms, you must expose the plants to the sun. It is quite rare for the trunks to develop branches.

**Repotting** Every second or third year in spring prune the roots by a third and repot into a well-drained container, choosing one that is larger than the previous one.

**Soil** Use a mixture of equal parts peat, leaf mould, loam and sharp sand. Cycads do well in good-quality loam to which some sand has been added. In the garden they grow in fertile, moist soil.

**Pruning** As a rule the fronds turn yellow and then fall every year or every second year. At the same time you can see new fronds developing from the centre of the trunk. They all emerge at the same time and you will not see others appearing later in the same season.

*Cycas revoluta: 90 years old; 70cm (28in) high; no particular style. Photographed in late autumn at an exhibition organized by bonsai growers in Taiwan.*

**Wiring** This is not practised. Cycads are miniaturized by root pruning.

**Watering** Cycads have natural water storage capacity in their trunks and generally require little water. Give a little water in winter and only a moderate amount in summer.

**Misting** Mist the foliage freely in summer. In winter mist only if the plant is in a warm, dry place.

**Feeding** Feed in spring and in autumn with a slow-release, organic fertilizer, applying a liquid and a solid fertilizer alternately.

### PESTS
**Glasshouse red spider mites** See page 32.

**Scale insects** See page 33.

### DISEASES
**Damping off**
*Symptoms* The roots and the collar rot. The stems are spotted with black, then rot and collapse.
*Treatment* Maintain a warm temperature and ensure good air circulation. Do not give too much water. Apply nitrogen and potassium to the soil. If necessary, use a fungicide.

# ENKIANTHUS

Ericaceae. Deciduous or evergreen. This genus of 10 shrubs and some trees is native to east Asia and the Himalayas, where they grow in woodland and scrub. They must be grown in lime-free soil. They bear racemes of bell-shaped flowers in late spring, and the lance-shaped, toothed, alternate leaves turn red in autumn.

## PROPAGATION

**Seed** Sow seed in late winter or early spring in a greenhouse in a mixture of ericaceous compost and peat. Cover the seeds lightly with sieved soil. Keep moist in a dark place. Germination occurs within three weeks. As soon as the seeds have germinated, move into the light and keep the compost damp. Take care that there is no damping off. Plant out straight away into growing pots with good drainage. Put a layer of finely sieved ericaceous compost on the surface of the compost. Keep in a cool, shaded position as long as the shoots are soft. As soon as they harden, expose them to air and light.

**Cuttings** In late summer take semi-ripe cuttings and keep them in a greenhouse. Root development requires heat.

**Simple layering** In early to mid-spring layer in cool, moist soil.

## CARE

**Sunlight** These plants like good light throughout the year but they should be shaded from direct summer sun.

**Temperature** Protect from frost. They do best in fairly humid conditions.

**Ventilation** There are no special requirements, but they do not like strong winds.

**Container** Choose a medium-deep container; unglazed ones look best.

**Regular maintenance** Remove any leaves that do not fall at the end of autumn.

**Growth** These are slow-growing plants.

**Repotting** Repot in early spring every year or every second year, after you have pruned the roots by a third.

---

**SPECIES**

***Enkianthus campanulatus*** (Furin-tsutsuji) A deciduous tree that can grow to 10m (33ft) in Japan but only to about 3m (10ft) in Europe. It is an upright shrub, with red branches, and elliptic, acute, dentate leaves that are green on top and red underneath.
***Enkianthus perulatus*** (Dodan-tsutsuji) Also native to Japan, this compact, deciduous shrub grows to 2m (6ft). It has elliptic, acute oval leaves, bright green on top and with long veins underneath, and pendent, white, umbellate flowers, which appear before the leaves (in mid- to late spring).

---

**Soil** Use a mixture of two parts leaf mould, one part loam and one part sharp sand. Enkianthus need a compost containing leaf mould and cannot tolerate lime. They need moist, cool, humus-rich, but well-drained soil.

**Pruning**
*Pruning sub-branches* At the end of summer prune sub-branches with clippers; wait until the flowerheads have withered and before new shoots have hardened too much.
*Pruning branches* In early autumn shorten long branches.

**Wiring** Wire from spring until autumn. Do not wire stems too tightly because this could result in the sap being cut off and the flowers failing.

**Watering** Water freely as soon as the leaves appear, continuing until autumn; then reduce the amount of water given throughout winter.

**Misting** Do not mist when the plants are in flower.

Shakan

Tachiki

Han-Kengai

Sekijôju

Sôkan

Kabudachi

Sôju

Sambon-Yose

STYLES

Enkianthus perulatus: *15 years old; 20cm (8in) high; Tachiki style. Photographed in mid-spring.*

**Feeding** In spring and autumn apply a slow-release, organic fertilizer. It is best to use a liquid fertilizer when the tree is in flower.

These plants are not much affected by pests and diseases.

## PESTS
**Aphids** See page 33.

**Scale insects** See page 33.

## DISEASES
**Sooty mould**
*Symptoms* Black scabs may be seen on the leaves and stems, and there will be sticky deposits.

*Treatment* Clean the leaves with a sponge soaked in water and spirit. Kill the insects with insecticide.

**Chlorosis**
*Symptoms* The leaves turn yellow and new leaves are discoloured.
*Treatment* Apply nitrogen, iron, magnesium and zinc to the soil. Do not give too much calcium, sodium or water and do not expose to cold. Keep out of draughts and away from noxious gases. Place in the light.

# SYZYGIUM, STOPPER

Myrtaceae. Evergreen. This is a large genus, originally containing more than 1000 species of tender evergreen trees and shrubs, many of which have been reclassified as *Acmena*, *Syzygium*, *Myrciaria*, *Luma* and *Ugni*, among others. They bear simple, rather leathery, opposite leaves and cymes or panicles of saucer-shaped flowers. The best known member of the genus is probably *Syzygium aromaticum* (syn. *Eugenia aromatica*), the dried flower buds of which are used to produce the spice known as cloves. *Syzygium jambos* (syn. *Eugenia jambos*), a tree native to China, southeast Asia and Australia, produces fruits that smell strongly of rose water. The genus was named after Prince Eugène of Savoy (1663–1736).

## PROPAGATION

**Seed** Sow seed in spring in a heated greenhouse with bottom heat. If you have one, use a propagator.

**Cuttings** Root greenwood cuttings in early summer or semi-ripe cuttings in mid- or late summer, both in a heated greenhouse in good light. Use a soil mix of equal parts sharp sand and special cuttings compost. Pot up the following spring.

## CARE

**Sunlight** These plants like good light all year round. They will withstand full sun but should be shaded from direct sun at the height of summer.

**Temperature** These tender plants need warmth all year round, especially in the growing season. Protect from frost. The temperature should not fall below 18°C (64°F).

**Ventilation** Protect from draughts but place them where air can circulate freely. They prefer humid conditions.

**Container** Choose a medium-deep container, in a colour that will complement the colour of the flowers. The shape – round, oval or rectangular – will depend on the shape of the tree.

**Regular maintenance** Remove any yellowing leaves from the tree and tidy away any leaves that fall on the compost. Brush the trunks to remove any moss. Do not let moss or algae grow on the surface of the compost.

**Growth** These are moderately slow-growing plants, although branches will grow quickly early in the year.

**Repotting** Repot in early to late spring every second year; older trees should be repotted every third year. At the same time, prune the roots by between one-third and one-half and remove all damaged, dead or wrongly positioned branches. Repot into a slightly large container.

*This close-up of the trunk of* Myrciaria cauliflora *(syn.* Eugenia cauliflora) *shows how the bark peels from the branches, revealing darker colours on the older wood.*

Chokkan

Shakan

Han-Kengai

Kengai

Tachiki

Sharimiki

Bunjingi

Neagari

Nejikan

Hôkidachi

Sabamiki

Sôkan

Kabudachi

Sôju

Sambon-Yose

Kyûhon-Yose

Yose-Ue

Nanahon-Yose

STYLES

*Eugenia uniflora* (Surinam cherry, pitanga) Native to Brazil, this is a small tree or shrub, growing to 10m (30ft). The ovate leaves are purplish-red when young, turning green as they mature. The fragrant flowers are followed by round, ribbed, edible fruits, which are glossy red or yellow.

*Myrciaria cauliflora* (syn. *Eugenia cauliflora*; jaboticaba) Native to Brazil, this tree is, as the specific name suggests, a cauliflorous plant – that is, the flowers are produced directly from the wood of the branches or trunk (as in *Cercis*). The plants grow to 13m (43ft). It bears edible, spherical, white to purplish fruits.

*Syzygium aromaticum* (syn. *Eugenia aromatica*; clove). This tree, to 15m (50ft), is native to Indonesia. It has a conical habit, with dark green leaves. lighter below, and pink flowers, followed by purplish fruit.

*Syzygium paniculatum* (syn. *Eugenia australis, E. myrtifolia, E. paniculata*; brush cherry) This species is native to Australia. It is a small tree or large shrub, to 10m (30ft), which has glossy leaves, reddish-bronze when young. The edible fruits are white or red to reddish-purple.

Myrciaria cauliflora *(syn.* Eugenia cauliflora*): 20 years old; 40cm (16in) high; Tachiki style. Photographed in mid-autumn.*

**Soil** Use a mixture of two parts leaf mould, two parts loam and one part sharp sand. Eugenias like humus-rich, well-drained compost.

**Pruning**
*Pruning sub-branches* From early spring to mid-autumn prune sub-branches with clippers. You will need to do this three or four times depending on the speed of growth of your plants. Cut carefully at the base of a new shoot.
*Pruning branches* This should be done when plants are repotted. Remove any poorly placed or damaged branches. Apply wound paint to the cuts.

**Wiring** This can be done all year round on sub-branches and branches that have hardened. Leave the wire on for no more than three months and replace if necessary the following year. Protect the bark with raffia.

**Watering** Water freely as soon as the leaves appear. Make sure that the water has been completely taken up before watering again so that the soil never becomes waterlogged. Increase the frequency of watering in summer and winter, but give less water in spring and autumn.

**Misting** Mist every day in winter to increase the humidity around the plants. Mist daily in hot, windy weather. Increase humidity by standing the container on a bed of gravel in a tray of water.

**Feeding** Every two weeks from early spring to early summer and from early autumn to early winter apply a slow-release, organic fertilizer, alternating liquid and granule fertilizers. Throughout winter apply fertilizer every six weeks.

## PESTS AND DISEASES

### PESTS
These plants are largely trouble free.

**Whitefly**
*Symptoms* These tiny insects, can be seen on the undersides of leaves, which become covered with honeydew and sooty mould.
*Treatment* Spray with an insecticide such as malathion, permethrin or heptenophos and permethrin. Organic gardeners will prefer to try the parasitic wasp *Encarsia formosa*.

# SPINDLE TREE

Celastraceae. Deciduous or evergreen. This is a large genus, containing 170 species of trees and shrubs, which are mainly native to Asia and Europe, although some are found in North and Central America, Australia and Madagascar. The deciduous species do best in sun, while the evergreen species prefer partial shade. Forms with variegated foliage need sun to maintain the variegation.

## PROPAGATION

**Seed** Sow seed as soon as it is ripe. Use new, humus-rich compost and stand the containers in good light.

**Cuttings** Take softwood cuttings of deciduous species and semi-ripe cuttings of evergreen species in late summer and plant them in a freely draining compost. Place them in a cold frame or in the shelter at the foot of a garden wall.

**Young nursery stock** Choose a plant with a well-developed central stem and with a good distribution of branches and stems to make your work easier (see also page 18).

## CARE

**Sunlight** All species need good light and plenty of sun if they are to develop fully. Variegated species require good light if the variegation is to be maintained. Like most plants, however, they will appreciate shade from strong summer sun.

**Temperature** Euonymus are hardy plants and will withstand extremes of both heat and cold. Young plants will need protection from very cold winter weather, but established deciduous plants will withstand temperatures of -5 to -7°C (19–23°F). Evergreen euonymus will withstand winter temperatures to about 5°C (41°F).

**Ventilation** The deciduous species that are often seen in hedgerows withstand wind quite well, although young plants should be protected from exceptionally strong and cold winds.

**Container** Use a medium-deep pot; it can be round, oval or rectangular. Choose a container whose colour harmonizes with the autumn tones of the foliage.

**Regular maintenance** Remove any leaves from deciduous species that have not fallen

### SPECIES

*Euonymus alatus* (winged spindle) This hardy, deciduous species is native to China and Japan. It is a dense, rather shrubby plant, which grows to 2m (6ft) or more high. It has dark green, toothed, ovate leaves, which turn dark red in autumn. The almost spherical, reddish-purple fruits open to reveal orange-covered seeds. This species is reliably hardy and is often used in hedgerows.

*Euonymus europaeus* (common spindle tree). A deciduous shrub, growing to 7m (21ft), this is native to Europe and West Asia. It is the parent of many attractive cultivars, including 'Red Cascade', which has fiery leaves in autumn.

*Euonymus hamiltonianus* subsp. *sieboldianus* (syn. *E. yedoensis*) This hardy form is native to Korea and Japan. It is an upright, deciduous shrub, growing to about 6m (20ft). The mid-green, ovate leaves turn yellow and pink in autumn. The four-lobed fruits open to reveal the orange-red seeds.

by the end of autumn. Brush the trunk once or twice a year and remove any moss that appears on the trunk.

**Growth** These are fairly fast growing.

**Repotting** In early spring every year or every second year, when the buds have started to swell, repot into new, humus-rich, moist compost that is either neutral or slightly acid. Cut off about one-third of the roots and pot up into a slightly large container than before.

Shakan

Han-Kengai

Tachiki

Neagari

Ishitsuki

Takozukuri

Sabamiki

Sôkan

Sôju

**Soil** Use a standard compost that contains about 20 per cent humus and 30 per cent coarse sand.

**Pruning**

*Pruning shoots* Pinch out new shoots in spring as they emerge but before they have hardened.

*Pruning sub-branches* Prune out new sub-branches with clippers as they begin to emerge and before they have developed too much. Repeat the process once or twice more during the growing season.

*Pruning branches* At the end of winter cut out any dead, damaged or crossing branches and remove any branches that are out of proportion with the overall plant. The aim is to create a smooth, domed crown.

*Leaf pruning* If the leaves seem to be too large, completely leaf prune the plant in early summer.

**Wiring** Wire in spring and remove the wire in autumn. If necessary, repeat the process the following year. Take care that the wire is not so tight that the stems are damaged.

**Watering** Water freely but allow the plant to take up all the water before watering again. In spring and summer water frequently and regularly, but in winter these plants need less water, and do not water at all during frosty weather, in case the roots are damaged.

**Misting** In dry or windy weather mist the leaves (or hold them under a shower) to clean the foliage of dust and insects. In warm weather make sure the soil is moist

*Euonymus alatus (winged spindle): 40 years old; 65cm (26in) high; Sôkan style. Photographed in mid-autumn.*

so that evaporation maintains the humidity around the plant.

**Feeding** From early spring to early summer and from early to late autumn apply a slow-release, organic fertilizer. Give an extra feed at the end of autumn to boost the plant before winter sets in.

## PESTS AND DISEASES

*Euonymous fortunei* var. *radicans* (syn. *E. radicans*) is especially resistant to dust, smoke and pollution.

### PESTS
**Red spider mites** See page 32.

**Scale insects** See page 33.

**Mealy bugs** See page 33.

**Bark beetles** See page 34.

**Aphids** See page 33.

### DISEASES
**Mildew** See page 34.

**Rust** See page 35.

# BEECH

Fagaceae. Deciduous. The genus contains 10 species of deciduous trees, which are native to the temperate areas of the northern hemisphere. They are long-lived and hardy trees, although they generally do best in areas with long, fairly warm summers. The trees have smooth, grey bark and spreading crowns. The shoots are slender and the buds are narrowly ellipsoid. In spring the leaves are light green, turning darker in summer and to shades of brown and orange in autumn. Some of the leaves stay on the tree throughout winter, not falling until the new shoots burgeon in spring. Such leaves are called marcescent. The edible nuts or beech masts occur mainly on established trees. All the species and many of the cultivar can be grown as bonsai.

## PROPAGATION

**Seed** Sow seed in autumn. It does not take long to germinate. If it is impossible to sow the seeds in autumn, keep them stratified in dry sand until spring and sow them then. Plant them in a tray at a depth of 2.5cm (1in) in a mixture of peat and coarse sand (make sure the compost is not too acid). Do not over-firm the soil to allow air to circulate.

**Grafting** The method used for the beech is inarching (approach grafting). In this method the scion is not severed immediately but left joined to the parent plant until the union is complete. The scion and the stock can come from the same tree. If the graft is made in early spring, it will have taken by late autumn. The top of the rootstock is cut off – cut as close as possible to the stock to avoid too large a swelling – and the cut is painted with a wound-sealing compound so that the scar quickly becomes inconspicuous. The compound also prevents pests and diseases from entering the tree. After grafting, the beech needs protection from wind and frost and should be treated as a tree that has just been repotted. See pages 21–3 for more information on inarching.

**Young nursery stock** You can often find young beeches with interesting trunks in nurseries. In spring apply bonsai techniques to these specimens, pruning the branches and roots and putting them in a pot. They will have to be worked on for two or three years before they are real bonsai. See also page 18.

See pages 21–3 for more information on inarching. See also page 18.

### SPECIES

***Fagus crenata*** (syn. *F. sieboldii*; Japanese beech) This hardy tree is native to Japan. It has a longer bole, a whiter trunk and smaller foliage than *F. sylvatica*.

***Fagus sylvatica*** (common beech) This tree, which can grow to 25m (80ft), is found from central Europe to the Caucasus. It has oblong, dentate leaves with prominent veins.

***Fagus sylvatica*** f. ***pendula*** (weeping beech) The branches hang down naturally and may even touch the ground.

## CARE

**Sunlight** The beech tolerates full sun, but in summer, especially in very hot, sunny gardens, it is better to place it in a slightly shaded position.

**Temperature** In their natural habitat beeches occur naturally on high ground where it is cooler. These plants do not like intense heat, and they generally do best in areas with a moderate, temperate climate and long, warm summers. Bonsai specimens react badly to severe winters and spring frosts. If the temperature falls below -5°C (23°F), the roots and container must be protected with a covering of wool, straw or dead leaves, or the plant, with its container, should be buried up to the base

Shakan

Chokkan

Tachiki

Kabudachi

Sôkan

Netsunagari

Korabuki

Yose-Ue

Sôju

Tsukami-Yose

STYLES

of the trunk. In extremely cold weather bonsai beeches can also be brought inside into a cold room, provided that it is not too bright. However, like all hardy species, the bonsai beech is able to withstand most of the conditions found in gardens in temperate regions.

**Ventilation** In many gardens beech, especially *Fagus sylvatica* f. *purpurea*, is used for hedging, so it is known to stand up well to wind. Young specimens (less than five years old) and repotted trees should be protected from a strong wind.

**Container** For aesthetic reasons, beeches are not put in decorated pots. Choose a container that is not too shallow; old, single specimens need a container 4–8cm (1½–3in) deep. A group bonsai, on the other hand, can be planted in a shallow dish or even in a simple tray.

Fagus crenata *(syn. F. sieboldii; Japanese beech): 150 years old; 55cm (22in); Tachiki style. Photographed in mid-spring. Although the trunk appears initially to be in the Chokkan style, it is more characteristic of the Tachiki style nearer the top. It is possible to see the persistent (marcescent) leaves on this venerable tree as well as the new, young shoots.*

**Regular maintenance** Beeches have marcescent leaves. Clear away any leaves lying at the foot of the trees, but leave any others that are still attached on the

*This close-up reveals the characteristic of beech trees: that old leaves persist until new shoots emerge.*

branches. In fact, you should remove any dead or damaged material to discourage the occurrence of diseases or pests, and keep the tree well ventilated, including its foliage, and never let the soil become waterlogged.

**Ventilation** In many gardens beech, especially *Fagus sylvatica* f. *purpurea*, is used for hedging, so it is known to stand up well to wind. Young specimens (less than five years old) and repotted trees should be protected from a strong wind, however.

**Growth** Beeches are slow-growing trees. The foliage grows slowly, so leave it to grow until the end of spring before cutting it.

**Repotting** Repotting is always done in spring, just as growth starts and before the new shoots have opened. Repot every two or three years, depending on the age of the tree. Old trees – that is, those over 50 years – are repotted every four or five years. Cut away between one-half and two-thirds of the root hairs, and place the tree in a new slightly larger pot.

**Soil** Use a mixture of equal parts loam and sand. Beeches are tolerant of a wide range of conditions, including chalky soils, but they will do best in cool, sandy, clay soil that drains well. They do not like compacted, poorly draining soil.

**Pruning** The branches and leaves are pruned at the same time as the beech is repotted and the roots are pruned.
*Pinching back* New shoots on beech trees are vigorous and must be pinched back.

Beeches do not produce secondary buds. The spacing between the nodes tends to become wider and there is a danger that cuts made in pruning will be visible, and it is for this reason that young shoots should be pinched back while they are still soft, leaving one or two leaves. This process should be done in late spring when the previous year's dead leaves have fallen as the new shoots begin to emerge.
*Leaf pruning* This is a tricky operation that is carried out in summer on healthy trees. It is done only every second year. It takes it out of the tree, but after leaf cutting the beech will be all the lovelier in autumn, with smaller leaves produced by an artificially created second spring. It is also possible to strip a tree completely, but this should not be done in the same year it has been repotted.
*Pruning branches* Branches should be lightly pruned, preferably after repotting. The beech is a slow-growing tree and is pruned only once in the season. Cuts should be made at a slant, leaving two or three leaves on each section of branch, and just above a leaf bud, to encourage a good spread of new branches.
*Structural pruning* This should be done in winter when the tree's outline can be clearly seen. Any main branch that is spoiling the aesthetic effect of the tree should be cut out. Some wound-sealing compound should be applied to each cut to guard against pests and disease.

**Wiring** A beech bonsai is mainly sculpted into shape by pruning, but wiring can be used if you want to train the tree into a fixed style. When you remove the wire, use wire cutters, taking care that you do not

*The close-up shows how new buds of* Fagus crenata *(syn.* F. sieboldii*) burst. Note that the wire is wrapped in paper to protect the delicate stems.*

Fagus crenata *(syn.* F. sieboldii)*; 15–30 years old; 70cm (28in) high; Yose-Ue style. Photographed in early-winter.*

damage the tree; if the bark is cut through, apply a wound-sealing compound. Beech bark is easily damaged, so wrap raffia or paper around the wire. The beech is wired between spring and autumn for a maximum of three months. Until you achieve the style you are aiming for, repeat the process annually.

**Watering** Water freely from late spring to late summer. Give less water from late summer and in autumn.

**Misting** Beeches do best in a humid atmosphere and should be misted from early spring to late summer. If trees are small and the weather is dry, mist in morning and evening.

**Feeding** fertilizer can be given in granule, powder or liquid form. Feed from early spring, after the buds have opened, until the end of autumn, when the tree becomes dormant, but not in mid- or late summer.

## PESTS AND DISEASES

### PESTS

**Beech-leaf miner**
*Symptoms* The leaves have round holes in them which get bigger. The weevil (*Rhynchaenus fagi*), which appears when the leaves are forming, is 2–3mm (?in) long. This pest feeds on leaves.
*Treatment* Use insecticide in spring when leaves are developing.

**Gall midges**
*Symptoms* Red galls about 1cm (½in) long on the leaves are caused by the tiny red, white or yellow maggots. The leaves ripen and fall to the compost.
*Treatment* Remove and burn affected leaves. Spray with carbendazim.

**Felted beech coccus**
*Symptoms* 'Tufts of wool' seem to be attached to the bark. If you look closely you can see insects (*Cryptococcus fagi*) with a white, waxy carapace adhering to the bark.
*Treatment* Because only trees that are in poor condition are infested, improving the conditions in which the tree is kept should be sufficient.

**Bark beetles**
*Symptoms* A great many small holes can be seen on the bark. Branches gradually die and the tree falls.
*Treatment* These brown-black insects interfere with the circulation of the sap and tend to attack trees that are not in the best condition. Cut out dead branches immediately and burn them. If the tree is heavily infested, use an insecticide.

### DISEASES

**Canker**
*Symptoms* Where there are scars or clefts between branches sores develop, deepening, cracking and swelling and causing the branch to die. Golden-coloured gum oozes from the affected area. Adjacent branches form excrescences as a defence mechanism. When the canker encircles stems or branches, die-back occurs.
*Treatment* Cut out and burn diseased branches, applying wound paint to the cuts. Spray with a copper-based fungicide in late summer to early autumn. Badly affected trees should be burned completely.

**Chokkan**

**Bankan**

**Shakan**

**Kengai**

**Han-Kengai**

**Tachiki**

**Bunjingi**

**Sharimiki**

**Fukinagashi**

**Hôkidachi**

**Sekijôju**

**Neagari**

**Ishitsuki**

**Takozukuri**

**Nejikan**

**Sabamiki**

**Kabudachi**

**Sôkan**

**Korabuki**

**Netsunagari**

**Ikadabuki**

**Sôju**

**Gohon-Yose**

**Sambon-Yose**

**Nanahon-Yose**

**Yose-Ue**

**Kyûhon-Yose**

**Yamayori**

**Bonkei**

**Tsukami-Yose**

**Kusamono**

**Plantations saisonnières**

**STYLES**

# FIG

Moraceae. Deciduous or evergreen. This is a very large genus of about 800 trees, shrubs and woody climbers, which are native to tropical and subtropical areas. The species exhibit a wide range of characteristics, but the alternate leaves are usually simple or lobed.

## PROPAGATION

**Seed** It is practicable to raise *Ficus* from seed only in a greenhouse inside a propagator.

**Cuttings** Take cuttings in mid- or late summer in a cold frame. Take cuttings that are 5–10cm (2–4in) long. Cut off the top, remove one or two pairs of leaves from the lower part of the slip and plant in a mixture of equal parts sand and peat. Remove the glass as soon as roots have formed. Repot in spring the next year. Cuttings can also be made by standing slips in water.

**Air layering** This can be done in spring (see page 20).

## CARE

**Sunlight** These plants love light. *Ficus microcarpa* needs more light than the other species.

**Temperature** *Ficus* tolerates heat but does not like fluctuations in temperature. Of the species, *F. carica* withstands cold best (it can be grown outdoors in a sheltered garden in Britain). The other species should be kept in winter in a temperature that does not fall below 13°C (55°F).

**Ventilation** Keep out of draughts.

**Container** Choose a medium-deep pot when the plant is young; old specimens need much deeper containers. It can be glazed or unglazed, decorated or undecorated. Old trees are usually planted in rectangular containers.

**Regular maintenance** Do not cut off any aerial roots that develop. Remove any shoots growing out of the trunk and any yellow leaves. Wipe the foliage with a sponge soaked in a water to remove dust.

**Growth** These plants grow fast and steadily. You can quite quickly achieve spectacular specimens.

**Repotting** Every second year (every third year in the case of old trees), in mid- to late spring, prune the roots by a half and repot into a larger container.

**Soil** Use a mixture of equal parts ericaceous compost, loam, coarse sand and leaf mould. *Ficus* likes warm, medium-damp, slightly calcareous soil, which should be permeable, deep, cool and rich. It is possible to use peat instead of ericaceous compost.

**Pruning**
*Pruning sub-branches* During the growing season cut sub-branches back to two or three pairs of leaves as soon as they have produced five or six.
*Pruning branches* In late winter prune out branches that are damaged, overlong or broken. Cuts will ooze, and the liquid they produce is rubber. Apply a wound-sealing compound to large cuts.
*Leaf pruning* It is possible to remove all the leaves from a healthy plant. Give less water after leaf stripping. Alternatively, cut only large leaves off the tree.

**Wiring** This can be done at any time of year. Wait until the branches have hardened. Remove copper wire after six to eight weeks.

**Watering** Keep the roots dry in winter. Give a moderate amount of water during other seasons, with a little more in summer.

**Misting** Mist the foliage daily to create the humid heat that these plants prefer.

**Feeding** In spring and autumn feed with a slow-release, organic fertilizer. If the bonsai is in prime condition, it can be fed once in winter. Use a liquid and a solid fertilizer alternately.

Ficus microcarpa *(syn. F. retusa; curtain fig): 150 years old; 110cm (43in) high; Tachiki style. Photographed in late spring. This is a fine specimen, with aerial roots that twine around the main trunk.*

## SPECIES

*Ficus benjamina* (weeping fig) The well-known houseplant is native to Asia, Australia and islands in the southwest Pacific, when it can grow to 30m (100ft). It has bright green, oblong, evergreen leaves and a supple, elegant habit. The upright trunk is grey.

*Ficus carica* (common fig) This deciduous species yields the highly prized fruit. It is native to western Asia and the east Mediterranean and grows to about 3m (10ft). The leathery leaves have three or five lobes.

*Ficus microcarpa* (syn. *F. retusa*; curtain fig, Indian laurel, Malay banyan) This tree, which is closely related to *F. benjamina*, resembles the banyan and grows to 30m (100ft). The bright green, evergreen leaves are elongated, and the tree puts out aerial roots, which may root when they reach the ground.

*Ficus natalensis* subsp. *leprieurii* (syn. *F. triangularis*; Natal fig) This shrub or tree, to 20m 70ft), has broadly obovate or obdeltoid, leathery, evergreen leaves and relatively small fruits. It is native to Zambia to Senegal.

*Ficus neriifolia* This is a small tree, deciduous for a short period in spring, which is native to the Himalayas and eastwards to China. It has entire leaves, red when young but maturing to dark green above, lighter green below.

*Ficus religiosa* (sacred fig, peepul). This deciduous or semi-deciduoud tree, to 8m (25ft), is native to China, Thailand and Vietnam. The leathery leaves are dark, glossy green.

*Ficus rubiginosa* (syn. Port Jackson fig) Native to eastern Australia, this is an evergreen tree, which grows to 15m (50ft). It has leathery leaves, which are at first hairy, later smooth and lighter below.

## PESTS AND DISEASES

### PESTS
**Eelworms** See page 34.

**Thrips**
*Symptoms* There are dry, grey patches on the leaves, and spots appear on these. The plant will be weakened, and the leaves eaten. The insects may be seen beneath the leaves.
*Treatment* Spray with malathion or with heptenophos and permethrin.

**Vine weevils**
*Symptoms* These are a very serious pest of all container-grown plants. The first sign may be the total collapse of the plant, but inspection will show that the roots have been eaten by the brown-headed, white larvae. Adult weevils eat the edges of leaves.
*Treatment* At the first sign of attack remove the plant from the pot. Remove and kill the larvae. Prune the roots and repot in good soil. Spray with contact insecticide from late spring to midsummer. Under glass, use the parasitic nematode *Heterorhabditis megedis*.

### DISEASES
**Anthracnose**
*Symptoms* There is a form of this fungal disease that is specific to *Ficus*. Yellow patches appear on the edge of the leaves and spread all over the surface. Specks of black can be seen on these patches. The foliage becomes discoloured and crumpled. The diseased parts wither and drop off.
*Treatment* Make sure the soil is not too damp and keep the temperature constant.

Cut out and burn diseased leaves. Spray with a fungicide such as Bordeaux mixture as leaves open and again, in summer.

**Scorching**
*Symptoms* Pale brown patches appear on the leaves, which become papery and tear. The foliage is shrivelled, distorted and may have holes in it. Badly affected leaves will drop.
*Treatment* Take care not to mist the foliage or to water while the sun is on the tree; keep out of strong, direct sun and protect from cold, drying winds. Keep away from noxious gases. Do not use a fertilizer that is too rich in nitrogen. Water from the base to avoid getting drops of water on the foliage.

**Grey mould**
*Symptoms* This fungal disease (botrytis) causes dead and discoloured patches to appear on stems and leaves. A grey, velvety mould forms on leaves and stems, and spreads rapidly in damp, overcrowded conditions and when plants are kept in poorly ventilated rooms. The leaves wither, then fall. The side branches become cankered.
*Treatment* Provide good ventilation. Be careful not to overwater or to expose the plant to changes in temperature. Cut out and burn the diseased branches and remove and burn any leaves that all. Spray with a fungicide containing benomyl, thiophanate-methyl or carbendazim.

# GARDENIA

Rubiaceae. Evergreen. This is a genus of about 250 shrubs and trees, mostly from tropical and subtropical areas of Asia. The glossy leaves are simple and leathery, but gardenias are usually grown for the fragrant flowers.

## PROPAGATION

**Cuttings** Choose strong, lateral shoots and try to take them off with a heel. Cuttings can be grown in a greenhouse virtually at any time of year, but midwinter is a good time. Plant the cuttings in ericaceous compost and keep in a warm place at 22°C (72°F) until they have rooted. Pot up in spring.

**Layering** Air layering or simple layering work best in spring in a light, warm room.

**Young nursery stock** Choose a plant with a good trunk and prune the branches (see also page 18).

## CARE

**Sunlight** Gardenias need a lot of light but keep them out of direct sun. In areas with warm summers they can be stood outside.

**Temperature** They need warmth during the growing season but during dormancy gradually reduce the heat. In winter the temperature should not fall below 12–15∞C (54–59∞F).

**Ventilation** Protect from draughts but make sure plants are in well-ventilated rooms, especially during dormancy.

**Container** Select a fairly deep bowl; unglazed containers are usually used.

**Regular maintenance** Remove the flowers as soon as they start to go yellow. The flowers do not last long, but by way of compensation their scent is delightful.

**Growth** These are slow-growing plants.

**Repotting** Every second year, in late spring when the new buds are appearing, prune the roots by a half and repot into a larger container.

**Soil** Use a mixture of equal parts ericaceous compost, loam, leaf mould and

### SPECIES

***Gardenia augusta*** (syn. *G. florida, G. grandiflora, G. jasminoides*;) Cape jasmine, common gardenia, opera flower) This tender shrub is native to China, Taiwan and Japan and grows to 12m (40ft). It is of regular habit, and has evergreen, glossy, bright green leaves and white, highly scented, double flowers. Most *Gardenia augusta* trees that are grown as bonsai come from natural material collected in Japan and China.

sharp sand. Gardenias like warm, humus-rich soil.

**Pruning**
*Pruning sub-branches* When flowering is over cut the branches of old trees back hard. On younger trees, cut back side branches to leave just three leaves as soon as they have produced six or seven.
*Pruning branches* At the end of winter cut out any branches that mar the overall appearance or that are damaged or diseased. Apply a wound-sealant compound to any large cuts.

**Wiring** Wait until new shoots have lignified or apply wire before the buds have hardened. Protect the bark with strips of raffia.

**Watering** Give only a little water in winter, but do not allow the soil to dry out. In summer water moderately. Just before flowering slightly increase the amount of water given to encourage blooming.

**Misting** Mist the leaves daily except when the tree is in flower. Gardenias need a lot of moisture in the atmosphere. If necessary, stand the container on a gravel-covered tray to improve humidity.

**Feeding** Apply fertilizer after flowering and in autumn. It is best to use a slow-release, organic liquid fertilizer. If the leaves turn yellow, add a little nitrogen to the fertilizer.

Chokkan

Shakan

Tachiki

Han-Kengai

Sharimiki

Neagari

Fukinagashi

Sabamiki

Sôkan

Kabudachi

Korabuki

Sôju

Bonkei

Plantations saisonnières

STYLES

Gardenia augusta (common gardenia): 15 years old; 14cm (5½in) high; Shakan style. Photographed in mid-autumn. Most of the Gardenia augusta plants grown as bonsai are found growing wild in Asia and then trained to grow in containers.

## PESTS AND DISEASES

### PESTS

**Scale insects** See page 33.

**Greenfly** See page 33.

#### Whitefly

*Symptoms* These tiny insects, resemble minute moths and can be a real pest in greenhouses, where they are seen on the leaves, which are covered with honeydew and sooty mould.

*Treatment* Spray with an insecticide such as malathion, permethrin or heptenophos and permethrin. Organic gardeners will prefer to try the parasitic wasp *Encarsia formosa*; do not use insecticides for other pests if a biological control has been introduced to the greenhouse.

#### Snails

*Symptoms* In spring stems, leaves, buds and flowers are eaten.

*Treatment* Collect up the snails and dispose of them. Avoid excessive moisture and remove decaying organic material. Scatter methiocarb or metaldehyde pellets.

### DISEASES

#### Chlorosis

*Symptoms* The leaves gradually turn yellow, discoloured parts wither and the foliage gradually drops off.

*Treatment* Take care not to apply too much calcium and water, and do not let the tree get too cold. Keep plants out of draughts and away from noxious gases. Keep in a well-lit position. Apply iron, magnesium, zinc and nitrogen to the soil.

# MAIDENHAIR TREE

Ginkgoaceae. Deciduous. The name of this monotypic genus should be spelt 'ginkyo', which is the Latin transcription of the Chinese name *Yin-Kuo* (silver apricot). It is a ancient tree, a living fossil, which can grow to a height of 30m (100ft) and is native to China. In Japan it was planted near Buddhist temples. It is a dioecious species. The outline is pyramid shaped. The straight, ash-grey trunk has fissures running down the bark. The branches are spreading and horizontal. The top of a male tree is conical, while female trees have a wider crown with more deeply incised leaves, which turn yellow a month later than leaves on the male tree. The light green leaves turn golden-yellow in autumn, giving rise to the name 'tree of the forty golden crowns'. The ginkgo was for a long time classified as a conifer, but is now recognized as a separate though closely allied genus. The leaves are shaped like a rounded fan, sometimes with a central indentation dividing it into two lobes (*biloba*). Catkin-like inflorescences are male. The fruit is like a yellow plum, but is poisonous and foul smelling. When it is old, the ginkgo may grow aerial roots like stalactites.

## PROPAGATION

**Seed** Collecting seed from an isolated female tree will not yield results because the seed will not have been fertilized, so you need a fertilized tree. Keep the nut stratified for a year after harvesting. Sowing takes place in the second spring after harvesting. Soak the nut in hot water before sowing it so that the shell will split. Leave the seedlings for a year before transferring to a growing pot. Keep sheltered.

**Cuttings** Take semi-ripe cuttings in summer. It is best to use short lateral shoots. Cut off the tip and dip the bottom end of the slip into hormone rooting compound, and plant in a mixture of equal parts of sand and peat.

**Air layering** This air layering method produces twisted trees. Strip the bark from the part of the branch to be layered. Wrap sphagnum moss around it and envelop that with polythene, bound at either end with raffia to keep it closed. Mist. When the layer has taken, remove the polythene and moss and sever the layer from the tree. Pot up and treat as a tree that has just been repotted.

**Side grafting** In summer graft low on the trunk so that later on the earth will hide the graft union. The incision made into the rootstock is wider deeper down. The following spring the graft should have taken. Cut off the rootstock above the scion, pot up and treat as a tree that has just been repotted. *G. biloba* 'Pendula' is the cultivar most commonly grafted.

**Young nursery stock** Select a tree with an interesting trunk and a lot of branches (see page 18).

(see page 18).

### SPECIES

There are several cultivars of *Ginkgo biloba*: 'Aurea' has yellow leaves; 'Fastigiata' forms a narrow pyramid; 'Laciniata' has wide leaves, divided and indented; 'Pendula' has a rounded crown and the tips of the branches turn down; 'Princeton Sentry' is a male tree with a narrow, upright habit; 'Variegata' has leaves variegated with yellow.

Tachiki

Sôkan

Hôkidachi

Kabudachi

Ikadabuki

Netsunagari

STYLES

# CARE

**Sunlight** The ginkgo likes full sun. However, in summer young specimens and trees that have just been repotted should be kept in partial shade.

**Temperature** The ginkgo does not like frost. In winter protect the plant from severe cold and frost, covering the roots, the container and the trunk. Alternatively, keep it sheltered in a cold room.

**Ventilation** The ginkgo is not sensitive to atmospheric pollution and stands up to wind. However, shield trees that have been repotted for six weeks.

**Container** The ginkgo needs deep soil. Choose a round, hexagonal or square, fairly deep bowl, glazed or unglazed. Cobalt blue or brown are suitable.

**Regular maintenance** Regularly remove any dead material from the tree and compost to guard against diseases and pests. Mist the leaves to clean them and allow them to respire.

**Growth** At first these tree grow slowly, speeding up later.

**Repotting** Repot the ginkgo about every three years after new shoots have started to grow. Prune the roots by a half.

**Soil** Use a mixture of equal parts leaf mould, loam and sand. The ginkgo adapts to ordinary soil as long as it is deep and contains some clay and some loam.

**Pruning**
*Pinching back* Pinch out all unwanted growth on the trunk and large branches. Pinch out the tips of shoots and pick off two or three leaves from each branch. When a second set of buds appears, pinch out and pick off again, cutting back to one or two pairs of leaves. New shoots are then allowed to develop.
*Leaf pruning* Cut the leaves as soon as they have hardened on each branch.
*Pruning branches* The branches are pruned in spring when repotting takes place. Eliminate any superfluous branches. Prune other branches back to about a third of their length.
*Structural pruning* In winter cut out any branches that detract from the outline of the tree. Apply a wound-sealing compound to the cut.

**Wiring** As a rule, gingkoes are not wired, and he shape is mainly created by pinching back the head and the shoots and pruning the leaves and branches. Occasionally, however, a ginkgo can be lightly wired in

autumn, with the copper wire being removed at the end of summer.

**Watering** Allow the soil to dry out between waterings, and wet it thoroughly each time you water. Never water during frosty weather. Water daily in summer, but not in full sun. In autumn it is best to water the tree in the morning.

**Misting** Mist plants thoroughly from mid-spring to early autumn to keep the trunk, branches and foliage free of dust and pollution.

**Feeding** Feed with an organic fertilizer in spring and in autumn. Do not feed in mid- or late summer or for two months after repotting. Increase the amount of fertilizer given in the last autumn feed to set the tree up for winter.

*Ginkgo biloba (maidenhair tree): 20 years old; 30cm (12in) tall; Kabudachi style. Photographed in mid-autumn. In early autumn the leaves take on this golden-yellow hue, which gives rise to the tree's nickname of 'the tree of the forty golden crowns'.*

## PESTS AND DISEASES

### PESTS
Gingkoes make hardy bonsai specimens and are not usually attacked by pests.

### DISEASES
**Honey fungus** See page 35.

# HOLLY

Aquifoliaceae. Deciduous or evergreen. This is a genus of more than 400 species of long-lived shrubs and trees, which are found throughout the world. In ideal conditions a holly tree might live to be 200 years old and could grow to a height of 25m (80ft). Holly trees tend to be conical with straight trunks and spreading branches, which curve upwards at the tip. They are bushy and produce branches right from its base. The alternate leaves are oval and are entire, spiny or semi-toothed. The foliage is usually dark green and glossy, but several cream, silver and gold variegated forms are available. Insignificant pinkish-white, scented flowers appear in late spring or early summer.

## PROPAGATION

**Seed** Pick the berries in late autumn and leave them in a heap to rot. Wash the seeds, dry them and stratify in sand. Sow the following autumn or spring in humus-rich, peaty soil, which must be kept damp, in partial shade. Germination cannot be guaranteed and can take up to three years. Prick out seedlings a year later.

**Cuttings** In mid- or late summer take cuttings from trees with evergreen leaves and plant under glass in a mixture consisting of two parts peat and one part sand. The following spring, remove the glass. It is best to take cuttings from the current year's growth, which roots better.

**Simple layering** Layer for two years in cool, peaty soil. After severing from the parent plant, protect the tender plantlets from extremes of weather. This is the most satisfactory method.

**Young nursery stock** See page 18.

## CARE

**Sunlight** *Ilex crenata* tolerates full sun, even in summer. Place other species in partial shade in summer, although they should be in sun for the rest of the year. Bear in mind that hollies are naturally woodland plants and will do best in partial shade. Variegated forms do best in good light.

Ilex serrata *(syn.* I. sieboldii; *Japanese winterberry): 30 years old; 50cm (2in) high; Korabuki style. Photographed in early winter.*

**Temperature** Hollies like humid warmth and react badly to intense cold. Protect your bonsai if the temperature falls below -5°C (23°F).

**Ventilation** These plants prefer shelter from really strong winds, especially if they are cold and drying.

**Container** Choose a medium deep pot. Cobalt blue or terracotta are the most appropriate colours and suit the foliage, but it does not matter if the container is glazed or unglazed.

**Regular maintenance** Remove all unwanted growth on the trunk. If there are

Shakan

Kengai

Tachiki

Han-Kengai

Bunjingi

Sekijôju

Ishitsuki

Sabamiki

Sôkan

Korabuki

Kabudachi

Ikadabuki

Netsunagari

Bonkei

Ilex serrata *(syn.* I. sieboldii*; Japanese winterberry): 40 years old; 60cm (24in) high; Korabuki style. Photographed in early winter.*

## SPECIES

***Ilex aquifolium*** (common holly, English holly) An erect, evergreen tree or shrub, not reliably hardy, growing to 25m (80ft). The spiny leaves are glossy dark green, and the bark is grey. Fruit appears in early autumn.
***Ilex crenata*** (box-leaved holly, Japanese holly) An evergreen shrub, to 5m (16ft) tall, this is native to Russia, Japan and Korea. It has glossy, dark green leaves without prickles, and shiny black (or yellow or white) fruit.
***Ilex serrata*** (syn. *I. sieboldii*; Japanese winterberry) A compact, deciduous shrub, native to Japan and China, and growing to 5m (16ft). It has dull green, downy leaves. The fruit stays on the tree throughout winter. This species is often used for bonsai.

too many berries, or they stay too long on the tree, remove some before they exhaust the plant.

**Growth** Hollies are slow-growing plants, getting to 6m (20ft) high in 10 years.

**Repotting** In early spring, before bud burst, each year or every second year, prune between one-third and one-half from the roots and pot up into a slightly larger container.

**Soil** Use a mixture of equal parts loam and leaf mould. Some people say that hollies like acid soil, but this is not correct. They thrive in fertile soil that is clayey, calcareous, light, cool or even sandy.

**Pruning**
*Pinching back* Pinch out some new buds as they form. Also pinch out any superfluous shoots as soon as you see them but leave the remaining shoots to develop well until the leaves have hardened.
*Pruning sub-branches* Shorten by 3–6cm (1¼-2½in). Prune away unwanted secondary laterals but allow the others to develop.
*Pruning branches* When you are repotting, shape the tree by pruning any branches that have grown the previous year.
*Structural pruning* When you prune out a main branch, make sure that the cut is concave. Apply a wound-sealing compound.

**Wiring** Wire from spring to summer. Shape young branches with raffia, and protect other branches with raffia when coiling wire around them. The branches break quite easily.

**Watering** Water more freely from the start of flowering until the fruit appears in order to obtain good fruit formation. At other times, moisten the soil well and allow it to dry out between waterings.

**Misting** Mist plants thoroughly. Hollies do best in high humidity.

**Feeding** In spring and autumn apply a slow-release, organic fertilizer. In autumn reduce the amount of fertilizer.

## PESTS AND DISEASES

If a holly is badly positioned, without good light and freely circulating air, or if it has too much water, toadstools may grow on it. You will then have to use a fungicide to combat possible rot.

### PESTS
**Tortrix moth** See page 33.

**Leaf miners** See page 33.

### DISEASES
**Leaf spot** See page 35.

# JASMINE, JESSAMINE

Oleaceae. Deciduous or evergreen. This is a genus of about 200 species of shrubs and woody climbers, which are found in tropical and subtropical areas of southern Europe, north Africa and western Asia. They have alternate, pinnate leaves, but are mostly grown for their beautifully fragrant flowers, which are borne in cymes. Most species produce black berries.

## PROPAGATION

**Cuttings** Take softwood cuttings from branches that have grown that summer, and plant in early or midsummer. They can also be planted in autumn. Keep the cuttings in a greenhouse or under glass and leave them undisturbed for about two years.

**Simple layering** Do this in spring.

**Young nursery stock** See page 18.

## CARE

**Sunlight** Jasmines like light, but although they should be in a sunny position, they do not like direct summer sun. Provide some shelter at the height of summer.

**Temperature** These plants are not reliably hardy and should be protected from severe frost.

**Ventilation** Jasmines are not fussy plants but will do best in a slightly sheltered position.

**Container** Choose a small pot. The decoration should be selected to harmonize with the flowers.

**Regular maintenance** Cut off roots that grow from nodes on branches as soon as they appear, and remove shoots and suckers. Pick off the flowers as soon as they have faded.

**Growth** These are fairly slow-growing plants.

**Repotting** Repot once a year, preferably in early spring, before the flowers open or in autumn after the flowers have gone. Prune the roots by between one-third and one-half, and pot up into a larger container.

**Soil** Use a mixture of two parts loam, one part leaf mould and one part sharp sand. These plants are not fussy about the type of soil, but winter-flowering jasmine thrives in light, slightly moist, friable, nutritious soil.

**Pruning**
*Pinching back* Pinch out all superfluous shoots and allow others to develop. Prune faded shoots to one or two pairs of leaves.

Jasminum nudiflorum *(winter-flowering jasmine): the flowers appear before the leaves in late winter to early spring.*

Kengai

Tachiki

Shakan

Han-Kengai

Sekijôju

Neagari

Ishitsuki

Sôkan

Kabudachi

Ikadabuki

Netsunagari

*Jasminum humile* (Italian yellow jasmine) An evergreen, erect shrub, to 4m (12ft). The yellow flowers are borne in clusters from late spring until autumn.

*Jasminum nudiflorum* (winter-flowering jasmine) A deciduous, erect shrub, native to northern China, with arched green branches that curve back towards the ground. The dark green leaves are divided into three leaflets. The bright yellow flowers, which are in bloom from late winter to early spring, are borne on the previous year's wood before the leaves appear.

*Jasminum officinale* (common jasmine, jessamine) This deciduous, climbing shrub is native to the Caucasus, the Himalayas, Afghanistan and China. It is not reliably hardy. The white flowers, borne in cymes from summer to autumn, are intensely fragrant.

Repeat in midsummer.

*Pruning sub-branches* Prune branches you have allowed to grow back to two or three pairs of leaves. Prune again in early autumn, leaving three or four pairs of leaves.

*Structural pruning* Prune the main branches, shortening them or cutting them out completely, before flowering.

**Wiring** Wire from spring to summer, protecting the bark with raffia. Use raffia to train young branches. The branches of *J. nudiflorum* are brittle.

**Watering** Water plants copiously if they are in full sun. *J. nudiflorum* needs a lot of water, but this must not be allowed to stagnate at root level.

**Misting** Sprinkle water on the leaves during watering, but do not wet plants that are in flower.

**Feeding** Use a slow-release, organic fertilizer after flowering. Do not feed in mid- to late summer. In early autumn use fertilizer enriched with phosphate.

Jasminum nudiflorum *(winter-flowering jasmine): 20 years old; 18cm (7in) high; Sekijôju style. Photographed in late winter.*

## PESTS AND DISEASES

### PESTS
**Tortrix moth** See page 33.

### DISEASES
Jasmines are largely trouble free, although they react badly to pollution. If flower buds fail to develop, if flowers fade too quickly or if leaves turn yellow and fall prematurely, there are problems with watering.

**Phyllosticta blight**
*Symptoms* The fungal disease causes withered spots on the leaves with tiny black spots on them. Leaves eventually drop off.
*Treatment* Cut off and destroy infected leaves and spray with a copper-based fungicide.

**Jasmine yellow ring mosaic virus**
*Symptoms* The leaves gradually turn yellow, become distorted and may fall.
*Treatment* Destroy affected material. There are no chemical cures, but control aphids that carry the virus.

# CHINESE JUNIPER

Cupressaceae. Evergreen conifer. This hardy species is native to China and Mongolia, and in the wild it can grow to a height of 25m (80ft), although cultivated forms grown in Europe are not generally as tall. The species is less often grown than the many excellent cultivars that have been developed. It is a relatively short-lived species and is extremely variable. It is an upright conical tree to spreading shrub. Young needles, borne in twos or threes, are long and wedge-shaped; old needles are diamond-shaped and scale-like and held almost flat to the branches. The foliage is aromatic. Both adult and juvenile foliage can be found on the same tree. The brownish-red bark peels easily. Male trees bear yellow flowers; female trees produce green flowers in the leaf axils. The spherical cones are brownish-purple.

## PROPAGATION

**Seed** *Juniperus chinensis* is seldom grown from seed. If you collect the seed yourself, remove the seed from the flesh and sow in a cold frame in early spring. Germination may take five years and cannot be guaranteed.

**Cuttings** Take greenwood cuttings. Strip off the bark and remove lateral shoots from the lower part of the stem. Pinch out the tip of any slip that is too long. A new leader will grow as the roots form. The best time is from mid- to late summer. Plant the cuttings out in a mixture of sharp sand and peat. *Juniperus chinensis* will grow well from cuttings of young stems, but do not take cuttings after the bark on new wood has turned brown. If wished, dip the slips into hormone rooting compound before planting.

**Air layering** This technique can be done in spring. When the plant has come into growth, coil some wire around the branch (or trunk) to be layered, but do not fasten it so tightly that the sap cannot circulate. Peel off the bark immediately above the wire. Wrap damp sphagnum moss around it and enclose in polythene, sealed at both ends. It does not need much moisture. Roots will form in anything from three to six months. If the layering is done early in the season, it can be severed from the tree in early autumn. Pot up the new plant and treat it as a tree that has just been repotted. It must be protected from severe winter weather.

**Simple layering** Select a low, flexible branch. Strip off the bark from the section to be buried and remove any tufts of needles from it. Make one or two incisions in the wood to encourage rooting. Bury in a compost consisting of equal parts sharp sand, peat and loam. Water regularly, especially in summer. When new shoots appear, sever the layer and pot up.

**Side grafting** Make the graft in late winter. Select a straight, pencil-thick rootstock. The scion must be of the same diameter as the stock at the point of union. Bind the graft (grafting wax is not necessary) and keep moist by misting. Put in a warm place. Protect from wind. In about six months, when the graft will have bonded, the top of the rootstock can be cut off, potted up and treated as a tree that has just been repotted.

**Young nursery stock** Select a plant with an interesting trunk and firm, glossy needles (see also page 18).

## CARE

**Sunlight** *Juniperus chinensis* will tolerate full sun. It is not too demanding as regards climate, but these plants do grow better in the sun than in shady sites. Young trees should be placed in partial shade in summer.

**Temperature** *Juniperus chinensis* withstands both heat and cold. Even so, the needles tend to be frost-bitten in

Shakan

Kengai

Tachiki

Bankan

Han-Kengai

Bunjingi

Sharimiki

Neagari

Ishitsuki

Sekijôju

Nejikan

Sôkan

Kabudachi

Ikadabuki

Netsunagari

Bonkei

STYLES

Juniperus chinensis *var. sargentii: 40 years old; 15cm (6in) high; Bankan style. Photographed in late spring.*

## VARIETIES AND CULTIVARS

*Juniperus chinensis* 'Aurea' (Young's golden juniper) A columnar tree with golden-yellow foliage, which turns blue-grey as the tree matures.
*Juniperus chinensis* 'Japonica' This is a more prickly form, and its shoots stand up when it is old.
*Juniperus chinensis* 'Kaizuka' An erect shrub, with spreading branches and bright green foliage.
*Juniperus chinensis* 'Pyramidalis' A shrubby form with blue-grey foliage, which is prickly, unlike *J. c.* 'Stricta', which is otherwise similar.
*Juniperus chinensis* var. *sargentii* This is the variety most often used in the creation of bonsai.

winter, especially if they have snow on them. The plants stand up well to frost, although the leading shoot may freeze in winter.

**Ventilation** Protect young plants and recently repotted trees from strong, drying winds.

**Container** Choose a brown or terracotta, glazed or unglazed container. It should be quite deep, especially for older trees.

**Regular maintenance** From spring to the end of autumn regularly pick off any yellow needles from the tree. Mist the foliage and bark to cleanse them of dust and pollution. Keep the surface of the soil clean.

**Growth** Young plants grow quickly but slow down as they mature.

**Repotting** Repot in early spring every three to five years, depending on the age of the bonsai.

**Soil** Use a mixture of equal parts sharp sand, loam and leaf mould. This juniper tolerates any soil, but does best in ordinary, permeable, calcareous soil.

**Pruning**
*Pinching back* Between spring and autumn you need to pinch back new shoots between your thumb and index finger. Never use scissors to cut the needles. Pinch back well inside the foliage to improve the tree's development.

*Pruning sub-branches* In early and mid-spring and in early and mid-autumn prune quite hard to keep the foliage dense.
*Pruning branches* At the end of winter cut out any dead or damaged branches and any that detract from the overall appearance of the tree.

**Wiring** Wire in autumn and leave the wire in place for about eight months. Repeat every year until you have achieved

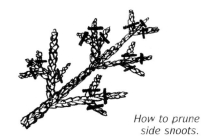

*How to prune side snoots.*

the shape you are aiming at. Make sure that you do not trap needles between the wire and the bark.

**Watering** This juniper needs plenty of water. Thoroughly moisten the soil, but let it dry out before watering again. Water daily in summer, less frequently in autumn, increasing the amount you give again in spring. Give more water to specimens that are exposed to drying winds.

**Misting** In summer mist the needles,

trunk and branches freely, with extra misting on the foliage.

**Feeding** Feed in spring and in autumn. Increase the amount given in the last autumn feed to set up the tree for winter. Do not feed in mid- or late summer nor if the tree is sickly or has just been repotted. Never feed with highly concentrated fertilizer because this might disturb the balance of branch and foliage growth.

## PESTS AND DISEASES

### PESTS
*Juniperus chinensis* is susceptible to the same pests as *J. rigida*; see pages 106–7.

### DISEASES
**Coryneum cardinale**
*Symptoms* This is a form of canker, infecting conifers, especially cypresses. The foliage turns yellow and brow and the branches wither. Black cankers develop on the bark with resin running from them.
*Treatment* Take care that you do not accidentally wound the tree. The fungal spores are air borne and infect branches through cuts. There is no effective chemical control. Remove and destroy all infected branches. Badly infected plants should be entirely destroyed.

Chokkan

Shakan

Kengai

Bankan

Han-Kengai

Tachiki

Bunjingi

Sekijôju

Sharimiki

Ishitsuki

Sabamiki

Nejikan

Sôkan

Korabuki

Kabudachi

Ikadabuki

Netsunagari

Sôju

Sambon-Yose

Nanahon-Yose

Gohon-Yose

Kyûhon-Yose

Yamayori

Yose-Ue

Tsukami-Yose

Bonkei

**STYLES**

# TEMPLE JUNIPER

Cupressaceae. Evergreen conifer. *Juniperus rigida* is native to Japan, Manchuria and Korea, where it will grow to a height of 8m (25ft) or more. These trees have a graceful outline, with branches arching at their tips, and side branches curving downwards. The slightly yellowish-green foliage has a light band on its upper face, which is formed by stomata. The foliage is stiff and needle shaped. The linear needles are narrow, concave and prickly. The round cones are green, turning purplish-black as they ripen.

## PROPAGATION

**Seed** Collect seed in late autumn. The fruits are picked like bilberries by 'combing' the tree. Dry the cones in a cool, airy place, then soak them in water for two days, before grinding and sieve them to get the seeds. Stratify these and sow in spring. They germinate after a year. If you buy seed, it may germinate in the second year, so leave the seed bed undisturbed until shoots appear.

**Cuttings** Take ripe cuttings before the wood has turned brown with or without heels. Strip off the bark and remove side shoots from the lower part. If the slip is too long, cut off the tip. When it has rooted, a new leading shoot will develop. Take cuttings in mid- or late summer and plant them in a mixture of sharp sand and sieved peat. Do not use hormone rooting compound but put a layer of good compost in the bottom of the tray. When the cutting has rooted, pot it up and keep it protected.

**Simple layering** This should be done in early spring. Wind some copper wire around the branch or trunk to be layered. Pull it tight but not so tight that the sap cannot circulate. Cut into the wood above the wire and strip the bark off the area above the wire. Wrap moist sphagnum moss around the area and enclose in polythene sealed at both ends. Mist to keep damp, but do not overdo it. In six months roots will have formed. If the layering has been carried out early in the season, the layer can be severed in early autumn and potted up. It will be established after a year, but until then protect it from strong wind and sun and from severe cold and drought.

**Young nursery stock** Select a tree with an interesting trunk and shape and with dense, sharp needles. Treat it as a tree that is to be repotted as far as pruning, wiring and potting up are concerned. (See also page 18.)

## CARE

**Sunlight** *Juniperus rigida* likes full sun, but do not expose young specimens and trees that have just been repotted to too much direct summer sun.

**Temperature** This juniper stands up to heat and cold, but the needles may turn brown in winter and the leading shoot may freeze. Protect plants from extreme cold.

**Ventilation** These plants are not affected by wind.

**Container** Choose a bowl of medium depth, transferring the tree to a deeper container as it gets older. A rectangular container in a shade of brown suits it best.

**Regular maintenance** Remove dead needles and twigs and yellow needles off the tree. Always take care to clean inside the tree to encourage the foliage to develop

### SPECIES

*Juniperus communis* (common juniper) This species, found widely throughout Eurasia, is a densely branching shrub or tree to 10m (33ft), largely similar to *P.*
*Juniperus squamata* (flaky juniper) Native to the Himalayas and China, this is a variable, prostrate or erect shrub with nodding tips to the shoots.

Juniperus rigida *(temple juniper): 110 years old; 45cm (18in) high; Sharimiki style. The bright green young shoots, which should be pinched out, can be seen clearly seen. It is also possible to see the way in which the jin technique has been used to give the tree an especially venerable appearance.*

## PESTS AND DISEASES

### PESTS
**Bark beetles** See page 34.

**Red spider mites** See page 32.

**Buprestrids**
*Symptoms* This is a group of insects whose larvae are wood borers. The insects are shiny and metallic looking and may be seen in summer. The larvae, which may live for 30 years, hollow out galleries in the wood, eventually causing branches to wither.
*Treatment* Cut out and burn infested branches. Spray with a systemic insecticide in summer.

**Leaf miners** See page 33.

**Aphids** See page 33.

**Blackfly** See page 34.

**Hard-shelled scale insects** See page 33.

### DISEASES
**Die-back**
*Symptoms* Twigs and branches turn brown and then wither.
*Treatment* Cut out diseased branches and spray with copper-based fungicide. Be careful that the fungicide does not damage the host plant.

**Rust** See page 35.

---

well. Pick dead leaves and wood off the compost. Mist well in summer to get rid of dust on the needles and trunk.

**Growth** When the bonsai is young it grows quickly and its roots develop rapidly. Once it is older the rate of growth slows considerably.

**Repotting** In mid- to late spring, every three to five years, prune the roots by half.

**Soil** Use a mixture of equal parts sharp sand, leaf mould and loam. This juniper has no special requirements but grows well in a calcareous, permeable soil.

**Pruning**
*Pinching back* Pinch back young shoots from spring to autumn. Do not cut the needles with clippers, because this will make them turn yellow and drop off. Even if you get scratched, pinch back well inside the tree. Remove shoots coming out of the trunk.
*Pruning sub-branches* In early spring shorten side branches by about a third, taking care not to cut the needles. Cut above a tuft.
*Pruning branches* At the beginning of winter carry out a structural pruning, removing any dead or damaged branches and those that detract from the overall appearance of the tree.

**Wiring** Coil wire around the branches to train them into the shape you want. Wrap raffia around the branches before wiring because the bark is brittle. Be careful that you not break or otherwise damage the branches. Put the wire in position in autumn and leave for eight to ten months. Repeat every year.

**Watering** This juniper should be allowed to dry out between waterings. It likes water, so soak the compost thoroughly each time you water as it absorbs a lot. Always check that it has taken up all the water before watering again.

**Misting** Mist well in summer to improve levels of humidity in the atmosphere around the *Juniperus rigida* and to cleanse it of dust and pollution. These plants like a humid atmosphere.

**Feeding** Feed with organic fertilizer once a month in spring and in autumn. Increase the amount given in the last autumn feed to set the tree up for winter.

# CREPE MYRTLE, CREPE FLOWER

Lythraceae. Deciduous or evergreen. The genus contains 53 species of tender trees and shrubs, which are native to tropical areas from Asia to Australia, including China and Japan. This deciduous species, which is native to China, is a tree or shrub and will grow to 8m (25ft) high and across. Its most striking feature is the exfoliating, reddish-brown bark, which peels away to reveal the whitish-grey trunk beneath. The ovate to obovate, entire leaves are borne in pairs or whorls. They are a glossy green in summer, turning red, brown and orange in autumn. The showy flowers, which may be white, pink or purple, are borne in panicles in late summer. The genus was named for the Swedish merchant Magnus von Lagerström (1691–1759), who was a friend of Linnaeus.

## PROPAGATION

**Cuttings** Take softwood cuttings in late spring or semi-ripe cuttings in summer. Dip the cuttings in hormone rooting compound before inserting them in compost in a warm, well-lit greenhouse; semi-ripe cuttings will need bottom heat. Use a standard cuttings compost to which some leaf mould and sharp sand have been added.

**Division** If a plant produces suckers, carefully separate these from the main stem, making sure that part of the root is attached. Pot in a warm, shaded place in good compost with added leaf mould and sharp sand.

## CARE

**Sunlight** This species requires sun all year round, although in very hot areas, it may need shading from direct summer sun.

**Temperature** This is a tender species, which will not survive winter frosts. Even if stood outside in summer, it should be overwintered in a conservatory.

**Ventilation** Although it will withstand warm breezes, it should be protected from strong, cold winds.

### CULTIVARS

Several cultivars of **L. indica** are available, including: 'White Dwarf', which is a shrub bearing abundant white flowers; 'Elegans', which is a vigorous form with small pink flowers; 'Rubra', which has pinkish-red flowers; and 'Violaceae', which produces reddish-purple flowers. The hybrid 'Miami' has deep pink flowers, and 'Natchez' has white flowers.

**Container** Choose a medium-deep container, which can be round, oval or rectangular. It does not matter if it is glazed or not. Select a colour that will complement the colour of the blooms and of the autumn leaves.

**Regular maintenance** Remove any yellow leaves from the tree and clear away leaves that fall onto the compost. Once or twice a year brush the trunk to remove any moss that is growing up it.

**Growth** *Lagerstroemia indica* will grow more quickly if it is kept in a warm, sheltered place.

Chokkan

Shakan

Tachiki

Sharimiki

Takozukuri

Sôkan

Sabamiki

Sôju

Netsunagari

STYLES

Lagerstroemia indica: *18 years old; 70cm (28in) high; Tachiki style. Photographed in late spring. The beautiful reddish-brown colour of the trunk is clearly visible. The bark generally peels away to reveal grey beneath.*

**Wiring** Put the wire in place in spring and remove it in winter. Repeat the process the following year if necessary.

**Watering** Water copiously from the moment growth begins in spring. Make sure that all water has been taken up by the roots before watering again. Water frequently in spring and summer and reduce the amount given in autumn and winter. In winter, in fact, give only sufficient water to keep the compost just moist.

**Misting** This species thrives in a humid atmosphere. Mist regularly to increase the humidity around the plant and mist the soil between waterings.

**Feeding** Apply a slow-acting, organic fertilizer from early spring until early summer and from early autumn to early winter. Give an additional feed at the end of autumn to boost the plant for winter.

**Repotting** Every second or third year in spring, when the buds begin to swell, pot up into good-quality, humus-rich compost. Prune between one-third and one-half of the roots, and if necessary repot into a container that is slightly larger than the one previously used.

**Soil** Use a mixture of five parts leaf mould, four parts loam and one part sharp sand. *Lagerstroemia indica* requires a rich compost, ideally without chemical additives.

**Pruning**
*Pruning shoots* Pinch out new shoots after flowering.
*Pruning sub-branches* At the end of winter cut the side branches fairly short, but take care that they are not damaged by late frosts, which could cause die-back.
*Leaf pruning* This is rarely done with this species.

## PESTS AND DISEASES

### PESTS
**Aphids** See page 33.

### DISEASES
**Powdery mildew** See page 34.

# LARCH

Pinaceae. Deciduous conifer. The genus contains about 14 species, which are native to the cold and high mountainous areas of the temperate zone in the northern hemisphere. They are long-lived trees, growing to about 50m (165ft) in height, and they have exfoliating bark. The distinguishing features of the tree are the needle-shaped leaves, which grow in clusters on short branches and singly on long ones. The small, egg-shaped cones stay on the tree for a long time.

## PROPAGATION

**Seed** Seeds can be gathered in autumn or winter depending on the climate in your area They ripen late. Leave the cones you have collected lying in the sun in winter. When they open up, shake them and the seeds will fall out. Take care: the cones close up again quickly. In early spring expose the seeds to warmth, turning them over several times, and keep them in medium humidity. Sow in mid- to late spring. They germinate slowly.

**Cuttings** You will get better results if you take cuttings on a damp, misty day. Always use hormone rooting compound. Do not take slips from old wood. The best time is late summer or early autumn, taking slips from leading shoots. However, larch cuttings are difficult to root, and you will get better results with another method.

**Simple layering** In spring select a low, flexible branch. Strip the section to be buried of foliage and make two or three incisions in the bark to encourage rooting. Bury the branch. Keep the earth moist. When you see new shoots, roots will have formed. Separate the layered branch from the parent plant, pot up and protect the young plant from extremes of wind, cold and sun.

**Grafting** Inlay grafting can be attempted towards the end of winter, but it is seldom used and good results cannot be guaranteed.

## CARE

**Sunlight** Larches tolerate and enjoy full sun. Provide bonsai with some shade from strong summer sun, however.

**Temperature** Larches grow at altitudes of up to 2400m (8000ft) and all species are fully hardy. They are not affected by cold.

**Ventilation** These trees stand up well to wind and need good ventilation.

**Container** Larches require a deep container because they need a good volume of well-drained, moisture-retentive soil and because they grow fast.

**Regular maintenance** Make sure you remove any dead material from inside the crown. In autumn the needles fall, so shake the tree gently to encourage the last ones and sweep the soil.

**Growth** Larches, especially *Larix kaempferi*, grow quickly and steadily.

**Repotting** In mid-spring, about every three years, prune the roots by half, and pot up into a larger container.

**Soil** Use a mixture consisting of equal parts leaf mould, loam and sharp sand. Larches thrive in cool, humus-rich, deep, clay soil; they do not like chalky soil.

**Pruning**
*Pinching back* Pinch back new shoots from the side branches in spring and right through the growing period. Remove any shoots coming from the trunk.
*Leaf cutting* This is not used on larches.
*Pruning branches* Cut back side branches that spread too far, taking them off just above a tuft of needles.
*Structural pruning* This is done on young specimens. You can prune the head of the larch when it has reached the height you want. In winter, when the needles have fallen, prune out any branches that spoil the tree's outline and any branches or side branches that are damaged.

**Wiring** The larch usually grows straight. When you want to train it either

Chokkan

Tachiki

Shakan

Sekijôju

Sharimiki

Ishitsuki

Sôkan

Sambon-Yose

Sabamiki

Kabudachi

Gohon-Yose

Sôju

Nanahon-Yose

Kyûhon-Yose

Yose-Ue

Kusamono

STYLES

*Larix decidua (European larch): 15 years old; 55cm (22in) high; Tachiki style. Photographed in early summer.*

## SPECIES

*Larix decidua* (common larch, European larch) This is a conical tree, native to continental Europe and growing to about 30m (100ft). In winter it sheds its needles, which are flat, narrow, soft and green. Egg-shaped cones start off red, turning brown.

*Larix kaempferi* (syn. *L. leptolepis*; Japanese larch) Native to Japan, this is a strongly growing, large tree, to 30m (100ft). It needs a damp climate and a light soil. It is conical in habit, with horizontal branches, bluish, thickly growing needles, which turn pinkish in autumn, and decorative, globular cones.

*Pseudolarix amaPbilis* (syn. *P. kaempferi*; golden larch) This monotypic genus is native to China and nowadays found naturalized in Italy. It is pyramidal in habit, with spreading branches. The needles, which are a soft green on the upper side and bluish with two bands of white underneath, turn golden in autumn. The cones are brick coloured. It needs lime-free soil.

often. However, larches can be misted occasionally in summer to clean the foliage rather than increase the humidity. *Larix kaempferi* will tolerate higher levels of humidity than other species.

**Feeding** Feed with a slow-release, organic fertilizer in spring and autumn. Increase the amount given at the last autumn application. Do not feed in mid- or late summer if the larch has just been repotted or if it is sickly.

emphasize its upright appearance or bend it by coiling wire around its trunk and branches in early summer. Remove the wire in autumn. Repeat annually if required.

**Watering** If the soil is well drained and permeable, water the larch frequently, especially in summer. The earth should be damp at all times because larches are native to moist mountainsides. Even so, take care that the soil does not become waterlogged.

**Misting** Larches prefer a fairly dry atmosphere and will wilt if the air is too moist, so there is no need to mist too

## PESTS AND DISEASES

### PESTS
**Gall-forming aphids** See page 33.
**Bark beetles** See page 34.
**Caterpillars** See page 33.

**Adelgids**
*Symptoms* The small insects (like aphids) suck the sap and stems. Honeydew is formed, on which sooty mould develops. In summer insects form colonies under white, waxy wool.
*Treatment* Spray with malathion in spring and again about three weeks later.

**Tortrix moth** See page 33.

### DISEASES
**Rust** See page 35.
**Honey fungus** See page 35.

**Die-back**
*Symptoms* Needles at the base of shoots turn yellow and drop off. Side branches wither.
*Treatment* Because die-back is usually caused by frost damage, fungal infection or a physiological complaint it is important to identify and treat the cause. Cut out and burn all infected stems and branches and make sure the plant is fed and watered appropriately.

**Canker**
*Symptoms* Stem canker causes lesions to appear on the branches, leading to malformations and withering. Only the Japanese larch is not susceptible to this disease.
*Treatment* There is no cure. Cut out and burn infected branches. Spray with Bordeaux mixture.

# BUSH CLOVER

Leguminosaceae. Deciduous. This is a genus of about 40 annual, perennials and sub-shrubs, which are native to rocky places in meadows, grassland and rocky places in tropical Asia and Australia and the eastern part of the United States. They have alternate, trifoliolobate leaves (that is, with three leaflets), and they have small, pea-flowers in late summer, making them useful in the mixed border. The colourful blooms are bright pinkish-red or purple. The name *Lespedeza* should actually be written *Cespedeza*, in honour of the Spaniard, Cespedez, who was governor of Florida at the end of the eighteenth century, but there was a spelling mistake.

## PROPAGATION

**Seed** Of the species, only *Lespedeza bicolor* is grown from seed. Seeds are sown in late spring in the open, but results are poor.

**Cuttings** Take cuttings in early summer. Plant in a mixture of equal parts peat and sand. Keep well protected during winter. Pot up the following spring.

**Simple layering** In spring remove the leaves from a fair length of a young branch, and bury the whole section in the compost. Roots form easily.

## CARE

**Sunlight** These plants like full sun.

**Temperature** Lespedezas like warmth and although full-grown plants are hardy, those grown as bonsai will suffer from frost. However, they will grow up again after being frosted if they are pruned right back at the end of winter. *Lespedeza bicolor* is the hardiest species.

**Ventilation** These plants have no special requirements. Take care when watering if they are in an exposed position so that the leaves do not get scorched.

**Container** The glazed container should be of medium depth.

**Regular maintenance** Cut off faded flowers as soon as they dry out, and remove any small dead branches.

## SPECIES

*Lespedeza bicolor* (ezo-yama-hagi) This upright shrub, which is native to northern China and Japan and is naturalized in the United States, grows to about 3m (10ft). It has arching branches. The leaves are dark green above and blue-green underneath, and the purple and red flowers are borne on the tips of the branches in late summer to early autumn.

*Lespedeza buergeri* (ki-hagi) This shrub, which grows to about 1m (3ft) is native to Japan and China. It has elliptic to ovate leaves and white or purple flowers.

*Lespedeza cyrtobotrya* (miyama-hagi) This is a scandent or woody-based shrub to 1.2m (4ft). It has obovate or elliptic leaves and clusters of pink-purple flowers. It is native to China and Korea.

*Lespedeza kiusiana* This small shrub is native to Japan and Korea. It has soft green foliage and pinkish-purple flowers in large panicles.

*Lespedeza thunbergii* (miyagino-hagi) Native to China and Japan, this is a woody perennial or sub-shrub 2m (6ft) tall and 2m (6ft) across, with arched branches, elliptical, light green leaves, which are silky underneath. Bright purple, butterfly-shaped flowers are borne in clusters from midsummer to early autumn and are followed by fruit that contains a single seed.

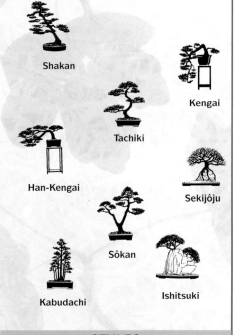

Shakan

Tachiki

Kengai

Han-Kengai

Sekijôju

Sôkan

Kabudachi

Ishitsuki

STYLES

Lespedez b color: *12 years old; 20cm (8in) high; SekijÙju style. Photographed in midsummer. The purple flowers appear in mid- to late summer and last until autumn.*

**Growth** These plants grow fairly slowly.

**Repotting** Repot annually in spring. Prune the roots by a third and pot up into a larger container.

**Soil** Use a mixture of equal parts loam and leaf mould. Lespedezas like garden earth that is permeable, sandy, light and dry.

**Pruning**
*Pruning sub-branches* Allow them to become quite long, then prune by a good third of their length; leave only two or three nodes.
*Structural pruning* At the end of winter, when all risk of frost is past, prune the lespedezas low to encourage new growth. It is important that the rootstock is not frost-bitten.

**Wiring** Wire from spring until the end of summer. Protect new branches with raffia.

**Watering** Do not overwater. Lespedezas like dry compost, but increase the amount of water given when flower buds are forming.

**Misting** Mist the foliage in summer to improve the humidity of the surrounding atmosphere and provide protection against possible insect infestations.

**Feeding** Give more fertilizer in spring than in autumn. Always use a slow-release, organic fertilizer. In autumn when the plant is in bloom use a weak solution of liquid fertilizer.

## PESTS AND DISEASES

### PESTS
**Aphids** See page 33.

### DISEASES
There are no known diseases that affect lespedezas. If the leaves turn yellow and fall prematurely, check watering: the plant may be being under or overwatered.

**Rhizoctonia**
*Symptoms* The fungal disease may cause rot on the collar or branches. A cottony white down may follow, then the tree drops.
*Treatment* Make sure there is not too much nitrogen in the fertilizer and do not overwater. Put in a well-ventilated place. Spray with a benomyl-based fungicide.

# PRIVET

Oleaceae. Deciduous or evergreen. This genus of about 50 shrub and trees is fund in woodland and scrub in Europe, north Africa, the Himalayas, southwest and east Asia and Australia. It is best known, perhaps, as a hedging plant, but there are species with variegated foliage and some that produce attractive (if unpleasantly scented) flowers. All are fairly tolerant of a range of conditions, but not all are frost hardy, and those grown as bonsai are best kept in a conservatory.

## PROPAGATION

**Seed** Harvest the fruit when they are ripe and leave them in a pile to rot down. Then mix them with soil and wait until the following autumn before planting them in good quality compost. Transplant the seedlings at the end of the first year. Wait for two years before beginning to prune and train the plantlet into a bonsai.

**Cuttings** In summer take semi-ripe cuttings or take hardwood cuttings in winter. Protect them from direct sun and frost until they are established.

**Grafting** This is not usually successful but try wedge or side-veneer grafting.

## CARE

**Sunlight** Position the bonsai near a window in the conservatory because these plants like plenty of light. In the early morning and afternoon they can withstand full sun, although they should be protected from direct summer sun, especially when they are close to glass.

**Temperature** Ligustrums need plenty of warmth in summer. *L. sinense* could stand outdoors in areas with very warm summers, but it will not survive outdoors in winter if temperatures fall below 12–14°C (54–57°F). *L. obtusifolium* and *L. ovalifolium* do best in warm conditions all year round.

**Ventilation** Protect plants from strong winds and from sudden changes in temperature.

**Container** Choose a container that is fairly deep and that, preferably, is glazed on the outside. Rectangular pots often look best, and shades of blue and green complement the foliage well.

**Regular maintenance** Remove any yellow leaves from the plant. Once or twice a year brush the trunk to remove any moss growing up it. Remove moss and algae from the surface of the soil.

**Growth** Ligustrums grow quite quickly, forming new branches rapidly.

**Repotting** Repot every second year, in spring. At the same time, carefully trim the roots, but take great care that you do not damage the tap root.

**Soil** Use a mixture of seven parts loam, two parts leaf mould and one part sharp sand. Avoid composts that are too acid.

**Pruning**
*Pruning sub-branches* At the end of winter cut back hard all side shoots, then continue to clip them throughout the growing season because they will go on growing. Flowers are borne on the current year's growth, so keep a look out for any buds that begin to develop. In winter cut back any stems that have grown too long.
*Pruning branches* At the end of winter cut out completely any dead or damaged branches or any that detract from the overall shape of the tree. Apply wound-sealing compound to the cuts.
*Leaf pruning* The leaves are so small that this is not worth doing.

**Wiring** The stems are so flexible that it is easy to train ligustrums. Wiring can be carried out all year round on side shoots and on hardened woody branches. Leave the wire in place for three months and repeat the process the following year if necessary. Protect the bark with raffia. Wire *L. ovalifolium* in spring.

**Watering** Water copiously. Allow the roots to take up all the water before watering again. Water more often in summer and

Yose-Ue

Kyûhon-Yose

Nanahon-Yose

Takozukuri

Sôju

Sekijôju

Nejikan

Sabamiki

Neagari

Hôkidachi

Tachiki

Han-Kengai

Shakan

Kabudachi

Ikadabuki

STYLES

Ligustrum obtusifolium: *20 years old; 30cm (12in) high; Nejikan style.*

## SPECIES

*Ligustrum japonicum* (Japanese privet). This evergreen shrub, native to China, Korea and Japan, grows to 3m (10ft). It has glossy, ovate, dark green leaves. Panicles of white flowers are borne in late summer and into autumn. There are several fine cultivars, including 'Rotundifolium', 'Texanum' and 'Texanum Argenteum'.

*Ligustrum obtusifolium* This hardy, graceful, deciduous shrub, native to Japan, grows to 3m (10ft). The leaves are dark green above, paler beneath, and they often become purple in autumn. White flowers are borne in panicles.

*Ligustrum ovalifolium* An evergreen (sometimes semi-evergreen) shrub, native to Japan, this bears oval, mid-green leaves and panicles of white flowers in midsummer. The flowers are followed by shiny black fruit.

*Ligustrum sinense* This hardy plant, native to China, is deciduous (sometimes semi-evergreen) and grows to about 4m (12ft). The light green leaves are lanceolate, and the panicles of white flowers are followed by purplish-black fruit.

winter, reducing the amount given in spring and autumn.

**Misting** In winter mist plants every day to increase the humidity around the leaves. If necessary, stand the container on a bed of gravel in a dish half-filled with water to maintain high levels of humidity.

**Feeding** From early spring until early summer and from early autumn until the beginning of winter apply a slow-release, organic fertilizer once a fortnight, alternating granules and liquid forms. From late autumn until the end of winter apply fertilizer every six weeks.

## PESTS AND DISEASES

### PESTS
**Aphids** See page 33.

**Scale insects** See page 33.

**Thrips**
*Symptoms* There are dry, grey patches on the leaves, and spots appear on these. The plant will be weakened, and the leaves eaten. The small insects may be seen beneath the leaves.
*Treatment* Spray with malathion or with heptenophos and permethrin. If necessary, repeat 10 days later.

### DISEASES
**Mildew** See page 34.

**Honey fungus** See page 35.

**Mosaic virus**
*Symptoms* The leaves become patterned with yellow and may eventually fall.
*Treatment* Once infected, plants cannot be cured and should be burned. The infection is transmitted by sap-sucking insects, so control aphids to prevent infection.

# LIQUIDAMBAR

Hamamelidaceae. Deciduous. The genus contains four species of large monoecious trees, which are found in Asia, North America and Mexico. They are grown for their fine, palmate leaves, which take on good autumn colours. Insignificant greenish-yellow flowers are borne in late spring, and the female flowers are followed by clusters of fruit.

## PROPAGATION

**Seed** Sow seed in a cold frame in autumn. The seed will take about a year to germinate and you may not think it worth the effort, although the young saplings grow quickly. They should be potted up in the first or second year.

**Air layering** Do this at the end of autumn, taking a side shoot of the current year's growth (see page 20).

## CARE

**Sunlight** Liquidambars need to be positioned in full sun all year round if they are to achieve the best autumn colour. However, shade plants from the hottest of the summer sun.

**Temperature** These plants do best with warmth in summer but will tolerate winter cold, including short periods of frost. *L. styraciflua* is the hardiest species.

**Ventilation** They will withstand strong winds and are suitable for seaside gardens.

**Container** Use a fairly deep container, which should be round or rectangular. Choose a colour that will harmonize with the autumn foliage.

**Regular maintenance** Clear away dead foliage and any dead leaves from the surface of the compost. Brush the trunk once or twice a year. Remove any moss that grows on the trunk.

**Growth** *L.styraciflua* is fairly slow growing; *L. formosana* grows more quickly.

**Repotting** Every two to four years, depending on the plant's age, pot up in spring, when the new shoots begin to swell. Prune the roots by between one-third and one-half, and repot into a larger container if necessary.

### SPECIES

*Liquidambar formosana* (syn. *L. formosana* var. *monticola*) Plants from Taiwan are said to be hardier than those from China. The tree grows to 10m (33ft) or more. The three-lobed leaves turn orange, red and purple in autumn.

*Liquidambar orientalis* (oriental sweet gum) This species, which is native to southwest Asia, is not reliably hardy. A slow-growing tree, it will get to about 6m (20ft). The mid-green, five-lobed leaves turn yellow and orange in autumn.

*Liquidambar styraciflua* (sweet gum) This is an upright, hardy tree, native to the eastern USA and Mexico, which will grow to 20m (65ft) or more. Attractive all year round, it is especially lovely in autumn, when the alternate leaves turn stunning shades of red. In winter the cork-like bark is visible. The leaves of 'Festival' turn shades of yellow, pink and peach in autumn. 'Worplesdon' has red autumn tints.

**Soil** Use a mixture of two parts loam and one part sharp sand. Liquidambars like moist, humus-rich, well-drained soil, and the autumn colours are best in acid to neutral ground.

**Pruning**
*Pruning sub-branches* Pinch out new shoots in spring, leaving two pairs of leaves.
*Pruning branches* At the end of winter cut away any damaged branches, applying a paint to stop the wound weeping.
*Leaf pruning* Carry out a complete leaf pruning in early summer every three years.

Chokkan

Shakan

Sekijôju

Tachiki

Hôkidachi

Sôkan

Ikadabuki

Sôju

Sambon-Yose

Gohon-Yose

Nanahon-Yose

Kyûhon-Yose

Yose-Ue

STYLES

Liquidambar styraciflua *(sweet gum): 5 years old; 25cm (10in) high; Kabudachi style. Photographed in early summer.*

**Wiring** *L. styraciflua* and *L. fomosana* have an upright habit, and the structure is achieved largely through pruning. *L. orientalis* will benefit from being wired. If necessary, add the wire in early summer and remove it in early autumn. Protect tender stems with raffia.

**Watering** Water freely but allow the compost to dry out before watering again. In spring and summer water more frequently than in autumn and winter.

**Misting** Liquidambars like high humidity. Mist the foliage in summer to increase the humidity of the surrounding atmosphere and provide protection against possible insect infestation.

**Feeding** Apply a slow-release, organic fertilizer once a month from early spring until early summer and from early until late autumn. Give an additional dose at the end of autumn to boost the plant before winter.

## PESTS AND DISEASES

Liquidambars are usually trouble free.

### PESTS
**Red spider mites** See page 32.
**Caterpillars** See page 33.
**Aphids** See page 33.

# CRAB APPLE, APPLE

Rosaceae. Deciduous. The genus contains about 35 trees and shrubs, which are found in woodland and scrub throughout Europe, Asia and North America. The genus includes commercially grown apples, *Malus* x *domestica*, as well as many trees that are grown for their ornamental value. All produce attractive blossom, which is borne in corymbs, usually in spring.

## PROPAGATION

**Seed** Pick the ripe fruit and leave in a cool place to rot. Wash the pips, dry them and stratify in sand. Sow in late autumn or early winter in light soil. Germination varies according to the species. Ornamental forms should come true to type.

**Air layering** Do this in spring (see page 20).

**Grafting** This method is the most widely used and most reliable. In early spring shield budding, side grafting, wedge grafting or inarching (approach grafting) can be practised. All methods produce good results. Seal well to make sure that the point of union is not conspicuous later on. It is possible to graft ornamental crab apples onto the usual fruit tree rootstocks.

## CARE

**Sunlight** The crab apple likes full sun all year round.

**Temperature** The crab apple tolerates frost well and can withstand hot weather.

**Ventilation** These trees tolerate wind.

**Container** Crab apples need a fairly deep pot. It can be decorated to harmonize with the flowers, and glazed blues or willow green or unglazed terracotta are appropriate.

**Regular maintenance** Remove a few apples so that the tree does not bear too many. If a lot of fruit is produced, remove about a third to avoid exhausting the tree. Remove any leaves that have not fallen in autumn in case they are harbouring parasites.

**Growth** Even when the tree is grown in a pot growth is fairly rapid.

*Fertilization by hand*

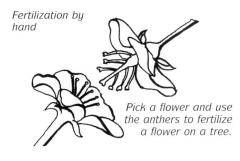

*Pick a flower and use the anthers to fertilize a flower on a tree.*

Malus baccata *var.* mandshurica *(syn.* M. cerasifera*):flowers in mid- to late spring. Flowers and leaves appear at the same time.*

Shakan

Kengai

Tachiki

Han-Kengai

Sekijôju

Sôkan

Kabudachi

Bonkei

Malus halliana (Hall's apple): 25 years old; 35cm (14in) high; Tachiki style. Photographed in mid-spring, at the beginning of flowering. The deep pink flower buds open to pale pink, sometimes white, flowers. The leaves on this species are rather shy.

# Malus

## SPECIES

***Malus baccata*** var. *mandshurica*
(syn. *M. cerasifera*; Manchurian crab
apple) Native to Japan and China, this
tree is 5–6m (16–20ft) tall, with oval
green leaves and white flowers. The
cherry-sized fruit is red or yellow
depending on the cultivar.

***Malus halliana*** (Hall's apple) Native
to China, this shrub grows to 5m
(16ft). It has a spreading habit, and
oval, purple-tinged, green leaves. Pink
flowers open in late spring, and small
edible fruit stays on the tree for a
good part of winter.

***Malus himekokoh*** Native to Japan,
this bears fruit with a wonderful taste.
They are about the size of a small
clementine.

***Malus sieboldii*** (syn. *M. toringo*)
Native to the mountainous areas of
Japan, this graceful tree grows to
about 3m (10ft) tall. The flower buds
are deep pink, but the flowers open
pale pink or white. The flowers are
followed by tiny red or yellow, edible
fruit.

**Repotting** In spring every year at bud
burst – every second year for old specimens
– pot up into a larger container after
pruning the roots by between one-third
and one-half.

**Soil** Use a mixture of equal parts loam
and leaf mould, to which some sand and
peat can be added.

Malus baccata *var.* mandshurica *(syn.* M.
cerasifera): *18 years old; 35cm (14in)
high; Tachiki style. Photographed in mid-
autumn. At the end of autumn the fruits,
become a wonderful, rich red colour;
unfortunately, they taste rather acid.*

## Pruning
*Pinching back* Pinch back the tips of new
shoots as they appear.

*Pruning when the fruit is setting* **1** *Trim the young shoot, leaving between three and five
buds.* **2** *The buds appear, making it possible for twigs to develop.* **3** *When the tree is a
little bigger begin wiring and trimming.* **4** *Do some more trimming to make it easier for
branches to develop.*

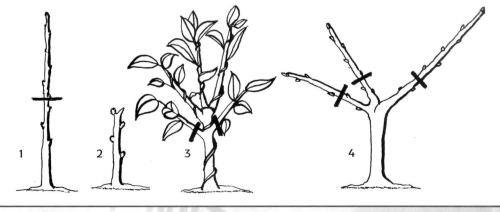

*Pruning sub-branches* After flowering (about midsummer) prune sub-branches back to two growth buds. Take out late-growing shoots.

*Pruning branches* Prune branches when repotting.

**Wiring** Wire from spring to autumn. Protect the bark with raffia.

**Watering** Water copiously while the flower buds are forming, give a little less water when the tree is in flower, then resume copious watering.

**Misting** Wet the whole tree when watering but not when there are flowers present. These plants are seldom misted.

**Feeding** In spring, after flowering, feed with a slow-release, organic fertilizer, in liquid form or in a powder form. In autumn feed less often but increase the amount given.

*Malus himekokoh: the fruit is larger than that produced by some crab apples, but it has an excellent taste.*

## PESTS

**Red spider mites** See page 32.

**Winter moth**
*Symptoms* Leaves are eaten between bud burst and late spring. Blossom and young fruits are also sometimes eaten.
*Treatment* After bud burst spray with derris, pyrethrum, permethrin or pirimiphos-methyl.

**Ermine moth** See page 33.

**Leaf miners** See page 33.

**Tortrix moth** See page 33.

**Greenfly** See page 33.

**Woolly aphids** See page 33.

**Scale insects** See page 33.

## DISEASES

**Powdery mildew** See page 34.

**Scab**
*Symptoms* Irregular greenish-brown blotches are seen on the leaves, and the fruit is blotched, discoloured and misshapen.
*Treatment* Pick off diseased or dead leaves and fruit, and spray with fungicide.

**Apple canker**
*Symptoms* The fungal disease causes brown crevices to appear on wounds or forks of branches. The crevice grows, cracks and girdles the branch, which withers and dies at the top. Defensive excrescences appear in the surrounding area. There are red grainy marks on the canker.

*Treatment* Cut out and burn diseased branches. Scrape out the canker. Dab the wound with a copper-based fungicide and seal it. Spray with a copper-based fungicide at leaf-fall.

**Brown rot**
*Symptoms* The fungus causes brown spots to appear on the fruit, followed by concentric rings of white pustules.
*Treatment* Remove and burn affected fruit. Protect fruit from damage.

**Fireblight**
*Symptoms* Flowers turn black and the leaves turn brown and wither. Cankers appear on the stems, oozing golden or white slime.
*Treatment* This is a serious bacterial disease. Cut out and burn affected branches and sterilize all tools. Do not apply fertilizer containing nitrogen and keep the soil relatively dry. In spring use a copper-based fungicide and repeat during the growing season.

**Crown gall**
*Symptoms* A hard or soft gall appears on the collar and upper roots. It takes the form of a white (later brown), cauliflower-shaped excrescence, which looks woody and cracked. Rot sets in, endangering the tree. There may be secondary infections.
*Treatment* Cut out and destroy infected branches. Improve the drainage so that compost is not waterlogged. Take care not to wound trees during cultivation so that bacteria can enter the plant tissue. Use clean tools.

**5** *The buds develop.* **6** *and* **7** *Each year stop branches from growing out of the trunk and continue to prune side branches.* **8** *The result will be a tree with a pattern of branches that is both skilfully arranged and aesthetically pleasing.*

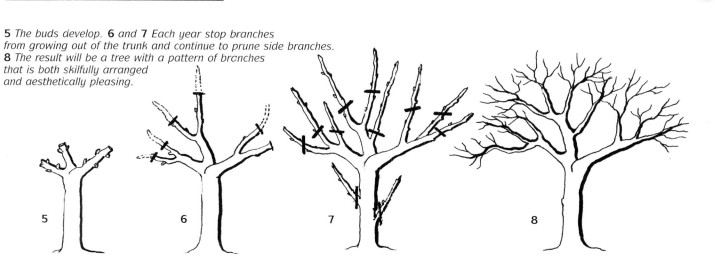

# MILLETTIA

Papilionaceae/Leguminosaceae. Deciduous or evergreen. The genus includes about 120 species of woody climbers, trees and shrubs, which are native to woodlands in Africa, Madagascar, India, east Asia. The leaves are pinnate, with lance-shaped leaflets, and pale purple, pink or white pea-like flowers are borne in panicles.

## PROPAGATION

**Seed** Collect the ripe seeds in their pods in mid-autumn and sow them straightaway in a warm place. Only a few seeds will germinate, and growth is slow.

**Cuttings** In summer take semi-ripe cuttings of the current year's growth. Cut off the growing tip. Dip in hormone rooting compound. Insert the cuttings in a mixture of equal parts peat and sand and keep them in a warm place sheltered from cold winds. Beware late night frosts. Bottom heat will be beneficial.

**Simple layering** Do this in spring and by autumn the layer will have put out roots. Pot it after cutting it free and keep in a warm place until the next spring.

**Grafting** A whip-and-tongue graft or an inlay graft carried out in a greenhouse in late winter or early spring may be successful. Bind and seal well with grafting wax. See also pages 21–3.

## CARE

**Sunlight** Millettias like the sun.

**Temperature** These species do best in warmth. They are not tender and must be protected from frost.

**Ventilation** Millettias tolerate wind, and they need to be in a well-ventilated position.

**Container** Select a pot that is deep or fairly deep. Millettias will not develop in a flat container. The pot can be decorated to harmonize with the flowers.

**Regular maintenance** In autumn remove any moss that is covering the base of the trunk and the surface of the soil.

**Growth** These plants grow slowly.

**Repotting** Every year or every second year in spring prune away a third of the roots and pot up into a slightly larger container.

**Soil** Use a mixture of equal parts loam and leaf mould. These species do best in cool, light but substantial soil. The compost must be free draining.

**Pruning**
*Pruning sub-branches* In late summer prune these with clippers after flowering and before shoots appear. Cut back well, leaving only three growth buds.
*Pruning branches* In autumn cut back the branches quite short.

**Wiring** In spring and summer use fine wire to train the branches and trunk into the desired shape. Do this every year.

**Watering** Water well, even in winter, unless there is frost. In summer water regularly, soaking if necessary, but allow

---

### SPECIES

*Millettia dura* A small tree of shrub, to 13m (43ft), which is native to East Africa. The leaves are downy beneath, and mauve flowers are borne in drooping panicles.
*Millettia grandis* This tree, to 12m (40ft), is native to South Africa. It bears purple flowers in spring.
*Millettia reticulata* This species, native to Taiwan and China, is similar to a small wisteria and is the most widely grown species of the genus. It is a long-lived climbing shrub, which becomes gnarled as it grows older. The branches are flexible and grow upwards. It produces a good branch structure, but it does not hook itself onto a surface, as wisteria do. It has small, shiny, leathery dark green leaves.

Shakan

Kengai

Tachiki

Han-Kengai

Sekijôju

Sôkan

Kabudachi

STYLES

Left: Millettia japonica: 18 years old;
70cm (28in) high; Neijikan style.
Right: Millettia reticulata: 10 years old;
25cm (10in) high; Sekijoju style.
Photographed in late spring.

the plant to droop between waterings to encourage it to flower again. Alternatively, leave it standing in water for a month at the height of summer.

**Misting** Mist the tree and the area around it to improve the humidity of the atmosphere around the plant.

**Feeding** Feed more in spring before flowering. In autumn it is best to use liquid fertilizer in smaller quantities.

## PESTS
**Scale insects** See page 33.

## DISEASES
**Mosaic virus**
*Symptoms* The leaves become patterned with yellow and may eventually fall.
*Treatment* Once infected, plants cannot be cured and should be burned. The infection is transmitted by sap-sucking insects, so control aphids to prevent infection.

# MULBERRY

Moraceae. Deciduous. The genus contains 12 shrubs and trees, which are monoecious or dioecious and which are native to Japan, North America and southern Europe. The leaves of several species are food for silkworms, which have been cultivated since 2700 BC.

## PROPAGATION

**Seed** Collect the fruit in mid- to late summer. Crush them and wash to separate the seeds from the squashed flesh. Dry the seeds and store between layers of sand or earth to stratify. Sow in mid- or late spring. Germination occurs within three weeks. Space the seeds well apart from one another when sowing, and watch out for cockchafer grubs. After they have germinated protect them throughout autumn and winter.

**Cuttings** In spring select a shoot produced in the current year. Remove the top and dip in hormone rooting powder. Set it to root in a mixture of equal parts peat and sand. Protect the cuttings from possible frosts and from cold winds.

**Air layering** Do this in spring (see page 20).

**Grafting** Use the bench grafting method in winter when mulberries cannot be propagated by other methods. This is the method used most widely by professional nurserymen. Shield budding is done early in the season when the bark of the rootstock lifts easily.

## CARE

**Sunlight** Mulberries like full sun. They need a lot of light.

**Temperature** Although hardy, mulberries dislike frosts and cold, preferring warmth all year round.

**Ventilation** The mulberry can withstand wind.

**Container** Choose a container that is fairly flat and preferably glazed. White, willow green, blue, green and beige are appropriate colours.

**Regular maintenance** Remove withered fruit from the tree if it does not fall of its own accord.

---

### SPECIES

*Morus alba* (syn. *M. bombycis*; white mulberry) There are several cultivars, and their shape varies. The type species has a spreading habit and grows to about 10m (33ft). The leaves are alternate, with deeply indented edges, often lobed, and they are light green, with a shiny upper surface, turning golden-yellow in autumn. The pinkish-white, round berries, which do not have much flavour, are ripe in late summer or early autumn.

*Morus nigra* (black mulberry) This species, which probably comes from southwest Asia, has a rounded crown and grows to about 12m (40ft). It has mid-green, heart-shaped, often double-toothed leaves, and in autumn oval green fruit, which later turn red, then purple, are borne.

---

**Growth** Mulberries are slow growing, making about 3m (10ft) in 20 years.

**Repotting** Repot in mid-spring every year. Prune a good third off the roots, and plant up into a larger container. Make sure the drainage is good.

**Soil** Use a mixture of two parts loam, one part leaf mould and one part sharp sand. Mulberries like light, sandy soil, and they dislike damp, heavy soil. If the soil is too fertile, growth finishes late in the autumn and the tree suffers from frosts.

**Pruning**
*Pinching back* Pinch back new shoots as soon as they begin to lengthen.
*Pruning sub-branches* After flowering cut back sub-branches, leaving just two growth buds. At the end of the autumn prune long sub-branches again, leaving only two or three growth buds.

Kengai

Shakan

Han-Kengai

Tachiki

Sekijôju

Sôkan

Kabudachi

Morus issaï: 15 years old; 30cm (12in) high; Tachiki style. Photographed in late spring. In Japan, its country of origin, this tree can grow to 10m (33ft).

*Pruning branches* In early spring, before the buds open, prune the branches short.

**Wiring** Wire in spring and summer. Wind raffia around the copper wire to protect the bark.

**Watering** Mulberries need a lot of water. It may be necessary to water twice a day in spring and autumn. Always allow the plant to dry out between waterings.

**Misting** Sprinkle water on the foliage when you are watering the plant. Do not mist for the short period when plants are in full flower.

**Feeding** Use a slow-release, organic fertilizer and feed more frequently in spring. In autumn, when the tree is bearing fruit, a liquid fertilizer is preferable.

## PESTS AND DISEASES

The caterpillar (silkworm) of the cultivated silk moth (*Bombyx mori*) does no damage.

### PESTS
**Scale insects** See page 33.

### DISEASES
**Honey fungus** See page 35.

# MURRAYA

Rutaceae. Evergreen. A genus of five species of aromatic trees, which are native to India, China and the Pacific islands. The trees, which are related to *Citrus*, have pinnate leaves, with alternately arranged leaflets. Single, white blooms, large and scented, are borne in panicles, and they are followed by inedible, oblong, orange-red berries, containing one or two seeds.

## PROPAGATION

**Cuttings** Take hardwood cuttings and leave on the leaves. Plant in moist sand under a cloche with good bottom heat. Pot up the following spring.

## CARE

**Sunlight** Murrayas need a lot of light but do not like direct sunlight.

**Temperature** These plants like warmth. In winter the temperature must not fall below 17°C (63°F).

**Ventilation** Keep the plants out of draughts but make sure that the air can circulate freely around them, which is essential.

**Container** Select a bowl somewhere between fairly flat and medium deep. It can be glazed or unglazed, oval or rectangular. Beiges and willow-greens go quite well with these plants.

**Regular maintenance** Remove yellow leaves and withered flowers and fruit as you notice them.

**Growth** These plants grow slowly. The trunk takes a long time to develop and then to expand in diameter.

**Repotting** Repot every second year in mid- to late spring. Prune the roots by a half and pot up into a larger container.

**Soil** Use a mixture of equal parts peat, loam, leaf mould and sharp sand. Murrayas like loamy, peaty soil and respond well to a dressing of leaf mould.

**Pruning**
*Pruning sub-branches* Throughout the growing season cut back side branches to

### SPECIES

*Murraya koenigii* (curry leaf) Left to grow naturally, this shrub, which is native to India and Sri Lanka, will grow to about 6m (20ft). The leaves have 11–21 leaflets, and the fragrant, white or cream flowers are borne in cymes.
*Murraya paniculata* (syn. *M. exotica*; orange jessamine, satinwood, Chinese box) This tree-like species, native to China and India, grows to a height of 3m (10ft). It has oval, evergreen leaves and scented, white flowers. It bears red fruit in late summer.

two leaves as soon as they have produced five or six.
*Pruning branches* In spring prune branches that are too long, broken or damaged or that are growing in an unsightly way.

**Wiring** Murrayas can be wired at any time of the year. Do not leave the wire in position for more than eight weeks.

**Watering** These plants need moisture. Water regularly, keeping the soil slightly damp throughout the year, but do not let it become waterlogged!

**Misting** Mist the foliage throughout the year to maintain high levels of humidity and to clean the tree.

**Feeding** In spring and in autumn feed with a slow-release, organic fertilizer. Alternate between liquid fertilizer and solid fertilizer. You can give a tree that is in perfect condition one application of fertilizer in winter.

Chokkan · Tachiki · Shakan · Han-Kengai · Fukinagashi · Sharimiki · Sôkan · Kabudachi · Sabamiki · Korabuki · Sôju · Tsukami-Yose · Yose-Ue · Bonkei

**STYLES**

Murraya paniculata *(syn. M. exotica; orange jessamine): 150 years old; 80cm (32in) high; Sabamiki style. Photographed in late autumn.*

## PESTS AND DISEASES

### PESTS

#### Whitefly
*Symptoms* These tiny insects, with wingspans to no more than 5mm (¼in), resemble minute moths and can be a real pest in greenhouses, where they are seen on the undersides of leaves, which become covered with honeydew and sooty mould.

*Treatment* Spray with an insecticide such as malathion, permethrin or heptenophos and permethrin. Organic gardeners will prefer to try the parasitic wasp *Encarsia formosa*; do not use insecticides for other pests if a biological control has been introduced to the greenhouse.

**Aphids** See page 33.
**Glasshouse red spider mites** See page 32.

#### Snails
*Symptoms* Leaves, shoots and buds are eaten and the tell-tale slimy trail will be seen.
*Treatment* Collect up the snails by hand and kill them. Do not let the compost get too wet. Remove all fallen leaves and decaying vegetable matter. If all other methods fail, use metaldehyde or methiocarb pellets.

### DISEASES
**Leaf spot** See page 35.

#### Downy mildew
*Symptoms* The fungi cause yellow patches on the upperside of the leaves and a white fur covers the underside. The leaves drop off.
*Treatment* Cut out and burn diseased leaves. Spray with a copper-based fungicide.

# HEAVENLY BAMBOO

Berberidaceae. Evergreen or semi-evergreen. This monotypic genus is native to India, central China and Japan. Plants, which grow to grow to a height of 2m (6ft), have a stiff, upright habit, and the close-set stems are somewhat reminiscent of the bamboo. These plants are grown for their foliage, graceful flowers and red berries, which appear only after very hot summers. It is not reliably hardy, although it can be grown in a sheltered position in the border in a warm garden. Container-grown plants can be stood outside during the summer, but are best taken under cover before the first frosts.

## PROPAGATION

**Seed** Stratify the berries after they have ripened. In spring sow under glass and keep the young shoots protected for the first year. Pot up the following spring, protecting the roots for the first few years.

**Cuttings** Take semi-ripe cuttings in summer and plant in a mixture of equal parts sand and peat. Provide bottom heat. Keep sheltered in winter.

## CARE

**Sunlight** Nandinas need sunlight and good light, but if they are outside, they should be placed in partial shade at the height of summer.

**Temperature** This is a plant for an unheated greenhouse and it likes warmth, shedding its leaves when it gets cold. Even if it is stood outdoors in summer, it is advisable to bring it into the greenhouse in winter. Decide from the start whether you want to cultivate it as an outdoor or indoor plant.

**Ventilation** Protect from wind outside and from draughts inside.

**Container** Choose a medium-depth pot; unglazed containers look best.

**Regular maintenance** Remove berries that form from the flowers as soon as they start to wilt because they exhaust the plant.

**Growth** These are slow-growing plants.

**Repotting** Every second or third year in spring prune the roots by a half, and pot up into a larger container.

**Soil** Use a mixture of two parts loam, one part leaf mould and one part sharp sand. These plants like light, cool, fertile soil and are quite happy in good garden soil. They respond well to a mulch of leaf mould.

**Pruning**
*Pruning sub-branches* During the growing period wait until the side branches have grown to four or five nodes. Cut back with clippers, leaving only one or two growth buds.
*Pruning branches* At the end of winter remove any dead or damaged branches and any that have grown too long.

**Wiring** This can be done in spring and summer but it is rarely done, the plants being shaped by pruning.

Sôkan

Kabudachi

Korabuki

Yamayori

Tsukami-Yose

Kusamono

Bonkei

Plantations saisonnières

**STYLES**

Nandina domestica *(heavenly bamboo): 14 years old; 20cm (8in) high; Sôkan style (three trunks growing from the same rootstock). Photographed in late autumn.*

**Watering** Water moderately and regularly to maintain a steady supply. These plants like moist soil, but it must be freely draining so that the roots never become waterlogged.

**Misting** Indoors, mist the foliage daily. Outdoors, mist leaves and branches in summer only.

**Feeding** Feed with a slow-release, organic fertilizer in spring and autumn.

## PESTS AND DISEASES

If these plants do not have enough light, the brownish-red shades in the foliage will tend to disappear and the internodal spaces will be large.

### PESTS
**Blackfly** See page 33.

**Glasshouse red spider mites** See page 32.

### DISEASES
**Mosaic virus**

*Symptoms* The leaves become patterned with yellow and may eventually fall.
*Treatment* Once infected, plants cannot be cured and should be burned. The infection is transmitted by sap-sucking insects, so control aphids to prevent infection.

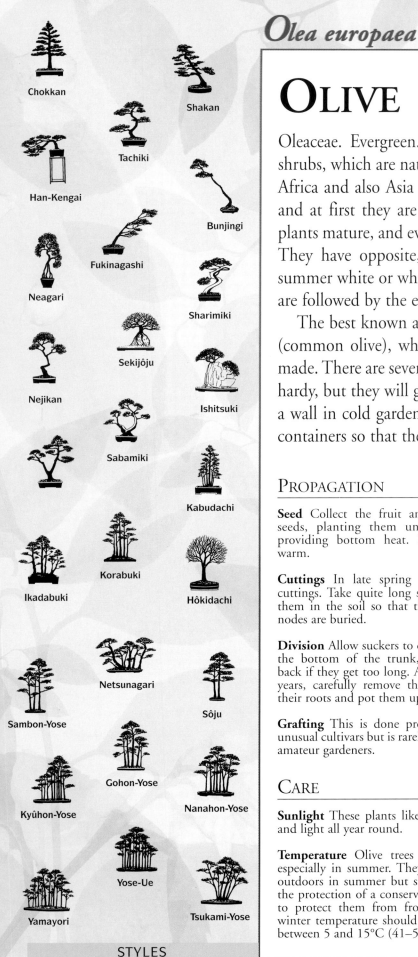

Chokkan

Shakan

Tachiki

Han-Kengai

Bunjingi

Fukinagashi

Neagari

Sharimiki

Sekijôju

Nejikan

Ishitsuki

Sabamiki

Kabudachi

Korabuki

Ikadabuki

Hôkidachi

Netsunagari

Sôju

Sambon-Yose

Gohon-Yose

Kyûhon-Yose

Nanahon-Yose

Yose-Ue

Yamayori

Tsukami-Yose

STYLES

# OLIVE

Oleaceae. Evergreen. The genus contains 20 long-lived trees and shrubs, which are native to fairly dry areas of the Mediterranean and Africa and also Asia to Australasia. The stems are smooth or spiny, and at first they are slender and pliable, becoming fissured as the plants mature, and eventually becoming contorted and almost black. They have opposite, leathery leaves, either entire or toothed. In summer white or whitish-cream flowers are borne in panicles. These are followed by the edible, spherical fruit.

The best known and most widely grown species is *Olea europaea* (common olive), which produces the fruit from which olive oil is made. There are several cultivars available. Olive trees are not reliably hardy, but they will grow outdoors provided they have the shelter of a wall in cold gardens. They are often grown as specimen plants in containers so that they can be protected under glass in winter.

## PROPAGATION

**Seed** Collect the fruit and remove the seeds, planting them under glass and providing bottom heat. Keep plantlets warm.

**Cuttings** In late spring take semi-ripe cuttings. Take quite long slips and insert them in the soil so that the first pair of nodes are buried.

**Division** Allow suckers to develop around the bottom of the trunk, cutting them back if they get too long. After about two years, carefully remove the suckers with their roots and pot them up.

**Grafting** This is done professionally for unusual cultivars but is rarely attempted by amateur gardeners.

## CARE

**Sunlight** These plants like plenty of sun and light all year round.

**Temperature** Olive trees need warmth, especially in summer. They can be stood outdoors in summer but should be given the protection of a conservatory in winter to protect them from frost. Ideally, the winter temperature should be maintained between 5 and 15°C (41–59°F).

**Ventilation** The trees withstand winds well, and they are suitable for seaside gardens.

**Container** Choose a medium-deep container in a neutral colour. Rectangular or round pots are most suitable.

**Regular maintenance** Remove any leaves that turn yellow and any that fall on the surface of the soil. Brush the trunk once or twice a year to remove any moss. Wipe the leaves with a damp cotton wool regularly so that the pores do not get clogged.

**Growth** Young plants grow relatively quickly, but mature trees grow more slowly.

**Repotting** Every two or three years in mid-spring cut back about a third of the roots and pot up into a slightly large container if necessary.

**Soil** Use a mixture of three parts leaf mould, two parts peat and two parts sharp sand. Olive trees prefer dry ground, growing in the wild in rocky, inhospitable ground, and a well-drained, fertile and deep soil is best.

**Pruning**
*Pruning shoots* Lightly pinch out shoots in early spring.
*Pruning sub-branches* Cut back all side

*Olea europaea (common olive): 15 years old; 35cm (14in) high; Hokidachi style. Photographed in early autumn. It takes several years before the trunk of an olive tree grown as a bonsai will begin to look like the contorted trunks of the trees seen growing around the Mediterranean.*

## SPECIES

*Olea europaea* (common olive) This slow-growing tree, native to the Mediterranean littoral, will grow to 10m (33ft). It has lanceolate leaves, dark green above and light greyish-green below. The fragrant white flowers are borne in terminal panicles.

branches between early spring and late autumn if they become too long for the overall shape of the tree.

*Pruning branches* In early to mid-spring cut out any damaged or unattractive branches, applying wound-sealing compound if necessary.

*Pruning leaves* Defoliating a tree is rarely useful because olives have small leaves.

**Wiring** This can be done all year round on hardened wood. Do not leave wire in position for more than three months, and if necessary repeat the process after four or six months.

**Watering** Water freely from the moment the buds open in spring. Allow the soil to dry out between waterings. Do not allow the soil to become waterlogged.

**Misting** If the weather is very hot and dry, mist around the foliage. If the tree is being grown indoors, mist the foliage but take care that the atmosphere does not become too humid.

**Feeding** Every three weeks give a slow-acting, organic fertilizer from early spring until early summer and from early autumn to the beginning of winter. Give an extra feed at the end of autumn to boost the tree before winter sets in. If the tree is in good condition, feed every six weeks throughout winter.

## PESTS AND DISEASES

### PESTS

**Scale insects** See page 33.

**Caterpillars** See page 33.

**Mealy bugs** see page 33.

#### Olive moth

*Symptoms* The shoots are eaten and the area where the caterpillars are feeding becomes covered with greyish-white webbing. The caterpillars may be visible.

*Treatment* If only a small area is affected, pick off the leaves or cut off the stems and destroy them. For serious infestations, spray with pyrethrum or primiphos-methyl. For plants grown under glass, try the bacterial solution of *Bacillus thuringiensis*.

#### Whitefly

*Symptoms* These tiny insects, with wingspans to no more than 5mm (¼in), resemble minute moths and can be a real pest in greenhouses, where they are seen on the undersides of leaves, which become covered with honeydew and sooty mould.

*Treatment* Spray with an insecticide such as malathion, permethrin or heptenophos and permethrin. Organic gardeners will prefer to try the parasitic wasp *Encarsia formosa*; do not use insecticides for other pests if a biological control has been introduced to the greenhouse.

#### Psyllids

*Symptoms* The edges of the leaves turn yellow and become thickened, and the leaves may be covered in honeydew and thus sooty mould. The damage is caused by minute suckers, which are specific to these trees (other species are susceptible to other species of psyllid).

*Treatment* Cut out and destroy affected leaves and shoots. Spray with pirimphos-methyl or demthoate in spring or when the infestation is first seen.

### DISEASES

**Mildew** See page 34.

# VIRGINIA CREEPER

Vitaceae. Deciduous. The 10 species in this genus are mostly woody climbing or trailing vines, native to North America and eastern Asia, with palmate leaves, clinging tendrils, inconspicuous flowers and dark blue or black fruit. The plants are grown for their glorious autumn leaf colour.

## PROPAGATION

**Seed** Collect the ripe fruit. Leave it to rot and collect the seeds. Keep layered between earth or sand and plant in spring in a mixture of sand and peat, protecting in a cold frame in autumn. The fruit is barely more than 5mm (¼in) across and the seed is tiny.

**Cuttings** Take softwood cuttings in early summer, hardwood cuttings in winter or greenwood cutting in late summer. If you plant several cuttings together, take care that they do not intertwine. In autumn cut back the cuttings. Pot up the following spring. Keep the soil cool, but protect the young plants from frost.

**Simple layering** Do this in spring in cool, humus-rich compost.

**Grafting** Try the inlay method in a greenhouse between midwinter and early spring. Select one-year-old scions. Remove the growth buds from the lower part of the rootstock. It is not necessary to apply grafting wax but you will get better results if you enclose the graft in a clay mixture to stop it from drying out.

**Young nursery stock** Choose a young plant with a upright main stem and an interesting overall shape (see also page 18).

## CARE

**Sunlight** These plants like full sun. They need a lot of light if the autumn leaves are

*Parthenocissus tricuspidata 'Lowii': 8 years old; 12cm (5in) high; Tachiki style.*

Shakan

Kengai

Tachiki

Han-Kengai

Sekijôju

Kabudachi

Sôkan

*Parthenocissus tricuspidata* (Boston ivy) This climber, to 20m (65ft) produces a large number of branches, with thin stems, and deciduous, three-lobed leaves, which are glossy green in summer, turning yellow-gold, red and purple in autumn. It bears flowers in mid- to late summer, followed by small, round, dark blue fruit in early to mid-autumn.

to take on their striking colours. In very sunny areas, stand in partial shade in summer.

**Temperature** They are tolerant of heat and fairly resistant to frost.

**Ventilation** Branches may snap if the plants are exposed to very strong winds.

**Container** Use a fairly deep pot. Glazed blue pots with or without decoration look attractive.

**Regular maintenance** Prevent moss from forming at the bottom of the trunk. These plants withstand pollution well.

**Growth** These climbers grow quickly and develop a large branch structure.

**Repotting** Repot annually, in early spring, into a larger pot. Prune the roots by a third.

**Soil** Use a mixture of equal parts loam and leaf mould. They like deep, not too moist soil but have no special requirements. Good garden earth will be suitable.

**Pruning**
*Pruning sub-branches* After flowering wait for new shoots to have about five growth buds, then use scissors to cut back to one or two nodes.
*Leaf pruning* Cut leaves from healthy trees in late spring or early summer, and then give less water.

**Wiring** Wire in spring and summer, but do not wire if the leaves are still soft; wait for a little while.

**Watering** Water freely but allow to dry out between waterings. The compost must be well drained so that it does not become waterlogged.

**Misting** Sprinkle water on the foliage and branches when you water the tree. Do not mist after stripping leaves or when the tree is in flower.

**Feeding** In spring and autumn apply a slow-release, organic fertilizer on a regular basis.

Parthenocissus tricuspidata *'Lowii': 10 years old; 20cm (8in) high; Kengai style. Photographed in mid-autumn.*

## PESTS AND DISEASES

### PESTS
**Scale insects** See page 33.

### DISEASES
**Downy mildew**
*Symptoms* The fungi cause yellow patches on the upperside of the leaves, and a white fur covers the underside. The leaves drop off.

*Treatment* Cut out and burn diseased leaves. Spray with a copper-based fungicide.

**Black rot**
*Symptoms* The fungus causes brownish-red patches to appear on the leaves. Black flecks form on these patches.
*Treatment* Remove and burn affected leaves. Spray with a copper-based fungicide.

Chokkan

Shakan

Kengai

Bankan

Tachiki

Han-Kengai

Bunjingi

Sharimiki

Ishitsuki

Sekijôju

Sabamiki

Sôkan

Kabudachi

Korabuki

Ikadabuki

Netsunagari

Sôju

Sambon-Yose

Gohon-Yose

Nanahon-Yose

Kyûhon-Yose

Yose-Ue

Yamayori

Bonkei

Tsukami-Yose

Kusamono

STYLES

# SPRUCE

Pinaceae. Evergreen conifer. Spruces were for a long time categorized with pine trees, but for more than a century they have been treated as a separate genus. The Latin word *picea* meant tree with resin, and *pix* meant resin or pitch. There are about 35 monoecious species within the genus, and they are native to the northern hemisphere, mainly to mountainous areas. Spruces differ from *Abies* (silver fir) in that they have pointed crowns, sloping branches and drooping side branches. The needles form thick, prickly, light green whorls. The cones hang from the tips of the branches; they have thin scales that do not hinge open as they ripen with age.

## PROPAGATION

**Seed** The cones are usually picked between early autumn and midwinter; *P. glauca* cones should be picked in late summer or early autumn. As soon as seeds appear at the edge of the scales, remove them. Allow the seeds to mature in the cones for as long as possible. Prepare the seeds for germination by leaving them in damp sand for about 10 days. Sow in cool soil in mid-spring. They will normally sprouted after three weeks. Keep the seedlings under glass, shading them from direct sun, and keeping the compost moist. Remove the glass in early summer. Pot up the following spring.

**Cuttings** Take cuttings from leading shoots between early and late summer. Rooting can take up to two years. Use a grafting knife to cut along the base of shoots grown that year. You do not need to remove the needles. Plant the cuttings in a warm, shaded place.

**Layering** Choose low, flexible branches. Strip the needles off the part to be buried. Make a slit in the stem to encourage root formation. Bury the branch and keep the soil moist. When new shoots appear sever the layer and replant in a growing pot. Treat as a freshly potted tree and protect from extremes of temperature.

**Grafting** This method is used particularly for *Picea glauca*. The graft can be attempted in either summer or winter, but it is a tricky procedure.

**Young nursery stock** Choose a young plant with a upright main stem and an interesting overall shape.

## CARE

**Sunlight** Spruces like full sun, but they also like shade.

**Temperature** Many species start growing early in the season and can be affected by night frosts. There is a similar risk with late frosts. These trees like a cool atmosphere.

**Ventilation** Spruces are happy in wind, especially *Picea jezoensis*.

**Container** Choose a shallow bowl because these are not deep-rooted plants.

**Regular maintenance** Remember to remove damaged or dead twigs and needles from inside the crown. Keep the soil clear of any dead material.

**Growth** *Picea glauca, P. jezoensis* and *P. orientalis* are slow growing. *P. abies* grows slowly at a high altitude, but faster at lower altitudes. The more slowly it grows, the more tapering its outline becomes.

**Repotting** Repot in mid-spring every third to fifth year, depending on the plant's age. Prune off a third of the root hairs. Pot up into a slightly larger container.

**Soil** Use a mixture of equal parts leaf mould, loam and sharp sand. Most species prefer a rich, moist but well-drained, neutral to acid soil; *P. omorika* (Serbian spruce) tolerates alkaline soil.

**Pruning**
*Pinching back* In mid-spring pinch back the new shoots on the side branches. Pinching back is practised only once a year.
*Leaf pruning* The needles are never cut.

## SPECIES

*Picea abies* (syn. *P. excelsa*; Norway spruce) This, the most widely grown spruce, is a large tree, native to Scandinavia and central and southern Europe at altitudes of up to 2000m (6600ft) and growing to 40m (130ft) of more. It is conical in silhouette, and its branches almost touch the ground. Its needles, which grow in spirals around the branches, are stiff, sharp, shiny and dark green. The slender, triangular cones are spindle shaped with red scales, and they hang down.

*Picea glauca* (white spruce) This tree, which is native to North America, has a straight, tapering trunk, long spreading branches and a pyramidal shape. It will grow to 25m (80ft). The needles are greenish-blue, and the cones are small and green, turning brown as they ripen. Trees have a strong smell of resin.

*Picea jezoensis* (jezo spruce) This spruce can grow to a height of 35m (115ft). It is distinguished by a long leading shoot. The needles are bright green on top and silvery white beneath. The tips of the branches turn back towards the tree. The red cones turn brown.

*Picea mariana* (syn. *P. nigra*; black spruce) This tree has a conical habit, and is upright and dense. The needles are dark greenish-blue; red cones turn brown.

---

*Pruning branches* In spring cut branches back hard, leaving only a few tufts of needles on each branch.

**Wiring** Wire spruces at the end of autumn or in early winter. Remove the copper wire about 10 months later. Repeat every year until the desired shape has been achieved.

**Watering** The soil must be well drained. Water copiously, and then allow to dry out.

**Misting** Wet the foliage as much as possible, especially in spring and summer. Spruces like a moist atmosphere.

**Feeding** Use a slow-release, organic fertilizer in spring and autumn. Increase the dosage at the last autumn dressing. Do not feed in mid- to late summer, nor if the bonsai is in poor condition.

Picea jezoensis *(jezo spruce): 10–40 years old; 60cm (24in) high; Yose-Ue style. Photographed in mid-spring. This outstanding group has been planted on a dish of reconstituted rock (made from synthetic resin and powdered rock).*

## PESTS AND DISEASES

### PESTS

#### Weevils
*Symptoms* The bark, stems and needles may be damaged, although not seriously. The weevils are dark with a long snout; the legless grubs are whitish.
*Treatment* Cut out and burn affected material. At the first sign of attack, spray or dust the foliage with pirimiphos-methyl. Make sure that the compost is not harbouring the grubs.

#### Long-horned beetles
*Symptoms* Flattened galleries can be seen at the base of the trunk. Black beetles may be present.
*Treatment* Burn branches affected. Spray with insecticide when the adults emerge.

#### Adelgids
*Symptoms* The small insects (like aphids) suck the sap and stems. Honeydew is formed, on which sooty mould develops. In summer insects form colonies under white, waxy wool.
*Treatment* Spray with malathion in spring and again about three weeks later.

#### Sawflies
*Symptoms* Needles produced in the current season are completely eaten and the new shoots are distorted.
*Treatment* Spray with an insecticide such as malathion or fenitrothion when the shoots begin to grow.

#### Pine gall mites
*Symptoms* Spherical or prickly galls are at the tips of new branches.
*Treatment* Remove and burn infected shoots and branches. Spray with carbendazim.

### DISEASES
**Honey fungus** See page 35.

#### Browning of needles
*Symptoms* The needles wither and black marks appear on the underside.
*Treatment* Use a fungicide. If you are planting a group, make sure the trees are not too close to one another.

#### Septoria
*Symptoms* The fungus causes the needles wither, and the branches grow in the shape of a crook. There are black marks on the withered parts.
*Treatment* Cut out and burn diseased branches. Spray with a copper- or zineb-based fungicide.

#### Canker
*Symptoms* The roots rot, and the leaves turn pale, then go yellow and wither. There may be a white dust on the rotted collar.
*Treatment* Drench soil with a zineb-based fungicide. Make sure that the compost does not become waterlogged around the roots and feed with a well-balanced fertilizer.

## STYLES (left column captions)

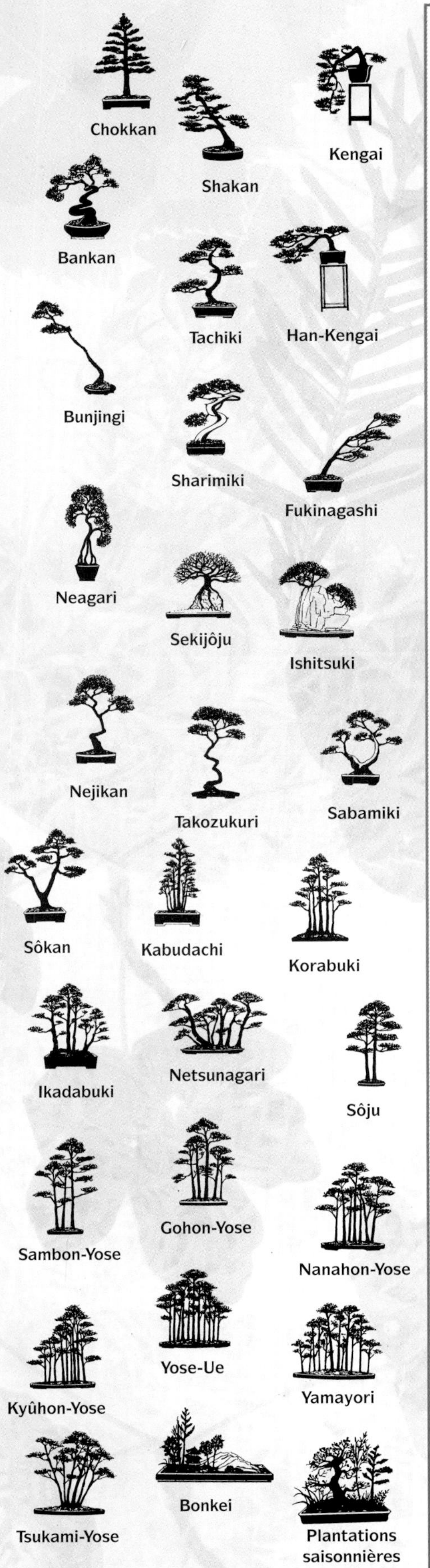

Chokkan

Shakan

Kengai

Bankan

Tachiki

Han-Kengai

Bunjingi

Sharimiki

Fukinagashi

Neagari

Sekijôju

Ishitsuki

Nejikan

Takozukuri

Sabamiki

Sôkan

Kabudachi

Korabuki

Ikadabuki

Netsunagari

Sôju

Sambon-Yose

Gohon-Yose

Nanahon-Yose

Kyûhon-Yose

Yose-Ue

Yamayori

Tsukami-Yose

Bonkei

Plantations saisonnières

**STYLES**

# PINE

Pinaceae. Evergreen conifer. This is a large genus, including more than 110 species, widely distributed in mountainous areas of the northern hemisphere from the Americas to Indonesia, and from the Arctic Circle to Central America. They are tall trees, usually with conical tops and often with fissured bark. They have long, scaly branches, with short side branches and needle-like, light to dark green leaves growing in clusters of from two five from a scaly sheath. Female cones take at least two years to ripen; male cones are like catkins. Pines are widely cultivated, and many forms of the most popular species have been developed, with foliage ranging from golden-yellow, through bluish-green to dark greyish-green.

## PROPAGATION

**Seed** Collect the seeds or pine nuts from the cones. Most of them are winged, except for *Pinus cembra* (Swiss pine), *P. koraiensis* (Korean pine) and *P. parviflora* (Japanese white pine). The length of time between ripening and germination varies according to species. Many species have cones that open when the seeds are ripe; others have to be dried so that the seeds are released. Collect the cones of *P. mugo* subsp. *uncinata* (mountain pine) in early winter. Dry them and store them in a cool, dark place. Pre-germinate the seeds and plant them in mid-spring. They will germinate in two months.

**Cuttings** This technique is rarely used because roots are slow to form. It can be done at the end of winter with cuttings taken from young trees. Take short slips from two-year-old branches and dip the slips in hormone rooting compound before planting them.

**Layering** Strip the needles from the section of the branch that will be buried. Make a 3cm (2–3in) long slit in the bark to encourage roots to form. Bury the section and keep the soil damp. When new shoots appear on the tip of the branch, roots have formed. Separate the layer from the tree and pot up. Air layering is also possible (see page 20).

**Grafting** Make a veneer graft or a wedge graft in winter in a greenhouse. *Pinus sylvestris* (Scots pine) makes an excellent rootstock for conifers with two needles. *P. nigra* (Austrian pine) is recommended as a rootstock for strong-growing species.

### SPECIES

*Pinus mugo* (dwarf mountain pine) This very hardy, large shrub or tall tree, native to central Europe, will grow to about 6m (20ft).
*Pinus sylvestris* (Scots pine) This is a conical tree, to 30m (100ft), with reddish-brown bark.
*Pinus thunbergii* (syn. *P. thunbergiana*; Japanese black pine) This fine tree has a conical habit, with purplish-grey bark and dark grey-green foliage. It will grow to 25m (80ft) or more.

**Young nursery stock** You can find a great many species in nurseries. Always look carefully at the trunk and the density of the branch structure before making your selection (see also page 18).

## CARE

**Sunlight** Grow pines in full sun. As a rule they need a lot of light and do badly in the shade.

**Temperature** Pines like warmth and do better in warm areas, even though they stand up well to intense winter cold and even to frosts.

**Ventilation** Pines like the wind and thrive in places with a lot of air movement. Guard against pollution, which harms them. *Pinus nigra* has the best resistance.

Pinus thunbergii *(syn. P. thunbergiana; Japanese black pine)*: 70 years old; 60cm (24in) high; Shakan style. Photographed in mid-spring.

*Pruning needles* Once a year in spring remove all new needles after they have appeared but before they harden. This will give dense foliage and small needles.
*Pruning branches* Cut the branches in mid-autumn just above a tuft of needles. Cut back the branch by about a third. Repeat in the autumn if necessary.

**Wiring** Wire in autumn and winter. Repeat each year if necessary. Do not squash the needles between the wire and the bark.

**Watering** Water regularly and copiously as long as the compost is free draining. From time to time keep the tree dry. Pines withstand hot, dry summers.

**Misting** Pines tolerate a dry atmosphere and do not have to be misted often. Misting has the primary purpose of cleansing plants of the damaging effects of pollution.

**Feeding** Feed with a slow-release, organic fertilizer from spring to late autumn. Do not feed in mid- or late summer, nor if the tree is sick or has just been repotted.

**Container** Pines need deep, well-drained soil, so choose a fairly deep pot with good drainage holes.

**Regular maintenance** Old needles turn yellow in autumn, and you should use tweezers to remove them. Always prune inside the crown and remove all damaged or dead material. Clear any dead material from the soil. Brush off moss that grows up from the soil onto the base of the trunk so that it does not become established.

**Growth** These are usually fast-growing plants, growing about 10m (33ft) in 20 years. *Pinus mugo* is one of the smaller growing species, and some dwarf cultivars are slow growing.

**Repotting** Repot in mid-spring every three to five years into a larger container.

Prune the roots by a third, taking care not to damage the main root.

**Soil** Use a mixture of equal parts leaf mould, loam and sharp sand. Pines have no special requirements. As a rule, mountain species growing on sandy soil are tall and slender, with straight trunks and short crowns, while those growing on calcareous soil have short, twisted trunks. The soil should be cool and damp for some species, poor and dry for others; mountain pines like cold, marshy soil. By and large, avoid soil with too much lime (except for *Pinus nigra*), and provide light soil.

**Pruning**
*Pinching back* In mid-spring once a year use your thumb and forefinger to pinch out the emerging clumps of needles are forming. Remove two-thirds of them.

## PESTS AND DISEASES

Pine trees suffer from the same pests and diseases as *Pinus parviflora* (Japanese white pine); see page 141.

*Pruning branchlets on* Pinus parviflora.

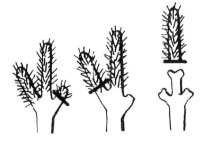

*Cut the branchlets close to the base and make the shoots all the same length.*

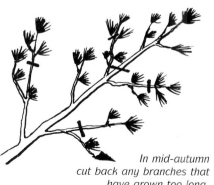

*In mid-autumn cut back any branches that have grown too long.*

# JAPANESE WHITE PINE

Pinaceae. Evergreen conifer. This is a small to medium-sized tree, which is native to Japan, where it is known as Goyo-Matsu. It is a popular choice for cultivating as a bonsai. The trees grow to 20m (65ft), and at first they are conical, becoming more flat topped as they age. The scaly bark is purplish-brown, and the soft greenish-blue foliage is dense and abundant. The needles, to 6cm (2½in) long, are borne in groups of five and have a bluish-white stripe on the inner surface. Male flowers are deep reddish-purple. Female cones are oval, to 7cm (3in) long, and have winged seeds. The needles of *P. parviflora* var. *pentaphylla* are also (as the name suggests) clustered in groups of five. They can be straight or twisted, and they are blue-green in colour and edged with two resin-coloured lines. The cones turn dark brown and stay on the tree for about seven years. There are several other cultivars and forms of *P. parviflora*, including the popular *P. parviflora* f. *glauca*, a small, spreading tree.

## PROPAGATION

**Seed** The cones are ripe when they are two years old. Gather them in early to mid-autumn. Leave them to dry in a warm place and they will open up. Collect the seeds and soak them in water. Those that sink can be planted. Apply a fungicide to the seeds and sow in spring after stratifying between layers of sand. They can also be planted at the end of autumn, when they will be naturally preserved in layers of earth during winter. The shoots are delicate after germinating and should be handled carefully. Repot the following spring.

**Simple layering** Choose a low, pliable branch. Remove needles from the section to be buried. Make a cut in the bark. Bury and keep moist. Sever the layer from the parent plant as soon as new shoots appear.

**Air layering** Strip the part of the branch to be layered of its leaves and make an incision in it. Hold the slit open with a twist of sphagnum moss. Cover the layer with damp moss, and enclose in a polythene tube that is closed at both ends. As soon as roots appear (in spring of the following year), sever the layer and pot it up, treating it as a bonsai that has just been repotted.

**Cuttings** Success cannot be guaranteed. At the end of winter, take cuttings from young plants, choosing short branches, two years old. Dip the cuttings in hormone rooting compound before planting them.

**Grafting** Try veneer or wedge grafting in winter in a greenhouse. It is possible to use *Pinus nigra* (black pine) as rootstock and *P. parviflora* (white pine) as the scion to try to accelerate the growth rate of the white pine, which is a slow grower. See pages 21–3 for more information.

## CARE

**Sunlight** Grow in full sun; these plants need a lot of light to grow well. A few dwarf cultivars need some shade during the summer months. If they are exposed to the sun, the needles will be small and the nodes will be closely spaced.

**Temperature** These pines can withstand intense cold and heat, but they prefer cool places.

**Ventilation** They will tolerate strong winds, but protect all forms with fine needles from drying winds.

Chokkan

Shakan

Kengai

Tachiki

Han-Kengai

Bankan

Bunjingi

Fukinagashi

Sharimiki

Neagari

Sekijôju

Ishitsuki

Takozukur

Nejikan

Sabamiki

**STYLES**

**Container** Use a fairly deep bowl to give sufficient room for the roots. The dense needles of *P. parviflora* var. *pentaphylla* give the wind something to catch, and a deep pot will hold it in position and prevent it from tipping up. This bonsai is often found in a cobalt blue container.

**Regular maintenance** Using your thumb and index finger, pick off old needles that turn yellow in autumn. Prune the inner foliage, and remove any dead or damaged parts from there or from the soil.

**Growth** *Pinus parviflora* is a slow-growing species.

**Repotting** Repot every three to five years, planting up into a larger container, which must always be fairly deep. In early spring

Pinus parviflora *var.* pentaphylla: *200 years old; 70cm (28in) high. Photographed in late spring. Although it is close to the Shakan style, this outstanding bonsai is actually in a non-classic style known as 'the hand of Buddha'. The highly individual shape of the tree (the curve of the trunk and the projecting upper crown) does, in fact, suggest the protective hand of Buddha. Placed at the entrance to a garden, a tree in this style is a sign of welcome. Only a few examples are known to exist.*

*Wires can be left on* Pinus parviflora *var.* pentaphylla *for about 10 months. Remove the wire before it marks the wood permanently or, worse still, becomes embedded in the bark.*

prune the roots by a third of their length, and remove old roots. Do not wash the roots but keep some of the old earth on the roots to help the plant to get re-established. Treat with especial care for three weeks after repotting.

**Soil** Use a mixture of equal parts leaf mould, loam and sharp sand. Good drainage is essential. The plants have no special requirements as regards soil.

## Pruning

*Pinching back* In mid-spring pinch back the candles by two-thirds before they open, using your thumb and index finger. If the crown is very dense, completely remove one bud in three. On the other hand, if you want it to thicken up, keep all three buds. First of all pinch out the slowest growing buds. Pinching back can be carried out over a three-week period. Finish with the fastest growing buds. This

*Pinch out the new shoots, using the nails of your thumb and index finger to cut through the stems.*

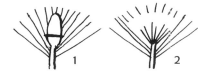

**Pines with one candle.**
1 *In mid-spring pinch off two-thirds of the candle before it opens.* 2 *The needles will grow shorter, hollow and pointed.*

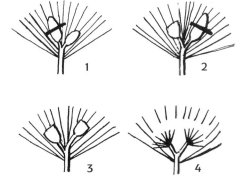

**Pines with two candles.**
1 *Pinch off two-thirds of the longer candle.* 2 *A week later trim two thirds of the other candle.* 3 *This will equalize the size of the candles.* 4 *When the needles appear they will be smaller and better balanced.*

will make the needles more equal in length.
*Pruning branches* In mid-autumn prune the branches that have grown most. Cut off a third of the branch above a cluster of needles, without cutting the needles.

**Wiring** Wire in mid-autumn and leave

Sôkan

Kabudachi

Ikadabuki

Korabuki

Netsunagari

Sôju

Sambon-Yose

Gohon-Yose

Nanahon-Yose

Kyûhon-Yose

Yose-Ue

Yamayori

Bonkei

Tsukami-Yose

Plantations saisonnières

Kusamono

*Pliers (see left) can be used to cut the wire, but removing it all is a delicate operation.*

**Pines with three candles.**
1 *Trim two-thirds off the shortest candle.*
2 *A week later trim two-thirds off the middle-sized candle.* 3 *Finally, trim two-thirds off the largest candle.* 4 *The candles should now be more equally balanced.* 5 *When the needles appear, they are shorter and more regular.*

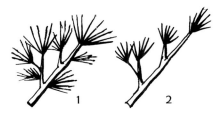

**Removing pine needles by hand.**
1 *In mid-autumn remove old needles by hand.* 2 *The tree should be cleaned and ready for winter.*

## PESTS

### Pine weevils
*Symptoms* Larvae damage the roots. The bark of the collar and the main branches may be so gnawed that the underlying tissues show through. Resin oozes from the sores. Galleries are hollowed out of the wood, and the needles are gnawed.
*Treatment* Cut out and burn affected parts. At the first sign of attack use an oil wash on young trees. Spray with pesticide in early or mid-spring.

### Bark beetles See page 34.

### Buprestrids
*Symptoms* This is a group of insects whose larvae are wood borers. The insects are shiny and metallic looking and may be seen in summer. The larvae, which may live for 30 years, hollow out galleries in the wood, eventually causing branches to wither.
*Treatment* Cut out and burn infested branches. Spray with a systemic insecticide in summer.

### Pine chafers
*Symptoms* The needles and branches are distorted and gnawed. Growth slows down and large brown beetles may be seen.
*Treatment* Search for and kill the larvae. Apply an insecticide such as pirimiphos-methyl.

### Leaf beetles
*Symptoms* The needles are gnawed, and the branches are misshapen. Growth is slowed down. Yellow beetles may be seen.
*Treatment* Spray with insecticide.

### Bombyx moth See page 33; this is rare on Scots pine.

### Hawkmoth and owlet moths
*Symptoms* The needles are gnawed by the caterpillars, and the caterpillars, which are nocturnal, can defoliate trees. High temperatures are favourable to their development.

*Treatment* Use pellets of bran, broken rice or grain mixed with insecticide.

### Bee hawkmoth
*Symptoms* A hollow in the trunk with resin running from it and sticking on the bark.
*Treatment* Remove the accumulation of resin. Spray with a lindane-based insecticide.

### Pine sawfly
*Symptoms* Presence of a brown cocoon on the trunk, the branches, the needles or in the soil. The needles are gnawed.
*Treatment* Cut out and burn affected branches. Spray with malathion, fenitrothion or pirimiphos-methyl.

### Woolly aphids See page 34.

### Scale insects See page 33.

## DISEASES

### Pine-leaf cast
*Symptoms* The needles on the lower branches turn yellow in winter and are covered with black spots in spring. They dry up, turn red and fall. Do not confuse this disease with a tendency for the needles to turn red at the tips if the feeding and transpiration of the tree are not in balance.
*Treatment* Remove and burn infected shoots and branches. Make sure that the soil is not too wet. As a precaution spray with fungicide in spring. From midsummer to early autumn use a combined fungicide.

### Red band disease
*Symptoms* This is a fungal disease. The needles have yellow patches on them in autumn. In spring red bands appear, which are scabs on the wounds.
*Treatment* During the growing season spray with a copper-based fungicide.

### Honey fungus See page 35.

### Rust
*Pinus parviflora* var. *pentaphylla* is not susceptible to rust; see page 35.

until early spring. Leave copper wire on the branches until the end of summer, but if it seems to be becoming embedded in the bark, remove it. If the tree is damaged in the course of doing this treat the wound with a sealing compound.

**Watering** Do not give too much water for best development. Excessive watering will do more harm than good. To get smaller needles, water more sparingly in spring. Give more water to trees that are planted on stone.

**Misting** Mist the foliage regularly in summer. This will refresh the bonsai and dislodge any parasites that might be on the foliage.

**Feeding** From spring to autumn, with a break in mid- and late summer, feed with slow-acting organic fertilizer. Apply a little at a time, but often (about once a month). Increase the amount given in the last autumn feed and add a little nitrate, which will feed the soil. Do not feed a tree that has just been repotted nor one that is sickly.

# PISTACHIO

Anacardiaceae. Deciduous or evergreen. The genus contains about nine dioecious trees and shrubs, which are native to warm temperate countries of the Mediterranean littoral, Mexico and central Asia to Japan. The plants are grown for their racemes of flowers and fruits. They are suitable for seaside gardens.

## PROPAGATION

**Seed** Sow seed in a heated greenhouse in spring. Fine specimens of *Pistacia chinensis* can be raised from seed, although the seedlings are tender.

**Cuttings** Take greenwood cuttings in late spring or early summer or semi-ripe cuttings in summer. Plant them in humus-rich cuttings compost and keep them in a warm, bright place.

**Layering** At the start of the growing season try either simple or air layering for *Pistacia lentiscus* or *P. terebinthus* or air layering only for *P. vera*.

**Grafting** *Pistacia vera* can be grafted onto rootstock of *P. chinensis* or *P. terebinthus*. This method is usually done in nurseries and by professionals.

**Young nursery stock** See page 18.

## CARE

**Sunlight** Pistachios need good light and plenty of sun all year round.

**Temperature** These plants need warmth all year, and they do best in areas with hot summers. *Pistacia terebinthus* and *P. chinensis* can withstand winter cold better than the other species, but even they should be regarded as tender in areas with cold winters. *P. lentiscus* and *P. vera* need winter temperatures of 7–18°C (45–64°F).

**Ventilation** These species tolerate winds and are suitable for seaside gardens.

**Container** Choose a moderately deep container in a natural colour. It can be rectangular, round or oval.

**Regular maintenance** Remove any yellow leaves from the tree and any that fall onto the surface of the compost. Brush the trunk once or twice a year to remove any

## SPECIES

*Pistacia atlantica* (Mount Atlas mastic, betoum) This evergreen tree, native to north Africa, grows to 20m (65ft). The leaves have 7–11 lanceolate leaflets. Clusters of purple flowers are borne in spring and are followed by oval fruits, which are at first yellow, later blue; they are not edible.

*Pistacia chinensis* (Chinese mastic) This is the only hardy species, but even so, it will not survive very cold winters. It is a deciduous tree, native to China, and will grow to 25m (80ft). The leathery, dark green, glossy leaves are composed of 10–12 leaflets. The panicles of red flowers are borne in mid- to late spring and are followed by spherical red fruit, which turn blue as they mature.

*Pistacia lentiscus* (mastic, lentisco) This evergreen tree or shrub, native to the countries of the Mediterranean littoral, will grow to about 3m (10ft). It has glossy, dark green, pinnate leaves. Brownish-green flowers are borne in panicles in spring or early summer and are followed by spherical red fruits, which mature to black.

*Pistacia terebinthus* (terebinth, turpentine tree) A deciduous tree or shrub, native to countries of the Mediterranean littoral, this will grow to 6m (20ft). The glossy leaves are dark green. Panicles of greenish-red flowers are borne in spring and early summer; they are followed by red to purple-brown, edible fruits.

*Pistacia vera* (pistachio, green almond) This plant, native to western Asia, is the source of the edible pistachio nut, but it is not usually grown as an ornamental species. It is deciduous and will grow to about 10m (33ft). The large leaves are glossy above, lighter below, and the greenish-brown flowers are borne in mid-spring. The long-stalked fruits are usually red.

Shakan

Kengai

Bankan

Tachiki

Han-Kengai

Sharimiki

Bunjingi

Fukinagashi

Neagari

Sekijôju

Ishitsuki

Nejikan

Hôkidachi

Sabamiki

Sôkan

Kabudachi

Korabuki

Ikadabuki

Netsunagari

**STYLES**

moss that is growing there. Sponge the foliage regularly to keep it clean.

**Growth** Growth is moderately slow in cultivation, although in their natural habitat all species grow quite quickly.

**Repotting** Repot every two or three years in mid-spring, although *P. chinensis* is not fussy. Prune the roots by a third and pot up into a slightly larger container.

**Soil** Use a mixture of two parts leaf mould, to one part loam and one part sharp sand. All species prefer well-drained, fairly dry soil.

**Pruning**
*Pinching back* In early spring lightly pinch back new shoots.
*Pruning sub-branches* Cut back side branches between early spring and late autumn, making sure that none of these gets too long.
*Pruning branches* Cut back straggly, diseased or damaged branches in early to mid-spring. Apply wound-sealing compound if necessary.

*Pistacia leutiscus: 20 years old; 55cm (22in) high; Shakan style. Photographed in mid-autumn.*

*Leaf pruning* Pruning the leaves is usually pointless as all species have small leaves.

**Wiring** This can be done all year on hardened branches and stems. Do not leave the copper wire in place for more than three months. If necessary, repeat the process from four to six months later.

**Watering** Water copiously from the start of the growing season. Make sure that all water has been taken up by the roots before watering again.

**Misting** Mist the foliage in summer. This refreshes the bonsai and dislodges any parasites that might be on the foliage. Do not mist in autumn and winter if the plants are in a cool place.

**Feeding** Apply a slow-acting, organic fertilizer every three weeks from early spring until early summer and from early autumn until early winter.

## PESTS AND DISEASES

### PESTS
**Whitefly**
*Symptoms* These tiny insects, with wingspans to no more than 5mm (¼in), resemble minute moths and can be a real pest in greenhouses, where they are seen on the undersides of leaves, which become covered with honeydew and sooty mould.
*Treatment* Spray with an insecticide such as malathion, permethrin or heptenophos and permethrin. Organic gardeners will prefer to try the parasitic wasp *Encarsia formosa*; do not use insecticides for other pests if a biological control has been introduced to the greenhouse.

**Scale insects** See page 33.

**Greenfly** See page 33.

### DISEASES
**Root rot** See page 35.

# PODOCARP

Podocarpaceae. Evergreen conifer. The genus contains about 100 species of trees and shrubs, which are found in Mexico and Central and South America as well as in Africa, Asia and Australasia. The trees can grow to 20m (65ft), while some of the lower growing species are useful ground cover. Podocarps are slow-growing plants, with leathery, rather stiff needles (like those of *Taxus*), usually in spirals, on horizontal branches and the densely arranged side branches.

## PROPAGATION

**Seed** Collect the seeds when they are ripe. Plant them in midsummer in a warm greenhouse, keeping them stratified until planting. Alternatively, plant them in late winter.

**Cuttings** Select cuttings from semi-ripe wood. Plant the slips in sandy soil in a cold frame. Shield from direct sun. After roots have formed, protect from winter frost. Pot up the following spring.

## CARE

**Sunlight** Podocarps like light and can be stood in full sun.

**Temperature** Podocarps need heat. They can be stood outdoors in summer in warm gardens, but must be taken under cover in winter, when the temperature should not fall below 13°C (55°F).

**Ventilation** Keep these plants out of draughts.

**Container** Choose a pot of medium depth. These plants look good in dark blue, glazed containers. Choose a shape that will suit the style in which the tree is grown.

**Regular maintenance** Take out any shoots growing out of the trunk. Be careful that no insects get in under the bark of the trunk, as it may become loose from time to time.

**Growth** These are slow-growing plants.

**Repotting** Every second to third year in late spring prune the roots by between one-third and one-half, and pot up into a larger container.

### SPECIES

***Podocarpus macrophyllus*** (big-leaved podocarp, Buddhist pine) This very hardy, conical tree, growing to 15m (50ft), is native to China. It has erect, almost vertical branches. The linear, spear-shaped leaves are dark green above, with two lighter bands beneath, and have an elongated rib running down the middle. The fruit is globular when it ripens.
***Podocarpus macrophyllus*** var. ***maki*** (shrubby podocarp) Native to Taiwan, then introduced into Japan, this variety is more compact than the type species. It has large horizontal branches, long leathery leaves, which are red when they first appear, then bright green above, glaucous underneath, and insignificant, pale yellow flowers. The fruit is green or purple.

**Soil** Use a mixture of equal parts loam, leaf mould, ericaceous to neutral compost and sharp sand. Podocarps like light, loamy, well-drained soil.

**Pruning**
*Pinching back* Pinch back the new shoots (candles) during the growing season.
*Pruning sub-branches and branches* Taking care not to cut the needles, use clippers to

*Pruning a podocarp.*

Chokkan, Shakan, Bankan, Kengai, Han-Kengai, Tachiki, Bunjingi, Sharimiki, Fukinagashi, Neagari, Nejikan, Ishitsuki, Sabamiki, Sôju, Sôkan, Bonkei

**STYLES**

144

Podocarpus macrophyllus *var.* maki *(shrubby podocarp): 8 years old; 15cm (6in) high; Shakan style. Photographed in early winter.*

prune excessively long branches above a leaf axil. If necessary, you can take off a few needles if they are too large.

**Wiring** Podocarps can be wired at any time of year. Wait until young branches have become woody before you wire them. Do not leave the wire in place for more than 10 weeks.

**Watering** Regular and moderate watering is essential. Keep the soil surface slightly moist. Make sure the compost drains well.

**Misting** Mist the foliage daily. Podocarps like humid heat and if necessary can be stood on a tray containing water and gravel in winter.

**Feeding** In spring and in autumn apply a slow-release, organic fertilizer. A perfectly healthy tree can be given one winter feed.

## PESTS AND DISEASES

If the podocarp is overwatered, its needles will turn grey, wither and fall. If it does not have enough light, the needles will grow too big and the tree will become etiolated. A properly tended podocarp should not suffer from any disease.

### PESTS
**Aphids** See page 33.

**Glasshouse red spider mites** See page 32.

**Scale insects** See page 33.

**Mealy bugs** See page 33.

**Snails**
*Symptoms* Shoots and needles are eaten and the trails of slime may be seen.
*Treatment* Collect up the snails by hand and kill them. Do not let the soil get too wet. If you must, and as a last resort only, use metaldehyde or methiocarb pellets.

### DISEASES
Usually trouble free.

# ELEPHANT BUSH

Portulacaceae. Evergreen. This genus now contains just a single species, many of the species originally categorized as *Portulacaria* having been transferred to the large genus *Crassula*. This species is native to South Africa, and it is much-branched, rather fleshy shrub, growing to about 3m (10ft). It is segmented and succulent. The glossy green leaves are about 2cm (¾in) long and are obovate. Tiny pink flowers are borne in small clusters in late spring.

## PROPAGATION

**Cuttings** In mid-spring take cuttings about 10cm (4in) long. Leave these to wilt in the sun or in the light for about three days. Insert in a mixture consisting of equal parts peat and sand. Do not water. After several days water lightly. Wait for small roots to form before watering more freely, but do not soak the soil.

## CARE

**Sunlight** Place in a well-lit position. These plants can be exposed to direct sunlight, but if they are stood outdoors in summer, shade them from direct sunlight.

**Temperature** These plants will do best if the temperature is constant. In winter can withstand temperatures down to 10°C (50°F) but not below.

**Ventilation** Keep these plants out of draughts but try to make sure that air can circulate around the foliage.

**Container** Choose a pot of medium depth. Blues, browns and natural colours look best with this tree.

**Regular maintenance** Remove any leaves that turn yellow. Remove all shoots growing out from the trunk and main branches.

**Growth** At first these plants grow fairly fast, but it will take three or four years for the trunk and branches to take shape.

**Repotting** Every second year in spring prune the roots by a third of their length and pot up into a larger container. Leave for a fortnight before watering again.

**Soil** Use a mixture of equal parts ericaceous compost, loam, leaf mould and

---

### SPECIES

***Crassula arborescens*** (silver jade plant) This shrubby succulent, frequently grown as a houseplant, is native to South Africa. It has an upright, branched stem and grows to about 4m (12ft) high in its natural habitat. The fleshy leaves are greyish-green and often have red margins. Star-shaped, pink flowers are borne in late autumn. It is not hardy.

***Crassula ovata*** (jade plant) The well-known houseplant is very similar.

---

sharp sand. These plants prefer a light, sandy soil. Add grit, sharp sand and leaf mould to good quality compost.

**Pruning**
*Pinching back* Pinch out the tips of new shoots as soon as they have reached the desired length.
*Leaf pruning* Pick the leaves off the old lower branches.
*Pruning sub-branches* Pinch out or cut off the tips of laterals, leaving only two or three pairs of leaves on each.
*Pruning branches* If it becomes necessary do this between mid-spring and mid-autumn to perfect the structure of the tree.

**Wiring** The shape is normally achieved through pruning, but for the Han-Kengaï and Kengaï styles the tree may be wired. Wait until the new shoots have become woody. Do not leave the wire on for more than six weeks and protect the bark with raffia.

**Watering** As a rule, keep watering to a minimum. Keep the plants dry in winter.

Chokkan

Shakan

Kengai

Tachiki

Han-Kengai

Nejikan

Ishitsuki

Sôkan

Sambon-Yose

Sôju

Yose-Ue

Bonkei

Plantations saisonnières

**STYLES**

Portulacaria afra *(elephant bush).*

### PESTS

**Scale insects** See page 33.

**Mealy bugs** See page 33.

### DISEASES

**Damping off**

*Symptoms* The roots are destroyed and the shrub stops growing. Wet rot may occur at the collar. The branches turn black in places, collapse onto the compost and die. The shrub wilts. There is a downy fluff on the stems.
*Treatment* Keep the plant warm and well aired, and do not give too much water. Apply nitrogen and potash to the soil.

**Downy mildew**

*Symptoms* The fungus causes yellow patches on the upperside of the leaves, and a white fur covers the underside. The leaves drop off.
*Treatment* Cut out and burn diseased leaves. Spray with a copper-based fungicide.

**Helminthosporium fungus**

*Symptoms* Yellow lesions, turning to brown, can be seen on the branches and they spread over the entire plant.
*Treatment* As a precaution spray with a captan-based mixture. Make sure that the soil is sterile when you pot up.

**Fusarium wilt**

*Symptoms* The fungus causes brown, cankerous lesions on the upper part of the branches, and these spread.
*Treatment* Check the condition of the soil. Disinfect if necessary.

**Anthracnose**

*Symptoms* In spring or during wet, mild summers, leaves curl and become discoloured before falling. Die-back may follow severe attacks.
*Treatment* Cut out and burn infected shoots and leaves. Spray with a copper-based fungicide.

**Leaf spot** See page 35.

In summer water moderately and bear in mind that they can last without water for about a fortnight.

**Misting** Mist the foliage daily to maintain a high level of humidity. If necessary, place on a container covered with a layer of gravel.

**Feeding** From late spring to early autumn, with a break in mid- to late summer, feed once a month with liquid fertilizer. Never feed in winter.

# ORNAMENTAL CHERRY

Rosaceae. Deciduous or evergreen. This is a very large genus, containing 430 shrubs and trees, which are found in temperate regions throughout the northern hemisphere and in South America. These trees have white, pink or red flowers, which may be solitary or borne in clusters or racemes. The fleshy fruit (drupes) contain, generally, one seed and are borne in autumn.

Ornamental cherries are widely grown in Japan, and the blossom is symbolically significant. They are attractive trees, varied in habit, but all bear white to pink flowers, some double, some semi-double, in mid-spring.

## PROPAGATION

**Cuttings** After flowering take one-year old shoots, cut off the growing tip and plant in humus-rich compost after dipping in hormone rooting compost. In the following spring put the plantlets in separate pots. Protect them from extremes of weather and pot them into their final container after two or three years.

**Air layering** Try this in spring when the new shoots begin to appear (see page 20).

**Grafting** Shield grafting should be attempted in summer.

**Young nursery stock** This method will give the best result. Choose a well-rooted plant with a good crown (see page 18).

## CARE

**Sunlight** Ornamental cherries do best in full sun.

**Temperature** These plants should be protected from winter frosts. They need a winter temperature of from 5 to 7°C (41–45°F).

**Ventilation** They are resistant to wind and do best in places where air can circulate freely.

**Container** Choose a moderately deep container and one whose colour harmonizes with the flowers.

**Regular maintenance** Remove flowers as they fade. After leaf fall, clear away the dead leaves, especially those that have fallen on the surface of the compost.

**Growth** These plants grow fairly quickly.

**Repotting** Repot every year in spring after flowering. Cut about a third of the roots back and pot up into a slightly larger container than before if necessary. Make sure the container can drain easily.

**Soil** Use a mixture of two parts leaf mould, two parts humus and one part sharp sand. These plants do not have particular requirements.

**Pruning**
*Pinching back* Before flowering pinch out some of the shoots so that the buds are evenly distributed over the branches.
*Pruning sub-branches* After flowering cut back any sub-branches that are crossing within the crown of the tree and remove any that did not bear flowers. This will ensure that there are plenty of flowers the following spring.
*Pruning branches* After flowering but before the leaves have fully developed carry out a thorough structural pruning, removing any dead or damaged branches. Apply wound-sealing compound if necessary.
*Leaf pruning* There is little point in carrying out leaf pruning because these plants have small leaves.

**Wiring** Wire from spring to autumn, protecting the bark with raffia and working carefully to prevent the stems from damage. The branches are delicate. Use weights or clamps if necessary to achieve the shape you want.

Shakan
Kengai
Han-Kengai
Bankan
Tachiki
Sharimiki
Bunjingi
Ishitsuki
Sekijôju
Sabamiki
Kabudachi
Sôkan
Ikadabuki
Netsunagari
Sôju
Sambon-Yose
Gohon-Yose
Nanahon-Yose
Kyûhon-Yose
Yose-Ue
Bonkei
Plantations saisonnières

**STYLES**

Prunus x subhirtella *(higan cherry):
30 years old; 65cm (26in); Sabamiki
style. Photographed in mid-spring.*

## SPECIES

*Prunus* 'Accolade' This spreading deciduous tree, which grows to about 8m (25ft), has oblong, dark green leaves. In mid- to late spring semi-double, pale pink flowers, to 4cm (1½in) across, open from deep pink buds and are borne in pendent clusters.

*Prunus cerasifera* (myrobalan, cherry plum) This hardy deciduous species, native to southeast Europe and southwest Asia, has a rounded habit. It early spring large white flowers, 2.5cm (1in) across, are borne amid the emergent leaves. Mature trees sometimes bear spherical, plum-like red or yellow fruit.

*Prunus* x *subhirtella* (higan cherry, rosebud cherry) A spreading deciduous tree, this will grow to 8m (25ft). The dark green, toothed leaves are bronze when young and yellow in autumn. The flowers, to 2cm (4in) across, are white or pink and are borne from autumn to spring. The flowers are sometimes followed by red fruits, which turn darker as they ripen.

*Prunus* 'Taihaku' (great white cherry). This is a vigorous cultivar, to 8m (25ft), with dark green leaves, which are bronze when young. Bright pink flowers, to 2.5cm (1in) or more across, are borne in late spring. The yellowish fruits follow.

**Watering** Make sure that the soil is moist and water regularly and generously, especially when the tree is coming into bloom. Make sure that all water has been taken up before watering again.

**Misting** Sprinkle water over the foliage in summer, but do not wet the leaves when the plant is standing in sunlight nor when the tree is in bloom.

**Feeding** Apply a slow-acting, organic fertilizer from the end of flowering until early summer and from early autumn to late autumn. Give an additional dose at the end of autumn to build up the tree before winter.

## PESTS AND DISEASES

### PESTS
*Prunus* 'Accolade' is resistant to many of the pests that affect other *Prunus* species.

**Bark beetles** See page 34.

**Bombyx moth** See page 33.

**Tortrix moth** See page 33.

**Scale insects** See page 33.

**Red spider mite** See page 32.

### DISEASES
**Rust** See page 35.

**Root rot** See page 35.

**Mildew** See page 34.

**Crown gall**
*Symptoms* A hard or soft gall appears on the collar and upper roots. It takes the form of a white (later brown), cauliflower-shaped excrescence, which looks woody and cracked. Rot sets in, endangering the tree. There may be secondary infections.
*Treatment* Cut out and destroy infected branches. Improve the drainage so that compost is not waterlogged. Take care not to wound trees during cultivation so that bacteria can enter the plant tissue. Use clean tools.

**Honey fungus** See page 34.

# ALMOND

Rosaceae. Deciduous. This upright, spreading tree, which is native to the mountains of central and western Asia and to northern Africa, grows to about 8m (25ft) tall. It has a thick trunk, which becomes gnarled and divided, angular branches and shiny green oblong leaves with finely toothed edges. The flowers appear before the leaves, sometimes in early or midwinter, but more often in late winter or early spring. They are white, pale pink or dark pink and are to 5cm (2in) across. The flowers are followed by ovoid, greenish-grey fruit, each of which contains an edible nut.

## PROPAGATION

**Seed** Collect the seeds in autumn. Stratify in a dry place and sow them in spring. Protect the plantlets from frost during the first year.

**Air layering** This should be done between late spring and midsummer (see page 20).

**Grafting** Shield-budding can be done in summer. Leave the graft alone for a whole year, then cut back the one-year-old stem at the end of winter. The upper growth bud from which the trunk extends must be on the opposite side from the point at which the graft is made so as to lessen any possible curve and subsequent swelling. Cut back the growth bud beneath the upper growth bud, which becomes a sucker as it develops.

**Young nursery stock** See page 18.

## CARE

**Sunlight** These trees like full sun and light.

**Temperature** Almond trees like warmth and are badly affected by cold. They must be protected in winter.

**Ventilation** The trees tolerate wind.

**Container** Choose a fairly deep bowl because almond trees like deep soil.

**Regular maintenance** Remove any shoots growing out from the trunk. Remove withered fruit from the tree.

**Growth** These are slow-growing trees.

**Repotting** Every year, either in early spring or after flowering, prune a good third off the root hairs and pot up into a larger container.

**Soil** Use a mixture of equal parts loam and leaf mould. Almond trees thrive in calcareous, deep, dry soil.

**Pruning**
*Pruning sub-branches* After the flowers have withered and before the new shoots have hardened, use clippers to cut back the side shoots to two or three growth buds.
*Pruning branches* Leave slow-growing branches that already have the following year's buds on them, and prune long branches at the end of summer. In mid-autumn prune all branches lightly.

**Wiring** Wire in spring and in summer.

*Pruning side shoots.*

When you put the wire in position make sure that you do not wound the tree or knock off developing flower buds. Protect delicate bark with raffia.

**Watering** Water freely just before flowering but reduce the water given while the tree is in flower.

Tachiki

Shakan

Han-Kengai

Sôkan

Kabudachi

Korabuki

**STYLES**

Prunus dulcis 'Amento': 10 years old; 35cm (14in) high; Tachiki style. Photographed in mid-spring. The photograph shows the beautiful flowers that, if they are pollinated, will produce fine fruits.

**Misting** Do not get the tree wet while it is in flower. After flowering sprinkle water over the plant while you are watering.

**Feeding** In spring and autumn feed with a slow-release, organic fertilizer. A tree that is in flower should not be fed. Increase the amount of fertilizer a little at the end of autumn to set the tree up for winter and to encourage good flowering, which is always early in the season.

Prunus dulcis 'Amento': this close up of the almond tree, photographed in early summer, shows the young fruits, which will mature during the summer and be ready for picking in early autumn, by which time the green colour will have intensified. The fruit is delicious.

## PESTS AND DISEASES

### PESTS
**Scale insects** See page 33.

**Tortrix moth** See page 33.

**Red spider mites** See page 32.

### DISEASES
**Rot** See page 35.

**Rust** See page 35.

**Scab**
*Symptoms* The fungus causes grey patches rimmed with red are seen on the leaves, the fruit and flower buds. Flowers and fruit wither and fail.
*Treatment* Cut out diseased leaves and branches. Spray with zineb-based fungicide.

# JAPANESE APRICOT

Rosaceae. Deciduous. This hardy tree, which is native to China and Korea and widely planted in Japan, grows to about 9m (28ft) tall. It has a rounded crown, grey-green bark and finely serrated, deciduous, oval leaves. The yellow or greenish fruit is edible but very bitter. From late winter to mid-spring it bears white, pale or dark pink or red flowers. Many cultivars have been developed with flowers of different colours.

## PROPAGATION

**Cuttings** In spring take a one-year-old slip, cut off the growing tip and plant it in good garden soil mixed with sand. The following year, put the plantlet in a pot and prune it. Repeat this process for two or three years.

**Air layering** Do this in spring (see page 20).

**Grafting** In summer graft by shield bud (see pages 21–3).

## CARE

**Sunlight** These trees do best in full sun.

**Temperature** Make sure that the trees are in a warm position. The branches will be damaged by frost although the trees will tolerate cold.

**Ventilation** Place the trees where air can circulate freely around them.

**Container** Choose a bowl of medium depth with pretty decoration that will complement the flowers.

**Regular maintenance** Pick some fruit if there is too much so that the tree is not exhausted. In autumn, after the leaves have fallen, carefully remove all dead leaves. Remove any shoots coming from the trunk.

**Growth** These trees grow strongly and quickly.

**Repotting** Repot every year in spring after flowering. Prune a third off the roots

---

### CULTIVARS

*Prunus mume* 'Beni-chidori' This shrubby, upright cultivar has fragrant, double, dark pink flowers to 1cm (½in) across.
*Prunus mume* 'Alphandii' (syn. *P. m.* 'Rosa Plena') This cultivar has double pink flowers, borne in abundance from the end of winter

---

and pot up into a larger container that has good drainage holes.

**Soil** Use a mixture of equal parts loam and leaf mould. A little sand may be added to the compost. *Prunus mume* likes deep, dry, calcareous soil.

**Pruning**
*Pinching back* As soon as they appear pinch out new shoots if there are too many and any unwanted shoots. Pinch back new growth on side branches to stop the branches growing too long. Pinching back is carried out just before the leaves mature.
*Pruning sub-branches* Pinch out the tips of side branches so that the branches will

Prunus mume *(Japanese apricot): 7 years old; 10cm (4in) high; Tachiki style. Photographed in early summer.*

---

Shakan

Kengai

Bankan

Tachiki

Han-Kengai

Bunjingi

Sharimiki

Sekijôju

Ishitsuki

Sabamiki

Sôkan

Kabudachi

Ikadabuki

Sôju

Sambon-Yose

Netsunagari

Gohon-Yose

Nanahon-Yose

Kyûhon-Yose

Yose-Ue

Plantations saisonnières

Bonkei

**STYLES**

Prunus mume *(Japanese apricot): 120 years old; Snarimiki style. Photographed in early summer. This remarkable specimen has a partially dead trunk, which has been sculpted and chiselled to make it appear older still.*

grow delicately and will not break in winter but will produce flowers the following spring. Side branches are pruned after flowering. If you are to achieve good results the work has to be carried out with great attention to detail.

*Pruning branches* When repotting study the tree's outline and prune out superfluous branches. Prune once a year, leaving only two or three leaves per branch after flowering.

**Wiring** Wire from the end of spring to autumn, protecting the brittle branches with raffia. It is not always necessary to coil wire around the branches. They can be trained by weighting, and the trunk can be shaped with a clamp, which should be used in conjunction with pruning.

**Watering** Water as soon as the surface of the soil is dry. Water copiously when the tree is in bud and in summer.

**Misting** Do not wet the tree when it is in flower. When you are watering in summer, sprinkle the leaves but not if the plant is standing in full sunlight.

**Feeding** After flowering until autumn apply a slow-release, organic fertilizer. After flowering until midsummer it is best to use liquid fertilizer. In autumn use fertilizer in a solid or powdered form.

## PESTS AND DISEASES

### PESTS
**Bark beetles** See page 34.

**Bombyx moth** See page 33.

**Tortrix moth** See page 33.

**Scale insects** See page 33.

**Red spider mites** See page 32.

### DISEASES
**Rust** See page 35.

**Rot** See page 36.

**Crown gall**
*Symptoms* A hard or soft gall appears on the collar and upper roots. It takes the form of a white (later brown), cauliflower-shaped excrescence, which looks woody and cracked. Rot sets in, endangering the tree. There may be secondary infections.
*Treatment* Cut out and destroy infected branches. Improve the drainage so that compost is not waterlogged. Take care not to wound trees during cultivation so that bacteria can enter the plant tissue. Use clean tools.

**Powdery mildew** See page 34.

**Bark beetle**
*Symptoms* Brown patches, red at the edges, appear on the leaves, which wither and fall after developing holes. Branches are blotched and distorted.
*Treatment* Cut out and burn diseased branches. Use a combined fungicide in mid- to late spring.

153

# POMEGRANATE

Punicaceae. Deciduous. The genus *Punica* contains just two species, *Punica protopunica* and *P. granatum*. Both are densely branched shrubs or small trees, native to eastern and western Asia and the Mediterranean basin. They have opposite, oblong leaves, and they bear flowers in clusters, and these are followed by spherical berries.

## PROPAGATION

**Seed** Pick the fruit when it is ripe and leave it to rot. Collect the seeds from inside. Wash and dry them. Stratify in sand and sow in spring in a warm place. They need bottom heat and a heated greenhouse for successful germination.

**Cuttings** Take semi-ripe cuttings in summer. Make sure the cuttings are kept damp and well ventilated. Pot up the following spring. Protect from cold and frost.

**Air layering** This can be attempted in spring.

**Young nursery stock** See page 18.

## CARE

**Sunlight** Pomegranates like full sun and need light, but keep the trees in partial shade at the height of summer.

**Temperature** These plants will not survive cold and frost and should ideally be grown in a conservatory.

**Ventilation** Pomegranates are not affected by wind and need a well-ventilated position.

**Container** Select a medium-deep pot.

**Regular maintenance** Remove a few flowers from overloaded branches. If the tree produces fruit, pick them before they fall of their own accord to avoid exhausting the tree.

**Growth** Young plants grow quite fast.

**Repotting** Repot every year or every second year in spring when the leaves are beginning to open. Prune a good third off the roots and pot up into a larger container.

### SPECIES

*Punica granatum* (pomegranate) This species, native to southeastern Europe to the Himalayas, is grown for its flowers and for its fruit. It grows to a height of 6m (20ft). It is of irregular habit, with slightly prickly branches, spindly sub-branches and oblong, deciduous leaves, which are shiny and glabrous. From early summer to early autumn it bears scarlet flowers with puckered petals. These are followed by orange-yellow or reddish fruit, which has several edible seeds in it. The variety *P. granatum* var. *nana* is free fruiting and very compact.

**Soil** Use a good quality potting compost or a mixture of equal parts loam and leaf mould. Sand can be added to the compost.

**Pruning**
*Pinching back* In early spring and late autumn pinch new growth back to two growth buds.
*Pruning sub-branches* After flowering prune side branches, leaving just two growth buds. Leave to grow. When they are about 8cm (3in) long prune the branches again, leaving only one growth bud.

**Wiring** Wire from the end of spring until summer. Protect the brittle branches with raffia. Repeat every year.

**Watering** Water copiously in summer, but make sure that the compost and container drain freely to avoid waterlogged compost. Water lightly in winter. Do not allow the trees to dry out.

**Misting** Mist trees regularly except during flowering.

Shakan

Kengai

Han-Kengai

Tachiki

Bunjingi

Sekijôju

Nejikan

Sôkan

Kabudachi

Ikadabuki

Sôju

Netsunagari

Sambon-Yose

**STYLES**

Punica granatum *(pomegranate): 20 years old, 25cm (10in) high; Tachiki style. Photographed in early summer.*

**Feeding** In spring apply a slow-release, organic fertilizer. During flowering in autumn give a little liquid fertilizer.

## PESTS AND DISEASES

### PESTS
**Greenfly** See page 33.

**Red spider mites** See page 32.

### DISEASES
**Rust** See page 35.

**Powdery mildew** See page 34

**Scab**

*Symptoms* Brown cankerous lesions are seen on the branches. The leaves are flecked with black and turn yellow and drop off. The fruit has black cankers on it and is cracked.
*Treatment* Cut off and burn yellow leaves and any diseased branches. Pick diseased fruit. Spray with a copper- or thiram-based fungicide.

# FIRETHORN

Rosaceae. Evergreen. The genus contains seven species of dense, thorny shrubs. They all have alternate leaves, glossy above and paler and downy beneath. The white flowers are borne in corymbs, and these are followed in autumn by orange or red fruits. There are vary many attractive and reliable cultivars available, with colourful berries.

## PROPAGATION

**Seed** Collect the seeds shortly before they are fully ripe and sow them in the open. Germination should occur the following spring. Seeds may also be kept for a year between layers of sand or earth and sown the following spring. Germination is temperamental and trees grown from seed can take up to five years to produce flowers and fruit.

**Cuttings** In early summer remove side branches that bear fruit in winter. Cut off the growing tip and plant. Roots will form rapidly. Pot up the following spring.

### SPECIES

*Pyracantha angustifolia* Native to southwest China, this dense shrub grows to about 3m (10ft) tall. It has a spreading habit and is sometimes prostrate. The oblong, semi-evergreen leaves can be slightly dentate at the tip, and they are shiny and dark green on top, greyish underneath. It flowers in late spring or early summer. The fruit, which is present from mid-autumn, is brick red to orange and stays on the tree throughout winter until early spring.

Pyracantha angustifolia: *12–25 years old; 60cm (24in) high; Yose-Ue style. Photographed in late summer.*

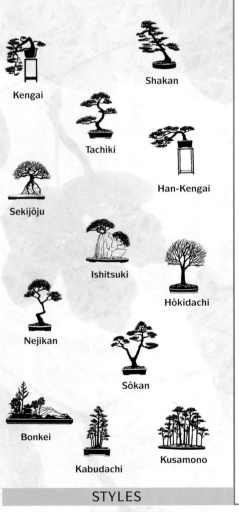

Kengai

Shakan

Tachiki

Han-Kengai

Sekijôju

Ishitsuki

Hôkidachi

Nejikan

Sôkan

Bonkei

Kabudachi

Kusamono

**STYLES**

*Pyracantha angustifolia: 15 years old; 25cm (10in) high; Neijikan style. Photographed in late spring.*

container. These plants do not like being transplanted, so leave some old soil on the roots to help them become re-established.

**Soil** Use a mixture of equal parts loam and leaf mould. Pyracanthas like deep, cool, light, loose soil. They need good drainage.

**Pruning**
*Pruning sub-branches* In summer, after flowering and before the new shoots harden, prune side branches with clippers. In autumn prune again to cut back late shoots.
*Pruning branches* At the end of winter shorten the branches with a view to shaping the tree.

**Wiring** Pyracanthas can be wired at any time during the year. Do not put the wire in place when the new branches are soft and do not leave wire on the tree for more than six months.

**Watering** Water copiously before and after flowering. If it is well drained, the pyracantha needs a lot of water.

**Misting** Sprinkle the foliage during summer watering, but do not wet it when the tree is in flower or bearing fruit.

**Feeding** Feed with liquid fertilizer in spring before flowering. In autumn feed with a slow-release, organic fertilizer once a month.

**Layering** Simple layering, done in spring, is the best method. Keep the soil moist.

**Young nursery stock** See page 18.

**Growth** Pyracanthas grow fairly fast in open soil but more slowly when they are container grown.

**Repotting** Every second year in spring prune the roots and pot up into a larger

## CARE

**Sunlight** Pyracanthas will do well in full sun but should be placed in partial shade at the height of summer.

**Temperature** *Pyracantha angustifolia* is not hardy and dislikes frost. If it is stood outdoors in summer, protect it under glass in winter.

**Ventilation** These plants can withstand wind as long as they are well watered.

**Container** Choose a medium-deep, glazed pot.

**Regular maintenance** Remove all yellow leaves to prevent insect infestations. If there is too much fruit, remove some after it has formed.

## PESTS AND DISEASES

### PESTS
**Greenfly** See page 33

**Woolly aphids** See page 34.

**Scale insects** See page 33.

**Ermine moth** See page 33.

### DISEASES
**Scab**
*Symptoms* Cankerous brown lesions are seen on the branches. The leaves are flecked with black, turn yellow and fall. The fruit has black cankers and is cracked.
*Treatment* Cut off and burn yellow leaves

and diseased branches. Pick diseased fruit. Spray with a copper- or thiram-based wash.

**Fireblight**
*Symptoms* New shoots and flower buds blacken and wither as if burned but cling to the stems. The affected parts shrivel. Oozing white-beige cankers may appear on the stems.
*Treatment* This is a serious bacterial disease. Cut out and burn diseased branches and sterilize all tools. Do not use a fertilizer containing nitrogen and make sure the soil is not waterlogged. Use a copper-based fungicide when flowering starts and during the growing season.

# OAK

Fagaceae. Deciduous or evergreen. This is a huge genus, with some 600 monoecious trees and shrubs, which are found in the temperate zones of the northern hemisphere. The bark is usually fissured, with downy or hairless shoots and alternate leaves.

## SPECIES

**Quercus petraea** (syn. *Q. sessili-flora*; sessile oak) Native to Europe, this deciduous tree grows to 45m (150ft). It has a straight, cylindrical trunk with furrowed, dark grey to blackish-brown bark. The large, mid-green leaves are broadly obovate and turn red in autumn. They may stay on the tree in winter. The acorns, which are borne singly or in clusters, are ripe in late autumn.

**Quercus pubescens** (downy oak) This is a deciduous tree, native to southern Europe to the Ukraine and growing to 20m (65m). It has a twisted trunk, with dark brown bark, and a rounded crown. The leaves have rounded lobes; they are grey-green and hairy underneath. The acorns are borne singly..

**Quercus robur** (syn. *Q. pedunculata*; pedunculate oak, English oak) A deciduous tree, native to Europe, which grows to 35m (115ft) or more. It is a very long-lived tree, with a straight, thick, short trunk and grey-brown bark. The trunk divides into sturdy boughs, which twist and bend. The familiarly shaped, lobed leaves are dark green. The acorns are borne singly or in clusters.

## PROPAGATION

**Seed** Collect ripe acorns in mid-autumn or as they appear. Dry them out a bit by turning them over occasionally, then keep them in barely moist sand or boxes of peat. Sow in early to mid-spring, 6cm (2¼in) deep, after all fear of frost has past. Germination takes place within six weeks. Protect the seedlings from the birds. Pot up the following spring.

**Cuttings** Choose wood that is one to three years old. Dip the slips in hormone rooting compound. Keep the cuttings in a warm place until roots have formed.

**Air layering** Choose a suitable shoot (see page 20) and enclose the layer in a double sheath, with polythene inside and foil

Quercus robur *(pedunculate oak): 30 years old; 90cm (36in); Tachiki style. Photographed in late spring.*

Shakan

Tachiki

Han-Kengai

Sôkan

Sekijôju

Kabudachi

## STYLES

outside, thus reducing moisture loss and retaining more heat.

**Young nursery stock** Select specimens with a tap root that is not too deep and with a well-developed root system (see also page 18).

# CARE

**Sunlight** *Quercus robur* needs a lot of light, but *Q. petraea* is more of a forest tree and should be placed in partial shade in summer. It is best to place *Q. pubescens* in a partially shaded site in summer and in full sun for the rest of the year.

**Temperature** These trees will withstand frost, although shoots may be damaged by late frosts, and like heat. *Q. petraea* likes a mild, damp climate.

**Ventilation** They will tolerate wind, but branches may break if the wind is too strong.

**Container** The main root goes deep, so select a suitable container.

**Regular maintenance** If there are any old dry leaves left on the tree in spring when the new leaves break, gently pick them off. Do not allow moss to develop on the base of the roots and trunk.

**Growth** *Quercus robur* and *Q. pubescens* are slow growing.

**Repotting** Repot every three years into a larger container. Prune the root hairs by a half but take care not to damage the tap root, although in young specimens it, too, must be reduced.

**Soil** Use a mixture of equal parts loam, sharp sand and leaf mould. Oaks thrive in light, well-drained, relatively dry soil. *Q. pubescens* grows in dry calcareous, poor soil, but other oaks like deep, fertile soil.

**Pruning**
*Pruning shoots* Allow the buds to burst. Cut with clippers when they fade and in summer cut before the new shoots harden.
*Pruning sub-branches* Use clippers to shorten the side branches, leaving only one or two pairs of leaves. Cut when the branches have produced about four or five pairs of leaves.
*Structural pruning* Before the growing season starts cut out any crossing branches. If this is done when the tree is young, it should gradually cease to be necessary.

**Wiring** If necessary, wire the oak from spring to autumn but shape the outline by pruning as far as possible.

**Watering** Water well in spring and summer, letting the compost dry out between waterings. Good drainage is essential.

**Misting** Mist in summer to cleanse the leaves of pollution and possible insect infestation.

**Feeding** Feed in spring and in autumn with a slow-release, organic fertilizer. Do not feed in mid- or late summer, nor after repotting, nor if the tree is in poor condition.

## PESTS AND DISEASES

### PESTS
**Chafer beetles**
*Symptoms* The leaves wilt and die and may be eaten. The roots will be eaten by the fat, white larvae, which have six legs and a brown head.
*Treatment* Dust compost with pirimiphos-methyl before planting. In spring spray with insecticide to kill the adult beetles.

**Buprestrids**
*Symptoms* This is a group of insects whose larvae are wood borers. The insects are shiny and metallic looking and may be seen in summer. The larvae, which may live for 30 years, hollow out galleries in the wood, eventually causing branches to wither.
*Treatment* Cut out and burn infested branches. Spray with a systemic insecticide in summer.

**Bark beetles** See page 30.

**Capricorn beetles**
*Symptoms* Holes appear in the bark with galleries running from them. Branches may wither and brown beetles may be seen.
*Treatment* Cut out and burn infested branches.

**Stag beetles**
*Symptoms* The trunk is gnawed by big white larvae and the brown beetles may be present. These insects only attack trees that are dying.

**Orchestres**
*Symptoms* Leaves are gnawed by the larvae.
*Treatment* Spray with insecticide.

**Goat moth** See page 33.

**Geometer moth** See page 33.

**Tortrix moth** See page 33.

**Leaf miners** See page 33

**Aphids** See page 33.

**Gall wasps**
*Symptoms* Hairy spherical galls appear on the shoots; they are caused by the tiny wasps, which live on the tree's tissues.
*Treatment* Cut out and burn the infested branches. No chemical treatment required and the damage done is rarely serious.

### DISEASES
**Damping off**
*Symptoms* This parasitic fungus affects seedlings sown under glass in crowded conditions. The seedlings rot at soil level and die.
*Treatment* Remove and burn dead seedlings. Water with a copper-based fungicide or Cheshunt compound. Do not allow water to stagnate and avoid excessive humidity. Allow water to circulate freely.

**Powdery mildew** See page 34.

**Leaf blight**
*Symptoms* White swellings appear on the leaves, which tear and shrivel.
*Treatment* Burn dead leaves. Spray with a copper- or thiram-based wash in spring and autumn.

**Canker**
*Symptoms* Where there are scars and gaps where the branches separate out, wounds form, swell and crack open; branches die. Neighbouring branches form excrescences as a defence mechanism. There are spots of red on the wood.
*Treatment* Cut out and burn affected branches. Scrape out the cankerous areas. Apply fungicide to the wounds, then treat with wound-sealing compound. Spray with a copper-based wash when leaves fall.

**Coral spot**
*Symptoms* A fungus (*Nectria cinnabarina*) causes die-back and orange-pink spots appear on dead.
*Treatment* Cut out and burn affected branches. Sterilize your tools. Check that the compost is not waterlogged.

**Leaf spot** See page 35.

**Anthracnose**
*Symptoms* In spring or during wet, mild summers, leaves curl and become discoloured before falling. Die-back may follow severe attacks.
*Treatment* Cut out infected shoots and burn. Burn affected leaves. Spray with a copper-based fungicide.

**Honey fungus** See page 35.

# OAK

Fagaceae. Deciduous or evergreen. This group includes some tender oaks, which are mostly native to the Mediterranean littoral. They are long-lived trees, mostly evergreen or semi-evergreen, which do best in a conservatory. Some of the hardy deciduous species, which have good autumn colour, are described on pages 158–9.

## PROPAGATION

**Seed** Collect ripe acorns and stratify them by placing them in sand before sowing them in spring. Alternatively, sow them in autumn in the open ground (in frost-free gardens) or in a cold frame. Mice can be a problem if acorns are planted in the ground. Protect seedlings until they are established.

**Cuttings** Take hardwood cuttings and dip them in hormone rooting compost. Plant them in cuttings compost and keep them in a cold frame until they are established.

**Grafting** Propagating cultivars can be achieved only by grafting, which should be done in mid-autumn or winter.

**Young nursery stock** Select specimens with a tap root that is not too deep and with a well-developed root system (see page 18).

## CARE

**Sunlight** These trees need plenty of sun and good levels of light all year round.

**Temperature** These species need warm, sunny summers if they are to do well. *Quercus coccifera* will survive outdoors in winter provided there are no prolonged frosts, but the other two species listed here should be taken under cover in winter, even if they are stood outdoors in summer.

**Ventilation** These trees withstand wind well and will survive in coastal gardens.

**Container** Choose a deep pot. It can be oval, circular or rectangular, but make sure that the colour harmonizes with the trunk.

**Regular maintenance** Remove any yellow leaves from the tree and any leaves that fall onto the compost. Once or twice a year brush the trunk to remove any moss that is growing on it.

### SPECIES

*Quercus coccifera* (kermes oak) This compact evergreen shrub, native to the Mediterranean, grows to 10m (33ft) high. It has smooth, grey bark, which cracks as it matures. The holly-like leaves are dark glossy green, and the acorns sit in spiny cups.

*Quercus ilex* (holm oak, evergreen oak) This is a large, variable tree, growing to 25m (80ft), which is native to the Mediterranean. It has corrugated bark and a good rounded crown. The glossy, dark green leaves are like holly leaves. This is a good choice for a seaside garden, but it is not hardy in gardens that are prone to frost.

*Quercus suber* (cork oak) This tree is found in the western Mediterranean, especially Portugal, and it is grown for its corky bark. The evergreen, ovate, toothed leaves and greyish and hairy beneath. The trees grow to about 20m (65ft) and become wide spreading. The acorns are oval and are borne in ones or twos.

*Quercus wislizeni* This evergreen tree or shrub, to 20m (65ft), is native to the USA. It has reddish bark and glossy, dark leaves.

**Growth** *Quercus ilex* grows fairly slowly; the other two species grow slightly faster, but even so, they are not fast-growing plants.

**Repotting** Every two or three years in

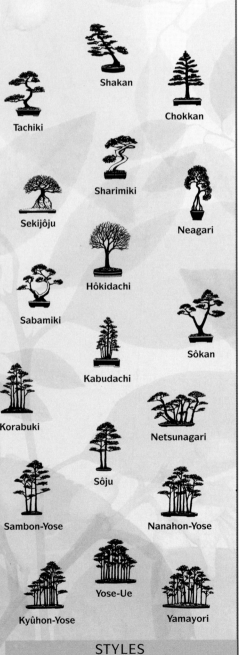

Tachiki

Shakan

Chokkan

Sharimiki

Sekijôju

Neagari

Hôkidachi

Sabamiki

Sôkan

Kabudachi

Korabuki

Netsunagari

Sôju

Sambon-Yose

Nanahon-Yose

Yose-Ue

Kyûhon-Yose

Yamayori

*Quercus coccifera (kermes oak): 12 years old; 30cm (12in) high; Tachiki style. Photographed in early autumn.*

### Pruning
*Pruning shoots* Lightly pinch out new shoots in spring.
*Pruning sub-branches* Between early spring and late autumn cut out side branches as necessary to create the desired shape. At the same time cut back any that are growing too long.
*Pruning branches* At the end of winter carry out a thorough overall pruning to create the desire shaped. At the same time cut out any damaged or diseased branches.
*Leaf pruning* The total leaf pruning of these oaks is rarely carried out because the leaves are comparatively small.

### Wiring
**Wiring** This can be done all year round on hardened shoots but do not leave the wire for more than three months. If necessary, repeat the process the following year.

### Watering
**Watering** Water freely from the moment growth begins in spring. Make sure that the roots have taken up all the water before the next watering. These plants will tolerate dry compost for short periods and do not like very humid conditions.

### Misting
**Misting** In summer mist around the foliage to keep the leaves clean and free from insects. Do not mist in autumn and winter. *Quercus suber* prefers more humid conditions than the other species mentioned, but do not mist in cold weather.

### Feeding
**Feeding** Apply a slow-acting, organic fertilizer every three weeks from early spring until early summer and early autumn to late autumn. Give an extra dose at the end of the autumn to boost the plants before winter.

## PESTS AND DISEASES

See page 159.

### Gall wasps
*Symptoms* These are a particular problem with oak trees. Small galls, known as oak apples, which may be solitary or in groups, grow out of the shoots in spring. They are caused by the tiny wasps, which live in the plant's tissues.
*Treatment* Remove and destroy the galls. The damage done to the plant is rarely serious, although the galls may look unsightly. There is no chemical treatment.

mid-spring plant up into well-drained compost. They have no special preferences for soil type as long as it is fertile and freely draining. Cut back the roots by about a third and, if necessary, pot into a slightly larger container.

**Soil** For *Quercus coccifera* use a mixture of five parts loam, two parts leaf mould and one part sharp sand; *Q. ilex* prefers a mixture of three parts loam, three parts leaf mould and four parts sharp sand; *Q. suber* prefers three parts loam to one part leaf mould and one part sharp sand.

# LADY PALM

Arecaceae/Palmae. Evergreen. This is a genus of 12 small, clump-forming palms, which are native to tropical and subtropical forests from southern China to Java. The plants tend to be slender and fairly upright. The stems, which are like bamboos or canes, sucker at the base. The leaves are dark green and palmate or digitate. The inconspicuous yellow flowers are dioecious. The egg-shaped fruit, which has the narrower end at the base, carries a single seed.

## PROPAGATION

**Division** Clumps can be divided at any time of year if they are being grown in a

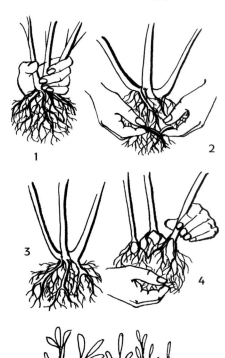

*Root development and new stems.*

greenhouse or in spring if the plant is kept outdoors.

**Suckers** Suckering shoots can be separated from the main plant.

**Seed** If available, sow seed at 27°C (81°F).

## CARE

**Sunlight** These plants tolerate light but prefer partial shade and will grow well in a poorly lit position.

**Temperature** The palms like warmth. In winter the temperature should not fall below 17°C (63°F).

**Ventilation** Keep plants out of draughts but in a well-ventilated room.

**Container** Select a shallow container or one that is between shallow and medium deep. It can be unglazed and brown, or glazed and cobalt blue, which is the most commonly seen colour.

**Regular maintenance** Cut the tips off the leaves if they turn yellow, though they will

Propagation by division of a clump
**1** *Shake off the earth from a clump of Rhapis and wash the roots.* **2** *Disentangle the root hairs.* **3** *Separate the roots belonging to each section of stem.* **4** *Pull the stems apart.* **5** *Each new Rhapis can be planted in its own pot.*

Sekijôju

Ishitsuki

Kabudachi

Sôju

Sambon-Yose

Gohon-Yose

Nanahon-Yose

Yose-Ue

Kyûhon-Yose

Kusamono

**STYLES**

Rhapis humilis *(reed rhapis, slender lady palm): 10 years old; 25cm (10in) high; Kabudachi style. Photographed in early winter.*

## SPECIES

***Rhapis excelsa*** (syn. *R. flabelliformis*; miniature fan palm, ground rattan cane) This small palm, native to southern China, has erect, slender, bamboo-like stems and grows to 5m (16ft). The dark green leaves are deeply lobed. Tiny cream flowers are borne in panicles.

***Rhapis excelsa*** 'Variegata' The lobes of the leaves of this cultivar have white stripes.

***Rhapis humilis*** (reed rhapis, slender lady palm) Native to southern China, this is a slender, smaller version of *R. excelsa*, growing to about 1.5m (5ft). It is an elegant plant, with dark green, evergreen leaves, which have up to 20 spreading leaflets.

continue to do so, and take care to cut obliquely to preserve the original shape (do not cut straight across). Remove suckers unless you want a group style. Wipe the leaves with a damp sponge.

**Growth** These plants grow slowly.

**Repotting** Repot every third year in early to mid-spring. Prune the roots by a half and pot up into a larger container.

**Soil** Use a mixture of equal parts loam, leaf mould, ericaceous compost and sharp sand. Rhapis have no special requirements, but the soil should be good loam with sand and leaf mould, or peat, added to it.

**Pruning** If you want to shorten a rhapis, you can cut the main stem, but only if side shoots have emerged. Other than this these plants are not pruned.

**Wiring** These palms are not wired.

**Watering** Little water is needed, and the shadier the position, the less water the plant will need. Keep the soil fairly dry but make sure that it does not dry out completely.

**Misting** Mist the foliage daily to maintain high levels of humidity.

**Feeding** In spring and in autumn feed with a small amount of slow-release, organic fertilizer.

## PESTS AND DISEASES

### PESTS

**Glasshouse red spider mites** See page 32.

**Thrips**
*Symptoms* There are dry, grey patches on the leaves, and spots appear on these. The plant will be weakened, and the leaves eaten. The small insects may be seen beneath the leaves.
*Treatment* Spray with malathion or with heptenophos and permethrin. If necessary, repeat 10 days later.

**Whitefly**
*Symptoms* These tiny insects, with wingspans to no more than 5mm (°in), resemble minute moths and can be a real pest in greenhouses, where they are seen on the undersides of leaves, which become covered with honeydew and sooty mould.
*Treatment* Spray with an insecticide such as malathion, permethrin or heptenophos and permethrin. Organic gardeners will prefer to try the parasitic wasp *Encarsia formosa*.

### DISEASES

**Rot** See page 31.

**Damping off**
*Symptoms* There is damp rot on the collar of the plant, the young roots rot, and the plant tissues disintegrate. The leaves droop and wilt.
*Treatment* Maintain a constant temperature and make sure that air can circulate freely around the plant but that there are no draughts. Do not overwater. Apply nitrogen and potassium to the soil.

**Fusarium wilt**
*Symptoms* This fungal disease causes leaves to turn brown, starting from the centre. The stems may also become discoloured, and the leaves may wither and fall.
*Treatment* Make sure the soil does not get too wet. Remove and destroy infected stems. In severe cases apply carbendazim, following the manufacturer's instructions.

**Leafspot** See page 35.

# RHODODENDRON

Ericaceae. Deciduous or evergreen. This is a large genus containing between 700 and 800 species, which are native to Asia, North America, Europe, Java, the Malay islands, Australasia, New Guinea and the Philippines. The plant forms are very diverse, and there are many named cultivars, some of which are known as azaleas.

## PROPAGATION

**Seed** Gather the seeds and keep in a dry place before sowing in late spring. Germination gets under way three weeks after sowing. Keep the soil moist. Leave the seedlings in position for two years before you repot, taking care to avoid mildew.

**Cuttings** Take cuttings in early summer. Plant them in a greenhouse or in a cold frame in sand and peat. Roots will have formed by mid-autumn. Leave under glass throughout winter before potting up in spring.

**Simple layering** The layering should be done in midsummer, and the following year, in early to mid-autumn, the layer can be severed and potted up.

**Young nursery stock** See page 18.

Rhododendron indicum: *8 years old; 12cm (5in) high; Sôkan style. Photographed in mid-spring. When both the leaves and flowers are miniaturized, the results can be startling.*

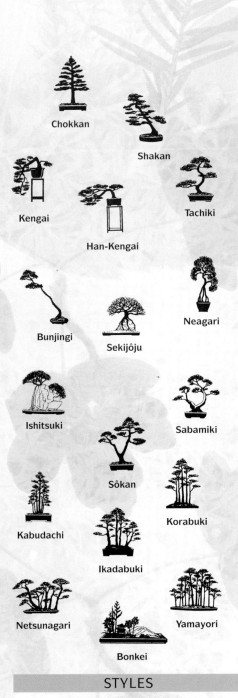

Chokkan, Shakan, Kengai, Han-Kengai, Tachiki, Bunjingi, Sekijôju, Neagari, Ishitsuki, Sabamiki, Sôkan, Korabuki, Kabudachi, Ikadabuki, Netsunagari, Bonkei, Yamayori

STYLES

164

*Rhododendron impeditum* This compact evergreen species, native to western China, has small elliptical leaves, green-grey on top and brownish underneath. It grows to about 1m (3ft) high. Slightly scented, mauve-blue flowers are borne from mid- to late spring.

*Rhododendron indicum* This shrub, to about 2m (6ft), is native to Japan. It is very variable in habit and may be prostrate. It usually forms quite a dense shrub, with dark green, evergreen or semi-evergreen leaves. The large flowers, which may be bright red to pinkish-red, are borne in late spring to early summer.

# CARE

**Sunlight** Place the plants in partial shade. Small-leaved varieties can withstand the sun better than other forms.

**Temperature** Rhododendrons like warmth and many react badly to frost. Keep them in a frost-free place over winter, but not indoors.

**Ventilation** The rhododendron stands up well to wind, but needs more water if exposed to cold, drying winds.

**Container** While the rhododendron is being developed it is best to use an unglazed bowl of medium depth. They are rarely grown in flat bowls.

**Regular maintenance** Pick off some flower buds if there are too many. After flowering remove faded blooms. Remove any shoots that form on the main trunk and any suckers. Keep the soil regularly swept as it is often covered by fallen leaves.

**Growth** The plants will grow slowly but steadily.

**Repotting** Repot after flowering every year for young trees and every second year for older trees. Prune the roots by a third and pot up into a larger container.

**Soil** Use a mixture of two parts ericaceous compost, one part leaf mould and one part peat. Rhododendrons need soil that is damp, cool, light, rich in humus and sandy. It can be acid, but must never be calcareous. The rhododendron becomes etiolated in soil consisting only of leaf mould.

## Pruning

*Pinching back* In spring, when the buds appear, pinch out leaf shoots above the flower buds to encourage flowers to form.
*Pruning sub-branches* At the end of summer, after the flowers have faded and

*Pruning a rhododendron.*

before the leaves harden, prune side branches with clippers, cutting back to two pairs of leaves.
*Pruning branches* When repotting, prune out dead branches or over-crowded branches to let air into the shrub.

**Wiring** Wire from spring to autumn. Rhododendron branches break easily and to harden them do not water for one day before wiring.

**Watering** Keep the compost damp. The roots dry out quickly and dry compost can be fatal for the tree. Water regularly throughout the year except in frosty weather.

**Misting** In summer mist the foliage every morning and evening. After repotting mist the leaves until the new roots have become established. Do not wet the flowers.

**Feeding** Give a weak solution of organic fertilizer in spring and autumn. Do not feed during flowering.

## PESTS

### Vine weevils
*Symptoms* These are a very serious pest of all container-grown plants. The first sign may be the total collapse of the plant, but inspection will show that the roots have been eaten by the brown-headed, white larvae. Adult weevils eat the edges of leaves.
*Treatment* At the first sign of attack, remove the plant from the pot. Remove and kill the larvae. Prune the roots and repot in sterile soil. Spray with contact insecticide from late spring to midsummer. Under glass, use the parasitic nematode *Heterorhabditis megedis*.

### Rhododendron leafhoppers
*Symptoms* The blue-green, orange-striped insects (*Graphocephala fennahi*), about 5mm (¼in) long, lay eggs in the flower buds. The insects themselves do not cause serious damage but transmit the virus causing rhododendron bud blast, a serious disease.
*Treatment* Cut out and burn affected branches. Spray with permethrin and heptenophos in late summer.

### Rhododendron lacebug
*Symptoms* In late spring or early summer the top surface of the leaves is covered with fine marbling, and brown or reddish-brown spots appear on the lower surface.
*Treatment* Prune out and burn affected leaves and branches. Spray with permethrin.

## DISEASES

### Rhododendron bud blast
*Symptoms* The buds turn grey-brown and infected buds develop bristly structures. The virus is transmitted by rhododendron leafhoppers.
*Treatment* Remove and burn infected shoots or, if necessary, the entire plant. Spray with Bordeaux mixture.

### Azalea gall
*Symptoms* The fungus causes pale green (later white), rather fleshy galls to develop on the flowers or foliage.
*Treatment* The fungus thrives in high humidity, so improve the circulation of air around the plants. Remove and destroy the swellings as soon as they are seen. Spray with Bordeaux mixture.

### Honey fungus See page 35.

### Chlorosis
*Symptoms* Leaves turn yellow or even white throughout the growing season. New leaves are small and discoloured.
*Treatment* This is a particular problem of rhododendrons and azaleas growing in alkaline soil. Add peat, pulverized bark or crushed bracken to the compost and use fertilizers that are sold specifically as lime-free. For iron deficiency (the most likely cause of yellow leaves) add chelated iron to the water.

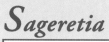

# SAGERETIA

Rhameae or Rhamnaceae. Evergreen. The name of the genus is derived from Sageret, a French agriculturist, to whom the Chinese dedicated this tree. It is native to central and southern Asia, Java and warm areas of North America. Most sageretias that are more than 10 years old come from the Republic of China, where they were collected as natural material, then grown in bonsai form. There are about 12 species of shrub in the genus, and all have stiff, slender branches, with or without thorns.

## PROPAGATION

**Seed** Collect the seed when it is ripe and stratify it. The following spring plant the seed in a propagating frame in a greenhouse and supply bottom heat. Keep the compost moist.

**Cuttings** Take cuttings from lateral shoots in spring. Cut off the growing tip and the bottom pair of leaves. Dip in hormone rooting compound if wished and plant in a mixture of sand and peat in a greenhouse or cold frame. Gradually harden off the new shoots by acclimatizing them to cooler conditions and pot up the following year.

## CARE

**Sunlight** These plants need good light all year round and in warm areas they can stand outdoors in summer, although they should be protected from direct summer sun. In winter they should be keep in a well-lit situation.

**Temperature** The shrubs like warmth, and in winter the temperature should not fall below 12°C (54°F).

**Ventilation** Protect these plants from draughts and from wind.

**Container** Choose a medium-deep container; unglazed pots look best.

**Regular maintenance** Remove shoots growing out of the trunk and all yellow leaves.

**Growth** Trunk formation is very slow, but the foliage and branch structure will develop quickly.

**Repotting** Every second year in mid- to late spring prune the roots by about one-half and pot up into a slightly larger container than before.

**Soil** Use a mixture of equal parts ericaceous compost, leaf mould, loam and sharp sand. Sageretias like good, cool, loamy soil.

Sageretia theezans: *25 years old; 30cm (12in) high; Shakan style. Photographed in early summer.*

## STYLES

Chokkan

Shakan

Kengai

Tachiki

Han-Kengai

Sharimiki

Fukinagashi

Ishitsuki

Nejikan

Sabamiki

Sôkan

Korabuki

Kabudachi

Sôju

Yose-Ue

Tsukami-Yose

Sageretia theezans: 150 years old; 45cm (18in) high; Shakan style. Photographed in late spring. This exceptional tree was produced from a plant collected from the wild in China.

## Pruning

*Pruning sub-branches* During the growing season prune new shoots, leaving two or three pairs of leaves on each branch.

*Pruning branches* Before growth starts, prune out any broken, damaged or unsightly branches. If you do not prune sagretias, white flowers appear in the leaf axils and exhaust the tree.

**Wiring** This shrub can be wired at any time of year but do not leave the wire in place for more than six to eight weeks. Wait until new shoots have hardened before you wire them.

**Watering** Give more water in summer than in winter. Make sure that the surface of the soil is always slightly damp. This shrub requires good drainage.

**Misting** Mist the foliage daily. In winter stand each plant on a tray filled with water and gravel to maintain high levels of humidity.

**Feeding** In spring and in autumn feed with a slow-release, organic fertilizer. Give liquid fertilizer and solid fertilizer alternately.

## PESTS AND DISEASES

If sagretias are overwatered, the leaves will wither and fall. They need light and constant warmth if the leaves are to be really green and well formed. They must be misted daily.

### PESTS

**Aphids** See page 33.

**Glasshouse red spider mites** See page 32.

**Snails**
*Symptoms* Shoots and needles are eaten and the trails of slime may be seen.
*Treatment* Collect up the snails by hand and kill them. Do not let the soil get too wet. If you must, and as a last resort only, use metaldehyde or methiocarb pellets.

**Vine weevils**
*Symptoms* These are a very serious pest of all container-grown plants. The first sign may be the total collapse of the plant, but inspection will show that the roots have been eaten by the brown-headed, white larvae. Adult weevils eat the edges of leaves.
*Treatment* At the first sign of attack, remove the plant from the pot. Remove and kill the larvae. Prune the roots and repot in clean soil. Spray with contact insecticide from late spring to midsummer. Under glass, use the parasitic nematode *Heterorhabditis megedis*.

### DISEASES

**Mildew** See page 34.

**Chlorosis**
*Symptoms* The leaves gradually turn yellow or white and new leaves are discoloured.
*Treatment* Do not give too much calcium or water and do not expose to cold. Keep out of draughts and away from noxious gases. Place in the light. Add iron, magnesium, zinc and nitrogen to the soil.

# WILLOW

Salicaceae. Deciduous. The genus contains about 300 trees and shrubs, most of which are dioecious. They are native to a wide range of habitats, from woodland and meadow to mountainous screes, throughout the world except Australia.

## SPECIES

*Salix alba* (white willow) The species, native to Europe, northern Africa and central Asia, grows to 10m (33ft). It has lanceolate, dull green leaves, bluish beneath. Male catkins are yellow and to 5cm (2in) long; female catkins are yellowish-green to 3cm (1¼in) long.

*Salix babylonica* (weeping willow) Native to China, Japan and Korea, this is a graceful, rounded, weeping tree to 12m (40ft), with greenish bark. The lanceolate leaves are mid-green, greyish beneath, and are borne on pendent green-brown shoots. Silvery-green catkins appear in spring; male catkins are to 5cm (2in) long, and female catkins are to 2.5cm (1in) long.

Salix babylonica *(weeping willow): 15 years old; 35cm (14in) high; Hôkidachi style. Photographed in mid-autumn.*

Tachiki

Kengai

Han-Kengai

Sekijôju

Ishitsuki

Hôkidachi

Sôkan

Kusamono

STYLES

## PROPAGATION

**Seed** The seed ripens in late spring or early summer and germinates directly it is sown. As soon as you have collected the seed, sow in damp, sandy soil. Grow on the plantlets for two years before potting up.

**Cuttings** Take softwood cuttings in early summer. Plant in a mixture of equal parts sand and peat and keep moist.

**Simple layering** Strip the section of branch to be buried and cut through the bark. Keep the sandy soil damp. Roots will form rapidly. Sever the layer and pot up in late spring or early summer.

**Young nursery stock** See page 18.

## CARE

**Sunlight** Place the plants in a sunny position but in summer provide some shade while maintaining good levels of light.

**Temperature** These plants are not fussy and will adapt to cool temperatures. Avoid excessive heat.

**Ventilation** Willows are not worried by wind and should be positioned where air can circulate freely around them.

**Container** Select a fairly flat bowl for an upright style. If it is in a cascade or semi-cascade style, a deep pot is necessary. Always make sure the pot has good drainage holes.

**Regular maintenance** Keep the inside of the crown well cleaned in summer. Remove all dead material from the tree and soil in autumn. Brush the trunk regularly to remove moss.

**Growth** These are fast-growing trees, although male trees are less vigorous than female ones.

**Repotting** Twice a year, in early spring and early summer, prune the roots by half and pot up into a larger container. Make sure the drainage is good.

**Soil** Use a mixture of equal parts loam, sharp sand and leaf mould. Willows need moist, marshy, light, cool soil.

**Pruning**
*Pinching back* In very early spring, before the sap begins to circulate, pinch back all shoots.
*Pruning sub-branches* Prune down to one growth bud. When repotting cut off any new long shoots. Prune again at the end of autumn.

**Wiring** Wire in spring and in summer. Wrap raffia around the wire to protect the branches. The tree's shape can be created by weighting it. After fixing the wire in place, gently direct the branches into position by hand.

**Watering** Water freely, provided the drainage is good. Keep the compost damp. In summer it may be necessary to stand the tree to soak in a basin of water.

**Misting** Mist plants thoroughly to maintain high levels of humidity. Misting also helps to protect plants against infestations of pests and cleanses the leaves of pollution. Mist frequently during the growing season.

**Feeding** In spring and autumn apply a slow-release, organic fertilizer. Do not feed in mid- to late summer.

## PESTS

### Gall mites
*Symptoms* In spring a white down, turning red in summer, appears on the underside of the leaves, which become misshapen. The catkins look like green galls.
*Treatment* Cut off and burn affected leaves and branches. There is no effective chemical treatment, but spraying with parathion or lindane-based insecticides might help.

### Capricorn beetle
*Symptoms* Holes in the bark have galleries running from them, and the wood of the trunk and branches gnawed by white grubs. The tree will eventually withers. The beetles are sometimes also seen.
*Treatment* Cut out infested branches. Push a copper wire through the tunnels to kill adults.

### Goat and leopard moths See page 33.

### Vine weevils
*Symptoms* These are a very serious pest of all container-grown plants. The first sign may be the total collapse of the plant, but inspection will show that the roots have been eaten by the brown-headed, white larvae. Adult weevils eat the edges of leaves.
*Treatment* At the first sign of attack, remove the plant from the pot. Remove and kill the larvae. Prune the roots and repot in clean soil. Spray with contact insecticide from late spring to midsummer. Under glass, use the parasitic nematode *Heterorhabditis megedis*.

### Bombyx moth, sawflies, gall-forming sawflies, leaf beetles
*Symptoms* The leaves are eaten by grubs or caterpillars and the parent insects may be may be present.
*Treatment* Spray with an insecticide based on parathion or lindane.

### Rosette-shaped galls
*Symptoms* The small leaves at the tips of shoot are shaped like artichokes and have tiny worms inside them.

*Treatment* Cut off and burn infested branches. Spray with an insecticide based on parathion.

### Aphids See page 33.

### Scale insects See page 33.

## DISEASES
### Powdery mildew See page 34.

### Canker
*Symptoms* This is a fungal problem. Where there are scars and where branching occurs, wounds open, swell, and crack. Branches die. Neighbouring branches form excrescences as a defence mechanism. Small red spots on wood.
*Treatment* Cut out and burn affected branches. Scrape out the cankers. Apply copper-based fungicide and cover with a wound-sealing compound. Apply a copper-based fungicidal wash when the leaves fall.

### Willow scab
*Symptoms* Black spots are seen on the underside of the leaves. Branches wither and bend. The spots start from the veins, then spread.
*Treatment* Cut out and burn diseased material. In early spring spray with a copper-based mixture as a precaution against scab.

### Black spot
*Symptoms* The fungus causes thick black scabs on the leaves.
*Treatment* Pick off diseased and dead leaves, and spray with a copper-based fungicide.

### Anthracnose
*Symptoms* In spring or during wet, mild summers, leaves curl and become discoloured before falling. Die-back may follow severe attacks.
*Treatment* Cut out infected shoots and burn. Burn affected leaves. Spray with a copper-based fungicide.

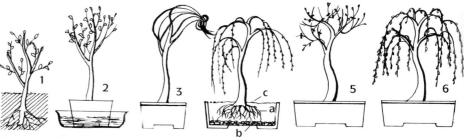

Training a willow
**1** *Grow on cutting.* **2** *Pot up the cutting and stand the container in a bowl of water.* **3** *Wire the long shoots in winter. The stems are pliable and can be fastened together to train them into an upward position.* **4** *(a) Old soil; (b) crocks; (c) new soil.* **5** *Prune all the side branches.* **6** *Repot in spring.*

# UMBRELLA TREE

Araliaceae. Evergreen. This is a very large genus, now containing more than 700 shrubs, sub-shrubs, trees and climbers; see also *Aralia* (pages 46–7). They are native to warm to tropical areas of southeast Asia, Central and South America and the islands of the Pacific. Many species are grown as houseplants.

## PROPAGATION

**Seed** Collect the seeds from the berries when they are ripe. Dry them, then stratify them. Plant them in spring in a greenhouse or cold frame in a mixture of peat and loam. Harden off the seedlings and pot up the following spring.

**Cuttings** Take semi-ripe cuttings in summer and give bottom heat. Keep in the greenhouse and protect plantlets from extremes of temperature.

## CARE

**Sunlight** Scheffleras need a lot of light. The more light they receive, the smaller the leaves will remain as they develop.

**Temperature** Good, constant warmth is essential. Make sure the temperature is no lower than 16 to 20°C (61–68°F) in winter.

**Ventilation** Keep out of draughts.

**Container** Choose a medium-deep pot. A glazed pot, in shades of blue or willow-green, is appropriate.

**Regular maintenance** Remove yellow leaves as they are seen. Do not cut out the aerial roots, which are essential to the plant's survival.

**Growth** These plants grow fairly fast and steadily.

**Repotting** Repot in early spring every second year. Prune the roots by a half and pot up into a larger container. The roots of schffleras that are planted on tufa can be shortened when the plants are growing rapidly.

**Soil** Use a mixture of equal parts ericaceous compost, leaf mould, loam and sharp sand. Schffleras do best in fairly dry soil.

| SPECIES |
|---|
| *Schefflera actinophylla* (syn. *Brassaia actinophyla*; Australian ivy palm) This tree is native to north Australia, New Guinea and Java, and it can grow to 12m (40ft). The branches turn white at the tips. The evergreen, oval leaves are borne in terminal rosettes. The pinkish-red flowers, borne in panicles, are followed by spherical, purple-black berries. *Schefflera arboricola* (syn. *Heptapleurum arboicolum*; parasol plant) Native to Taiwan, this plant forms a large shrub in the wild, although cultivated plants rarely get larger than about 1m (3ft) high. The branches are fragile, and the trunk is flexible. The glossy, dark green, palmate leaves have 6–16 stalked leaflets. The flowers are borne in panicles and are followed by orange berries which turn black as they ripen. |

**Pruning**

*Pruning sub-branches* In spring all branches can be reduced in length to encourage branching and keep the plant compact and dense. Remove withered or dead branches at the same time.

*Leaf pruning* Every two or three years in early summer prune the leaves to produce trees with small leaves. Take off about half the leaves (the remainder will turn yellow and fall).

**Wiring** Schffleras are not wired. The shape is produced solely by pruning.

**Watering** Give little water. Schffleras will produce smaller leaves if they are kept short of water. If they are planted over tufa, wet the stone regularly. Do not leave water standing in the container.

**Misting** Mist the leaves occasionally to clean them. When there is too much

Shakan

Neku

Tachiki

Han-Kengai

Neagari

Sekijôju

Ishitsuki

Nejikan

Sabamiki

Kabudachi

Sôju

Sôkan

STYLES

Schefflera arboricola (syn. Heptapleurum arboricolum; parasol plant): 10 years old; 30cm (12in) high; Kabudachi style. Photographed in early summer.

moisture, however, the leaves become too big and are out of proportion to the tree.

**Feeding** In spring and summer feed with a slow-release, organic fertilizer. Liquid fertilizer is best, but sometimes give solid fertilizer for a change.

## PESTS AND DISEASES

### PESTS
**Glasshouse red spider mite** See page 32.

**Aphids** See page 33.

**Scale insects** See page 33.

**Mealy bugs** See page 33.

### DISEASES
**Root and stem rot** See page 35.

**Alternariose**
*Symptoms* The fungal diseases causes small oily-looking spots on the leaves, sometimes ringed with red. Discoloured patches at the nodes of side branches may cause the branch to wither. Black spots are seen on the diseased areas.
*Treatment* Cut out diseased wood. Spray with a maneb-based fungicide.

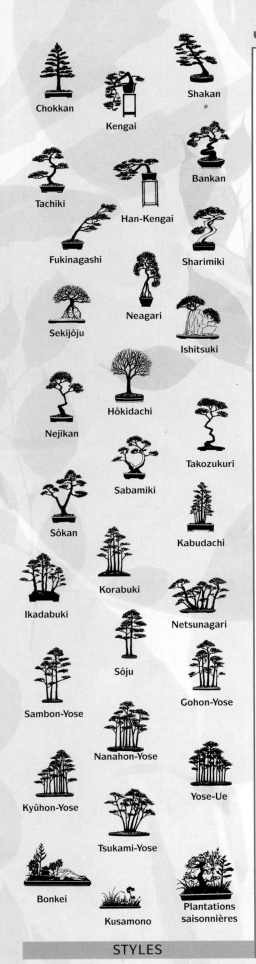

Chokkan

Kengai

Shakan

Tachiki

Han-Kengai

Bankan

Fukinagashi

Sharimiki

Sekijôju

Neagari

Ishitsuki

Nejikan

Hôkidachi

Takozukuri

Sôkan

Sabamiki

Kabudachi

Ikadabuki

Korabuki

Netsunagari

Sambon-Yose

Sôju

Gohon-Yose

Kyûhon-Yose

Nanahon-Yose

Yose-Ue

Bonkei

Tsukami-Yose

Kusamono

Plantations saisonnières

**STYLES**

# SERISSA

Rubiaceae. Evergreen. This monotypic genus is native to woodland in southeast Asia. It is a densely branched shrub, and its specific name derives from the unpleasant smell that arises from the crushed leaves. Several cultivars are now available.

## PROPAGATION

Like all tropical species the serissa is hard to propagate.

**Cuttings** Take softwood cuttings in spring or early summer or semi-ripe cuttings in late summer. Dip the ends of the slips into hormone rooting compound and plant them in a heated propagator. As soon as new shoots appear on the slips, the cuttings have taken.

## CARE

**Sunlight** Serissas are grown indoors but they need a lot of light, and this is especially true of the variegated forms. Keep out of full sun in summer.

**Temperature** The plants tolerate being hot in summer, when the temperature should be at least 18°C (64°F). They should be cooler in winter, with a minimum temperature between 15 and 19°C (59–66°F).

**Ventilation** Keep these plants out of draughts, which can do serious harm.

**Container** Serissas can be grown in fairly flat containers, especially if they are in a group style. The containers can be decorated provided that the pattern goes well with the bonsai. Old trees need pots that are 7–15cm (3–6in) deep.

**Regular maintenance** Serissas have evergreen foliage, but they constantly produce yellow leaves, which should be removed. Use clippers to remove any dead branches. It is most important to eliminate any shoots coming from the trunk or the base of the trunk. They are comparable to rose suckers.

**Growth** Although there is not much difference between the seasons, serissas have a period of dormancy in winter. They grow fast during the growing season (from mid-spring to early autumn).

Serissa foetida: *20 years old; 25cm (10in) high; Neagari style. Photographed in early summer.*

### SPECIES

*Serissa foetida* (syn. *Serissa japonica*) The shrub grows to about 60cm (2ft) tall. The small, leathery, ovate, leaves are dark green and borne in opposite pairs. The plant is sometimes called June snow because of its tiny, funnel-shaped, white flowers, which open from pink buds in summer, although there can be a few flowers all year long. It is a tender plant.
*Serissa foetida* 'Flore Pleno' This is a lower growing form, to about 45cm (18in), and it has double flowers.
*Serissa foetida* 'Variegata' The foliage has ivory variegation on the edge of the leaves. The grey trunk is rough and slender; it turns white as it grows older.

**Repotting** Report in early to mid-spring every second year, first pruning the root hairs by half. Repot before the flowers open.

**Soil** Use a mixture of equal parts loam, ericaceous compost and sand.

Serissa foetida: *10 years old; 18cm (7in) high; Nejikan style. Photographed in mid-autumn.*

## PESTS AND DISEASES

### PESTS
**Red spider mites** See page 32.

**Aphids** See page 33.

**Scale insects** See page 33.

#### Snails
*Symptoms* Shoots and needles are eaten and the trails of slime may be seen.
*Treatment* Collect up the snails by hand and kill them. Do not let the soil get too wet. If you must, and as a last resort only, use metaldehyde or methiocarb pellets.

#### Vine weevils
*Symptoms* These are a very serious pest of all container-grown plants. The first sign may be the total collapse of the plant, but inspection will show that the roots have been eaten by the brown-headed, white larvae. Adult weevils eat the edges of leaves.
*Treatment* At the first sign of attack, remove the plant from the pot. Remove and kill the larvae. Prune the roots and repot in good soil. Spray with contact insecticide from late spring to midsummer. Under glass, use the parasitic nematode *Heterorhabditis megedis*.

### DISEASES
**Root rot** See page 35.

#### Damping off
*Symptoms* The roots and the collar rot. The stems are spotted with black, then rot and collapse.
*Treatment* Maintain a warm temperature and ensure good air circulation. Do not give too much water. Apply nitrogen and potassium to the soil. If necessary, use a fungicide.

**Pruning** After repotting and root pruning, the branches and side branches are pruned, which produces a foul smell. The serissa is not pinched back.
*Leaf pruning* This is unnecessary because the leaves are already small and do not need to be reduced.
*Pruning branches* After repotting (between mid-spring and mid- to late autumn), young shoots are cut back to one or two pairs of leaves as soon as the side branches have grown longer. Serissas must be kept compact and bushy. Do not prune during flowering.
*Structural pruning* It may be necessary to prune the serissa hard back to the wood every two or three years.
*Flower cutting* Remove the flowers as soon as they fade to encourage new blooms.

**Wiring** The wood of the serissa is soft and the tree lends itself to any style. It is readily wired. Work from bottom to top, using fine wire. Avoid putting pressure on the branches so that you do not wound the bark. The wire is put in position in early summer and removed in early autumn, and the process is repeated annually until the desired shape has been achieved. Apply a wound-sealing compound if you wound the tree.

**Watering** More water is needed in summer than in winter. Water daily. Serissa like humidity. The roots dry quickly, but even so the compost must be allowed to dry out between waterings.

**Misting** Serissas come from the tropics and thrive in humid heat. It is important to mist the foliage daily but keep the water off the flowers because it would cause them to fade. A serissa can be placed in its pot on a layer of gravel. Any excess water drains down into the gravel, then gradually evaporates, thus creating a humid atmosphere.

**Feeding** Apply fertilizer (in liquid, powder or granule form) once a fortnight from the growing season until the dormant season. Do not feed in mid- or late summer, nor after repotting. Give slightly less fertilizer when the tree is in flower.

# SPIRAEA

Rosaceae. Deciduous or semi-evergreen. There are about 80 species in this genus, which are found throughout the temperate regions of the northern hemisphere, from Asia to North America. They are graceful shrubs, with toothed or lobed leaves. From early spring to late summer they bear terminal racemes of white or pink flowers.

## PROPAGATION

**Seed** Seed can be sown in spring under glass. They will germinate rapidly, but spiraeas are seldom grown from seed as they do not come true to type (the characteristics of the plant producing the seed are not completely reproduced).

**Cuttings** Take greenwood cuttings in early summer. Cut off the growing tip and plant in a mixture of equal parts sand and peat. The slips are delicate, so be careful with misting and shading. Remove flower buds from the slip.

**Division** Divide established plants in spring.

**Young nursery stock** See page 18.

## CARE

**Sunlight** Spiraeas need sun to flower but tolerate partial shade.

**Temperature** Spiraeas tolerate heat but should be protected from severe frosts.

**Ventilation** These plants stand up to wind and should be in a well-ventilated position.

**Container** Select a medium-deep bowl, which can be glazed or unglazed.

**Regular maintenance** Use scissors to cut off flowers as soon as they fade.

**Growth** Container-grown spiraeas grow slowly.

**Repotting** Every year or every second year in spring prune off a good third of the root hairs and pot up into a larger container.

**Soil** Use a mixture of equal parts loam and leaf mould. Spiraeas will grow in any soil, even poor or dry soil, but do best in

---

### SPECIES

*Spiraea japonica* This deciduous, clump-forming shrub is native to Japan and China. The mid-green leaves are coarsely toothed, and pink or white flowers are borne in terminal corymbs in late summer.
*Spiraea thunbergii* Native to China and Japan, this deciduous or semi-evergreen shrub has arching branches. The white flowers are borne in stalkless corymbs in early summer.
*Spiraea veitchii* An upright deciduous shrub, to 4m (12ft), is native to China. The white flowers are borne in dense corymbs in early to midsummer.

---

Spirea japonica: *5 years old; 10cm (4in) high; no particular style.*

---

cool, fertile soil that is not damp and stagnating or too rich in lime.

**Pruning**
*Pruning sub-branches* After flowering use clippers to prune the side branches, leaving only one or two growth buds on each. In early spring and at the end of autumn prune side branches, leaving only two or

---

## STYLES

Tachiki

Shakan

Kengai

Han-Kengai

Sekijôju

Ishitsuki

Kabudachi

Bonkei

Kusamono

Spirea japonica: 7 years old; 15cm (6in) high; Sekijôju style. Photographed in mid-autumn.

three growth buds. After flowering cut out dry twigs and old branches.

**Wiring** Spiraeas are not wired.

**Watering** Water freely and keep the compost nice and cool. Make sure that the pot has good drainage. Reduce the amount of water given when the tree is in flower.

**Misting** Sprinkle the foliage in summer when you are watering. Do not mist spiraeas when they are in flower.

**Feeding** In spring, before flowering, feed with a slow-release, organic fertilizer. Do not feed while the tree is in flower nor in mid- and late summer. Start feeding again in autumn, slightly increasing the amount given.

## PESTS AND DISEASES

### PESTS
**Greenfly** See page 33.

**Tortrix moth** See page 33.

### DISEASE
**Powdery mildew** See page 34.

**Rust** See page 35.

# LILAC

Oleaceae. Deciduous. The genus contains about 20 shrubs and trees, which are native to Asia and southeast Europe. The leaves are opposite and simple or lobed. Lilacs are grown for the panicles of fragrant flowers, which may be white, pink or purple. There are many cultivars.

## PROPAGATION

**Seed** Collect the seeds as soon as they are ripe (late autumn to early winter). Put them in bags and hang in a warm, dry place. They will shed their husks spontaneously. Clean the seeds and stratify in dry sand before planting in spring.

**Cuttings** Take greenwood cuttings in early spring. Strip the bark off the slips and plant them in spring in a mixture of sand and peat and put in a warm place.

**Simple layering** This is done in late spring. Roots will form quickly. Sever the layer in the autumn, pot up and protect from frost.

**Young nursery stock** See page 18.

## CARE

**Sunlight** The flowers will be best if the plants are in full sun, although lilacs will thrive in partial shade.

**Temperature** Lilacs can withstand cold, but do not like excessive frost. Late frosts may damage flower buds. They are happier in a warm position.

**Ventilation** Lilacs tolerate wind as long as it is not too strong.

**Container** Select a pot of medium depth, glazed or unglazed. The colour of the container should harmonize with the colour of the flowers.

**Regular maintenance** Pick or cut off withered flowers. Remove the fruit, which exhausts the tree. Remove shoots growing from the trunk.

**Growth** These are slow-growing plants.

**Repotting** Annually in spring before

### SPECIES

*Syringa* x *persica* (Persian lilac) This compact shrub, to 2m (6ft), has dark green, lance-shaped leaves. The fragrant, purple flowers are borne in panicles in late spring.

*Syringa vulgaris* (common lilac) This is a hardy, spreading tree or large shrub to 7m (22ft), often seen in gardens. The leaves are oval, smooth, light green and bright. In mid- to late spring it bears mauve or occasionally white, highly scented flowers in pyramidal panicles. 'Madame Lemoine' has lovely white flowers.

flowering prune the roots by half and pot up into a larger container.

**Soil** Use a mixture of equal parts loam and leaf mould. Lilacs grow in average soil, preferably cool, firm and clayey. It can be neutral with a little lime. Avoid an acid soil, and you should add lime to counteract too much acidity.

**Pruning**
*Pruning sub-branches* After flowering, prune side branches with clippers, leaving just one or two growth buds. In early spring and late autumn prune the side branches to two or three growth buds.
*Pruning branches* In winter prune out old branches and any that are growing untidily.

**Wiring** Wire in spring and in summer. Coil wire around the branches carefully so that you do not break them.

**Watering** Water freely in summer, more before flowering than during it. Keep the compost slightly damp.

Shakan

Kengai

Han-Kengai

Tachiki

Sekijôju

Ishitsuki

Kabudachi

Ikadabuki

Netsunagari

Bonkei

**STYLES**

*Syringa vulgaris: 5 years old; 15cm (6in) high; Shakan style. Photographed in mid-spring. The small size of the flowers is typical of the miniaturization of this shrub.*

### PESTS

**Gall mites**

*Symptoms* Small galls appear on the top surface of the leaves. They are caused by mites feeding, although the tree is not weakened.
*Treatment* Remove and burn affected leaves and stems. There is no suitable chemical control.

**Vine weevils**

*Symptoms* These are a very serious pest of all container-grown plants. The first sign may be the total collapse of the plant, but inspection will show that the roots have been eaten by the brown-headed, white larvae. Adult weevils eat the edges of leaves.
*Treatment* At the first sign of attack, remove the plant from the pot. Remove and kill the larvae. Prune the roots and repot in good soil. Spray with contact insecticide from late spring to midsummer. Under glass, use the parasitic nematode *Heterorhabditis megedis*.

**Moths**

*Symptoms* Brown holes are seen on the leaves. Silky threads are coiled around the stems and caterpillars can be seen.
*Treatment* Spray with insecticide.

**Tortrix moth** See page 33.

### DISEASES

**Bud rot** See page 35.

**Powdery mildew** See page 34.

**Leaf spot** See page 35.

**Virus disease**

*Symptoms* Wavy lines mark the leaves, which are misshapen and may have holes in them.
*Treatment* Once infected, plants cannot be cured and should be burned. The infection is transmitted by sap-sucking insects, so control aphids to prevent infection.

**Misting** Sprinkle the tree when you are watering in summer. Do not mist when the plant is in flower.

**Feeding** After flowering and in autumn feed with a slow-release, organic fertilizer. The lilac is greedy and needs feeding.

# YEW

Taxaceae. Evergreen conifer. There are up to 10 species in the genus, and they are found in forests in the temperate areas of the northern hemisphere throughout Europe, America and Asia. The trunks are covered in reddish-brown, often peeling or fissured bark. They are generally small conifers, about 20m (65ft) tall, with a wide spread. When it is young the trunk is straight and branches, with sparse foliage, rise at an oblique angle, and the top is rounded. As it grows older, the branches rise until they almost form a parallel trunk. The evergreen, needle-shaped, shiny foliage, dark green on the upper surface, and mid-green underneath, are arranged in spirals and have prominent ribs and are not prickly.

## PROPAGATION

**Seed** The fruit is ripe between late summer and mid-autumn. Pick it as soon as it is red, release the seed from the fruit under water, dry, then stratify until the following autumn. Use hormone rooting compound before you plant the seed. Germination will take place in or around late spring. Protect the seedlings from the sun and keep them moist. Plant out the saplings the following spring.

**Cuttings** Take semi-ripe cuttings in late summer or early autumn. Plant them in boxes placed in a greenhouse over winter. Roots form the following spring. If you want a pyramid-shaped tree, take your cutting from a leading shoot; for a spreading tree, take cuttings from lateral shoots.

**Layering** Choose a low, flexible branch. Strip needles off the part to be buried. Cut through the bark, bury the section and keep it moist. When young shoots appear, the layer is well rooted. Sever, pot up and protect from sun and frost.

**Grafting** In early to mid-spring, using veneer grafting. A few weeks later shorten the leading shoot slightly. As soon as the graft has taken, the top of the rootstock should be cut off and the grafted tree planted. See pages 21–3 for more information.

**Young nursery stock** Depending on the style you wish to achieve, select a pyramid-shaped or a spreading tree with a well-formed trunk, good branches, hard shiny needles and a good root system (see also page 18).

## CARE

**Sunlight** Yews adapt to sunlight and tolerate shade.

**Temperature** These are hardy trees from medium altitudes, and they like mountain temperatures. Nevertheless, they stands up well to heat if placed in partial shade.

**Ventilation** Yews are often used for hedging, and they stands up perfectly to wind.

**Container** The trunk of the yew tends to become big when it is old, and it will need a pot whose depth is in proportion to the diameter of its trunk. Young trees need fairly deep pots to help them stand up to wind.

**Regular maintenance** Make sure you clean inside the tree, removing all dead or damaged material. Keep the soil clear of any dead material. Pick off dead needles in autumn.

### SPECIES

*Taxus baccata* A broadly conical tree, growing to 20m (70ft). It is native to Europe, northern Africa and Iran.
*Taxus cuspidata* (Japanese yew) This shrub or small tree, native to Japan and China, has dark green leaves with spiny tips.

Chokkan

Tachiki

Fukinagashi

Kabudachi

Sabamiki

Sôkan

Yose-Ue

STYLES

Taxus cuspidata *(Japanese yew): 70 years old; 40cm (16in) nigh; Fukinagashi style. Photographed in late spring.*

**Growth** Yews are fairly slow growing.

**Repotting** Repot in spring every third or fourth year into a larger container. Reduce the roots by a third, cutting out any damaged or dead roots. The yew is temperamental about getting re-established after repotting, so leave some of the old soil around the roots.

**Soil** Use a mixture of equal parts leaf mould, loam and sharp sand. Yews grow well in any soil, but they prefer calcareous soil and really thrive on chalky soil.

**Pruning**
*Pinching back* Pinch back the young shoots on the side branches from spring to autumn. If you want to have fruit, do not pinch back until the tree has flowered.
*Pruning branches* The yew can be pruned in spring or in autumn. Prune side branches that are sticking out, cutting above a tuft of needles. It is possible to train yews into bonsai by pruning, as they are easy to mould into shape.

**Wiring** You will need to wire and prune to shape the tree. Wire from early autumn to early spring. Avoid wiring when the tree has new shoots.

**Watering** Water regularly in moderation. The roots must never be waterlogged.

**Misting** Misting is important in hot weather, especially if the tree is in a sunny position, but do not mist in full sun to prevent leaf scorch.

**Feeding** Because growth is slow, feeding is important. Feed in spring and autumn but never in mid- or late summer, nor if a bonsai has just been repotted or is in poor condition. Increase the amount of fertilizer given in the last autumn application.

## PESTS AND DISEASES

### PESTS
**Galls on buds**
*Symptoms* The buds turn brown, swell and drop off.
*Treatment* Spray with insecticide.

**Weevils**
*Symptoms* The needles are gnawed, and the bark on shoots withers at the tips. The tree turns yellow, withers and wilts. The roots are attacked and growth comes to a halt.

*Treatment* Spray with lindane-based insecticide from late spring to midsummer.

**Tortrix moth** See page 33.

**Scale insects** See page 33.

### DISEASES
**Rotting of roots and stem** See page 35.

# ELM

Ulmaceae. Deciduous or semi-evergreen. The genus contains 45 trees, which are native to the temperate areas of the northern hemisphere, from northern Mexico to central Asia. The trees grow in woodlands and hedgerows, and they have alternate leaves, asymmetrical at the base and dentate, often taking on attractive autumn colours. Clusters of tiny red or yellow flowers are borne in spring from axillary buds or in autumn from leafy buds. The fruit, in the form of winged keys, follows the flowers and is ripe in late spring or late autumn, depending on species. Many species and cultivars are available. *Ulmus parvifolia* can be grown as an indoor bonsai, and this is described on pages 182–3; the guidelines below are applicable to other elms and to *U. parvifolia* grown as an outdoor bonsai.

## PROPAGATION

**Seed** Most elm seeds are ripe in early summer, and they should be planted as soon as they have been gathered. The seeds of *Ulmus parvifolia* ripen in early to mid-autumn, and they should be allowed to dry out and be kept in a dry place throughout winter. Stratify them for about three weeks before they are planted.

**Air layering** This can be done in early summer (see page 20).

### SPECIES

*Ulmus parvifolia* (Chinese elm) The species, from China, Korea and Japan, has downy young shoots. The smallish, leathery, glossy, dark green leaves, which may, depending on the climate, be semi-evergreen or deciduous, fall after turning purple or orange in autumn and early winter. The trees grow to about 18m (60ft), and they have rounded crowns. The little red flowers are borne in early autumn, and these are followed by light green winged fruit. The species appears to be unaffected by Dutch elm disease, although, it is believed that no species has been entirely unaffected by the disease.

**Cuttings** Take greenwood cuttings in summer. Dip the slips in hormone rooting compound and plant in a mixture consisting of two parts loam and one part sharp sand. Make sure the atmosphere they are in is humid.

**Young nursery stock** You can find species of elm that are not susceptible to elm disease (*U. minor*, *U. parvifolia*) and that make fine bonsai specimens (see also page 18).

## CARE

**Sunlight** Elms like full sun and need a great deal of light.

**Temperature** Do not expose the bonsai to severe cold. Their frost resistance is limited.

**Ventilation** The trees stands up well to wind. They need to be positioned in a place where air can circulate freely around the crowns.

**Container** Select a relatively deep pot because elms like deep earth. Blue, willow green and ivory go well with these plants.

**Regular maintenance** Remove dead leaves in autumn. Prune branchlets growing off the main branches neatly. Brush the trunk.

**Growth** These plants grow quite fast.

Chokkan

Kengai

Shakan

Tachiki

Hôkidachi

Han-Kengai

Sekijôju

Ishitsuki

Nejikan

Sôkan

Kabudachi

Sôju

Sambon-Yose

Bonkei

STYLES

*Ulmus parvifolia (Chinese elm): 8–30 years old; 65cm (26in) high.*

**Repotting** Repot every second or third year, between early spring and summer, repot into a larger container. Prune the roots by between one-half and two-thirds.

**Soil** Use a mixture of two parts loam and one part sharp sand. These plants grow well in cool, moist, deep, fertile soil.

**Pruning**
*Pruning shoots* During the growing period prune new shoots down to one or two pairs of leaves.
*Pruning sub-branches* Branches will form wherever there is a leaf bud. Allow them to grow and pinch out the tip, then prune again, leaving only one pair of leaves. This will encourage a delicate network of branches to develop.
*Leaf pruning* The elm can be stripped of its leaves in early summer when it is well rooted and in perfect health. It will then produce dense, small foliage, a good network of branches and will look well in autumn.
*Structural pruning* At the end of winter, when you can get a good view of the tree's outline, cut side branches back fairly short, and prune out any main branches that might mar the tree's appearance.

**Wiring** Wire from early to midsummer. Remove copper wire in mid-autumn. Elms are seldom wired except for the main branches when the tree is young, the shape being mainly created by successive prunings.

**Watering** The elm likes moist soil. Water copiously in summer, cut down in autumn and still further in winter.

**Misting** In summer mist the foliage thoroughly to maintain the high levels of humidity in which elms do best.

**Feeding** Feed with a slow-release, organic fertilizer in spring and autumn. Do not feed in mid- to late summer, nor for six weeks after repotting, nor if the tree has been leaf stripped or is in poor condition.

## PESTS AND DISEASES

### PESTS
**Red spider mites** See page 32.

**Bark beetles** See page 34.

**Gall mites**
*Symptoms* Green, red or reddish-brown pimples appear on the upper surface of the leaves, and a thick down, which turns red in summer, appears on the underside. The leaves become misshapen.
*Treatment* Remove and burn affected leaves. There is no reliable chemical treatment.

**Leaf beetles**
*Symptoms* The leaves may be so eaten that only the ribs remain..
*Treatment* Spray with contact insecticide.

**Geometer moth** See page 33.

**Bombyx moth** See page 33.

**Greenfly and aphids** See page 33.

### DISEASES
**Black spot**
*Symptoms* Brown scabs on the leaves may cause premature leaf fall.
*Treatment* Cut off and burn the diseased leaves.

**Leaf blight**
*Symptoms* White swellings appear on the leaves, which tear and shrivel.
*Treatment* Remove and burn dead leaves. Spray with a copper- or thiram-based wash in spring and autumn.

# CHINESE ELM

Ulmaceae. Evergreen or semi-evergreen. The species, which was originally known as *Ulmus chinensis*, originated in north and central China, and in the wild this is a deciduous tree. However, when it is grown as an indoor bonsai, it will be evergreen. Even so, it should be allowed a period of rest in winter. There are several cultivars, which may also be treated as bonsai. *U. parvifolia* 'Frosty' is a slow-growing form, which a shrubby habit and small leaves, with white teeth. *U. parvifolia* 'Geisha' has a rather low, spreading habit.

## PROPAGATION

**Seed** The seeds ripen in early to mid-autumn, and they should be allowed to dry out and be kept in a dry place throughout winter. Stratify them for about three weeks before they are planted.

**Air layering** This can be done in early summer (see page 20).

**Cuttings** Take greenwood cuttings in late spring or early summer. Dip the slips in hormone rooting compound and plant in a mixture of two parts loam and one part sharp sand. Make sure the atmosphere they are in is humid and keep your plantlets warm and moist and in good light.

## CARE

**Sunlight** Place the plants near a window because they need good light, especially in the morning and later afternoon. Protect them from the midday summer sun so that the leaves do not get scorched.

**Temperature** These plants need warmth all year round, although they can be moved outdoors during the summer in warm areas. In winter they will tolerate temperatures of between 4 and 17°C (39–63°F), and will even withstand brief periods of temperatures of -3°C (27°F), but if they are subject to prolonged periods of cold weather they will lose their leaves.

**Ventilation** Position the plants where air can circulate freely around the crowns but do not place them in draughts or in cold, drying winds.

**Container** Select a relatively deep pot so that the root system can develop properly. Natural colours or shades of blue, green and cream often look best; choose a colour that will complement the bark.

**Regular maintenance** Remove any yellow or dead leaves as well as any that fall on the soil. Brush the trunk to remove any moss that is growing on it and remove any moss or algae from the surface of the soil. Cut out any dead branches.

**Growth** These plants grow quite fast.

**Repotting** Every year or every second year, between early spring and early summer, repot into a larger container. Prune the roots by about a third and remove any damaged roots at the same time.

**Soil** Use a mixture of five parts loam, three parts leaf mould and two parts sand.

**Pruning**
*Pruning sub-branches* At the end of winter cut back side branches very hard to maintain a good overall shape. Continue to cut back the side branches throughout the growing period, cutting just above a node to encourage a shrubby, bushy habit and a dense network of branches.
*Pruning branches* At the end of winter remove any dead or damaged branches. Take the opportunity to remove any branches that detract from the overall appearance of the plant, including any within the crown.
*Leaf pruning* If you have a form with small leaves this may not be necessary. See also page 180–81.

**Wiring** This can be done at any time of the year provided the wood has begun to harden. Do not leave the wire in place for more than three or four months, and repeat the process the following year if necessary.

Kengai
Chokkan
Shakan
Bankan
Tachiki
Han-Kengai
Bunjingi
Fukinagashi
Neagari
Sekijôju
Ishitsuki
Hôkidachi
Nejikan
Takozukuri
Sôkan
Sabamiki
Kabudachi
Korabuki
Ikadabuki
Netsunagari
Sôju
Gohon-Yose
Nanahon-Yose
Kyûhon-Yose
Yose-Ue
Yamayori
Tsukami-Yose
Bonkei

**STYLES**

Ulmus parvifolia *(Chinese elm): 30 years old; 45cm (18in) high; Nejikan style. Photographed in mid-autumn. The dense network of branches has been produced by frequent and regular pruning.*

**Watering** Water freely from the beginning of the growing season. Make sure that all water has been taken up by the roots before the next watering so that the soil never becomes waterlogged. Continue to water in winter, especially if the tree is receiving plenty of light.

**Misting** Mist daily in winter to maintain high levels of humidity around the foliage. If necessary, stand the container on a bed of gravel in a dish filled with water.

**Feeding** Every two weeks apply a slow-release, organic fertilizer from early spring to late spring and from early autumn to late autumn. Alternate liquid and granular formulations. From the beginning of winter to late winter apply a feed every six weeks as long as the tree has not lost its leaves.

## PESTS AND DISEASES

### PESTS
**Red spider mites** See page 32.

**Aphids** See page 33.

**Vine weevils**
*Symptoms* These are a very serious pest of all container-grown plants. The first sign may be the total collapse of the plant, but inspection will show that the roots have been eaten by the brown-headed, white larvae. Adult weevils eat the edges of leaves.
*Treatment* At the first sign of attack, remove the plant from the pot. Remove and kill the larvae. Prune the roots and repot in good soil. Spray with contact insecticide from late spring to midsummer. Under glass, use the parasitic nematode *Heterorhabditis megedis* but remember that once you introduce a biological control into your greenhouse or conservatory you should not use chemical controls for other pests.

**Snails**
*Symptoms* Presence of slimy trails and eaten leaves and young shoots.
*Treatment* Do not let the soil get too wet and remove dead and dying leaves. Pick off the snails and kill them. As a last resort scatter methiocarb or metaldehyde pellets on the soil.

### DISEASES
**Honey fungus** See page 35.

**Rust**
*Symptoms* Shoots are distorted and the upper surfaces of the leaves are covered with brown or orange-brown fungal spores.
*Treatment* Remove and burn all infected stems and branches. Improve the circulation of air around the plants. Spray with a fungicide containing mancozeb, propiconazole or myclobutanil.

# WISTERIA

Leguminosae/Papillionaceae. Deciduous. This is a genus of 10 species, which are native to China, Korea and Japan and the southern United States. They are climbing, woody plants, which can grow to more than 30m (100ft). The trunk becomes gnarled with age. The attractive, alternate, pinnate leaves are to 35cm (14in) long, but wisteria are really grown for their beautiful flowers.

## PROPAGATION

**Seed** Collect the pods in mid-autumn and open them. In spring plant the seeds in a greenhouse with bottom heat. Leave the shoots for two years before potting up. Not many seeds will germinate, and seedlings will grow slowly. You will have to wait for about 10 years for the wisteria to flower.

**Simple layering** Choose a long stem and bury it, with just the tip emerging. In autumn roots will have formed around the growth buds. Sever and pot up. Keep protected in winter.

**Grafting** This is the most commonly used method. Make a whip-and-tongue or an inlay graft in late winter or early spring. Select specimens that are four or five years old and that are already producing flowers. Make the graft as low as possible to keep the point of union inconspicuous. It is also possible to graft in autumn after leaf fall.

## CARE

**Sunlight** Wisterias like a sunny position.

*Wisteria sinensis 'Daruma'.*
*Photographed in late spring.*

**Temperature** Wisterias like warmth, and although they are hardy, the flowers may be damaged by late frost. If the temperature falls below -5°C (23°F) protect wisterias grown as bonsai.

**Ventilation** Wisterias can withstand wind and should stand in well-ventilated positions.

**Container** Choose a medium-deep, glazed or unglazed pot. If it is decorated, make sure that the decoration harmonizes with the flowers or the shape of the tree.

**Regular maintenance** After flowering wisterias produce pods. These are quite attractive, but if there are too many they exhaust the tree. They should be removed as soon as possible, leaving a few on the tree.

**Growth** Growth will be slow at first but plants will grow more quickly when the roots have settled.

**Repotting** Repot every year just after flowering. Prune away old or damaged roots, leaving only strong ones. Rearrange the roots and pot up into a larger container.

**Soil** Use a mixture of equal parts loam and leaf mould. Wisterias like cool, light,

Shakan

Han-Kengai

Bankan

Kengai

Sekijôju

## SPECIES

*Wisteria floribunda* (Japanese wisteria) This is a beautiful, hardy plant, growing to about 4m (12ft). The very fragrant, blue-violet to blue-purple flowers are borne in late spring or early summer with a second flush in late summer or early autumn.

*Wisteria sinensis* (syn. *Wisteria chinensis*; Chinese wisteria) A hardy, vigorous, long-lived climber, with long, twisted branches, which can get to 30m (100ft). The leaves turn from golden-yellow-green to pale green, and clusters of fragrant, blue-mauve flowers appear in late spring or early summer with a second flush in late summer.

*To ensure that a wisteria repeat flowers every year, soak it in late to midsummer. The rim of the container should stand slightly above the level of the water in the bowl.*

Wisteria sinensis *'Daruma': 30 years old; 50cm (20in) high; Shakan style. Photographed in spring.*

humus-rich soil. Soil that is too hard or impermeable can cause chlorosis. Good drainage is essential.

### Pruning

*Pruning sub-branches* After flowering and before the leaves mature, prune side branches with clippers. Do not prune at random, because this will harm the well-being of the tree and prevent flowering the following year. In autumn, after leaf fall, cut side branches short and remove unwanted new growth.

*Pruning branches* After flowering prune all superfluous branches.

### Wiring

Wire from spring to autumn. Coil wire into position when new buds appear. For twining stems use raffia when the leaves are beginning to mature. Always wire carefully, training stems in the same direction so that branches do not grow into one another.

### Watering

If the container is well drained, water copiously after repotting to encourage good root development. Otherwise, watering should be just adequate to keep the soil moist. In early summer water two or three times a day. In midsummer water once every second day; this will strengthen the leaves and help buds to develop. Place the pot in a basin of water and allow it to absorb as much water as it wants. Repeat three times at intervals of five or six days. Climbing stems will stop growing and the buds will produce flowers.

### Misting

Wisterias can be sprinkled during watering when they are not in flower.

### Feeding

After flowering alternate a liquid organic fertilizer with a slow-release, fertilizer in powder or solid form. Add phosphate if necessary. In autumn feed with a generous amount of liquid fertilizer, then with solid fertilizer. Wisterias need two or three times more fertilizer than other bonsai specimens.

## PESTS AND DISEASES

### PESTS
**Scale insects** See page 33.

### DISEASES
**Mosaic virus**

*Symptoms* The leaves become streaked with yellow. They may become distorted and fall.

*Treatment* Cut out diseased branches. Mosaic virus is transmitted by aphids, so use insecticides to control infestations.

# JAPANESE ELM

Ulmaceae. Deciduous. This is a genus of five or six hardy trees and shrubs, which are native to the Caucasus, Italy, Crete, Turkey, east Asia, Taiwan and Japan. They are similar to *Ulmus* (elm), but are not susceptible to Dutch elm disease, and are found in woodland and on scrubby land. They bear small, greenish flowers, which are followed by spherical fruits. The alternate, oval leaves have attractive autumn colours. These trees are not widely available but are worth searching out. *Z. serrata* is the parent of several fine cultivars.

*Zelkova serrata 'Makino': 70 years old; 45cm (18in) high; HÙkidachi style. Photographed in August.*

## PROPAGATION

**Seed** Sow the seed during the summer in which it was harvested. Keep the compost moist and protect from winter frosts. Prick out seedlings in spring. Alternatively, stratify the seeds, plant them in spring and pot them up the following year.

**Cuttings** Take cuttings in early summer. Lightly strip the bark off the slip and dip it in hormone rooting compound. Take off the head, and plant in a mixture of equal parts sand and peat.

**Air layering** Do this in early summer, when zelkovas cannot be propagated from seed or from cuttings.

**Young nursery stock** See page 18; *Zelkova serrata* and its cultivars are the most widely available forms.

## CARE

**Sunlight** Grow in full sun but provide some shade in summer.

**Temperature** These trees need warmth to do best. Protect zelkovas that are planted in shallow containers from the frost.

---

Sekijôju

Chokkan

Ishitsuki

Sôkan

Hôkidachi

Kabudachi

Nanahon-Yose

Gohon-Yose

Kyûhon-Yose

Yose-Ue

Bonkei

**STYLES**

## SPECIES

*Zelkova abelicea* (syn. *Z. cretica*) A hardy tree or shrub, native to Crete, which grows to 15m (50ft).
*Zelkova carpinifolia* (syn. *Z. crenata*; Caucasian elm) A hardy, slow-growing, long-lived tree, native to the Caucasus, Turkey and Iran, which grows to 30m (100ft). The dark green leaves turn orange-brown in autumn.
*Zelkova serrata* (syn. *Z. acuminata*, *Z. formosana*, *Z. keaki*; Japanese zelkova, saw-leaf zelkova) This tree, to 30m (100ft), has smooth grey bark, which peels to reveal orange beneath. The dark green leaves turn yellow, orange or red in autumn.

**Ventilation** Although zelkovas need good circulation of air around the foliage, they should be protected from cold, drying winds.

**Container** Most zelkova bonsai are grown in the 'broom' style (see below) in shallow containers, which are glazed on the outside in blue, willow green or beige or are unglazed terracotta.

**Regular maintenance** Keep the inside of the tree's crown well pruned to allow sun and air to get through to it. Remove dead leaves and twigs from the soil and from the tree.

**Growth** Zelkovas grow quickly, especially when grown in good soil and light.

**Repotting** Repot every second or third year in early spring. Prune the roots by half and pot up into a larger bowl. Provide good drainage.

**Soil** Use a mixture of two parts loam and one part sharp sand. Zelkovas like heavy soils with soft clay or cool, sandy, clay soils.

### Pruning
*Pruning shoots* Prune zelkovas from spring to autumn to keep only two or three leaves on the side branches. Remove new shoots.
*Pruning sub-branches* Each time branches form cut back the new branches, leaving only one or two pairs of leaves to achieve a good branch structure.
*Leaf pruning* A well-rooted healthy zelkova can be stripped of its leaves in early summer.
*Structural pruning* In winter prune out any main branches that mar the tree's shape and make sure that side branches are balanced.

**Wiring** Zelkovas are rarely wired and the shape is largely achieved by pruning. However, wiring can be used after leaf burst until mid-autumn. Wire the branches and train them by hand in the direction you want.

**Watering** Water freely in summer and allow to dry out between waterings. Give less water in spring and autumn, and water sparingly in winter.

**Misting** Mist the foliage in summer to clean off any pollution and insect infestations.

**Feeding** In spring and autumn apply a slow-release, organic fertilizer. Do not feed for six weeks after repotting. No fertilizer should be given in mid- to late summer nor to a sickly tree.

*This Zelkova serrata has become badly overgrown and needs pruning.*

*Pruning is carried out methodically with scissors.*

*After pruning the tree has regained its harmonious proportions. The process may be repeated several times during the growing*

Training a sapling into a 'broom' shape.
**1** *A sapling raised from a seed or cutting.* **2** *When the trunk is large enough, prune the main root.* **3** *Lop the trunk.* **4** *Cut the branches.* **5** *Prune the roots.* **6** *Prune the sub-branches.* **7** *A month or two before the sap rises, use raffia to tie up the branches into a broom shape.*

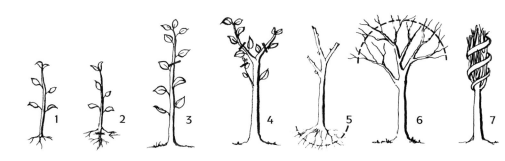

## PESTS AND DISEASES

Pests and diseases are similar to those of *Ulmus* (elm); see page 180.

# SUMMARY OF BONSAI CARE

## OUTDOOR BONSAI EVERGREEN

| GENUS OR SPECIES | REPOTTING (every 3–5 years) | PRUNING | WIRING | WATERING AND MISTING | FEEDING |
|---|---|---|---|---|---|
| *Cedrus* | Early to mid-spring | Shoots: spring to summer Branches: spring to autumn | End of autumn for about 10 months | Copious in spring and summer; reduce in autumn | From the onset of growth until mid-autumn |
| *Chamaecyparis* | Early or mid-spring | Shoots: growing season Sub-branches: early to mid-spring, early to mid-autumn | End of autumn for about 10 months | Copious, especially in summer | Mid-spring to mid-autumn |
| *Cryptomeria* | Mid-spring | Shoots: spring to autumn spring to autumn. Sub-branches: spring | From late spring to summer | Copious and frequent from | Mid-spring to mid-autumn |
| *Ginkgo biloba* | Early spring | Shoots: spring. Branches: early spring. Structure: late winter | From autumn to late summer | Copious but allow to dry out between waterings | Mid-spring to mid-autumn |
| *Juniperus chinensis* | Early spring | Shoots: spring to autumn. Sub-branches: early to mid-spring, early to mid-autumn | Autumn for about 8 months | Copious but allow to dry out between waterings | Spring and autumn |
| *Juniperus rigida* | Early to mid-spring | Shoots: spring to autumn. Sub-branches: early spring | Autumn for 8–10 months | Copious but allow to dry out between waterings | Spring and autumn |
| *Larix* | Mid-spring | Shoots: growing season. Sub-branches: mid-spring Structure: mid- to late winter | Early summer to autumn | Copious and frequent | Spring and autumn |
| *Picea* | Mid-spring | Shoots: mid-spring. Sub-branches: spring to early autumn | Late autumn for 9–10 months | Copious but allow to dry out between waterings | Spring and autumn |
| *Pinus* | Mid-spring | Shoots: mid-sprin. Branches: mid-autumn | Autumn and winter | Copious, but happier in a dry atmosphere | Spring and autumn |
| *Pinus parviflora* | Early or mid-spring | Shoots: mid-spring. Branches: mid-autumn | Mid-autumn to early spring | Regular and moderate; mist in summer | Spring and autumn |
| *Taxus* | Early spring | Shoots: spring to autumn Branches: spring or autumn | Early autumn to early spring | Regular and moderate | Spring and autumn |

## INDOOR BONSAI DECIDUOUS

| GENUS OR SPECIES | REPOTTING (every 3–5 years) | PRUNING | WIRING | WATERING AND MISTING | FEEDING |
|---|---|---|---|---|---|
| *Acer buergerianum* | Early or mid-spring | Shoots and branches: growing season Structure: late winter | Seldom used but any time in summer; protect with raffia | Copious in spring to autumn; reduce in winter | Spring and autumn |
| *Acer palmatum* | Early or mid-spring | Leaves: early summer. Shoots: early spring to early autumn Structure: mid- or late winter | End of spring for 6 months; protect with raffia | Moderate; allow to dry out | Spring to autumn |
| *Betula* | Early spring | Shoots: early spring to late autumn | Spring to summer; protect with raffia | Light and frequent; prefers a | Spring and autumn |
| *Carpinus* | Early spring | Shoots: spring. Branches: growing season Structure: late winter | Seldom used, but spring to summer | Copious; reduce in winter; mist in summer | Spring and autumn |
| *Celtis* | Early spring | Shoots: spring to late summer Sub-branches: growing season Structure: early to mid-spring | Spring to autumn; protect with raffia | Copious in hot weather but allow to dry out between waterings | Spring and autumn |
| *Euonymus* | Early to mid-spring | Shoots: spring. Sub-branches: growing season. Branches; end of winter Leaves: early summer every 2–3 years | Spring for 6 months | Copiously in spring and summer but less in autumn and winter | Spring and autumn |
| *Fagus* | Early spring | Shoots: late spring, Leaves: early summer every other year,. Branches: after repotting Structure: late winter | Spring to autumn for 3 months | Copiously but less in winter; | Spring and autumn mist frequently |
| *Liquidambar* | Mid-spring | Shoots: late spring. Sub-branches: growing season. Branches: late winter. Leaves: early summer every 3 years | Rarely done, but from early summer to early autumn | Copiously in spring and summer; less often in autumn and winter mist frequently | Spring and autumn |
| *Quercus* | Early to mid-spring | Shoots: early summer. Sub-branches: growing season. Structure: late winter | Spring to autumn but better to use pruning | Copiously in spring and summer; allow to dry between waterings | Spring and autumn |
| *Salix* | Twice a year (early spring and early summer) | Shoots: early summer. Sub-branches: after repotting and in late autumn | Spring and summer; protect with raffia | Copiously; keep compost slightly moist; mist frequently | Spring and autumn |
| *Ulmus* | Early spring to summer | Shoots: growing season. Sub-branches: growing season. Leaves: early summer | Rarely done, but from late early summer to mid-autumn | Copiously in summer; reduce in mid-autumn and winter | Spring and autumn |
| *Zelkova* | Early spring | Shoots: spring to autumn. Sub-branches: growing season. Leaves: early summer. Structure: late winter | Rarely done, but from leaf break to mid-autumn | Copiously in summer; allow to dry out between waterings; mist in summer | Spring and autumn |

# OUTDOOR BONSAI FLOWERING AND FRUIT TREES

| GENUS OR SPECIES | REPOTTING (every 2–3 years) | PRUNING | WIRING | WATERING AND MISTING | FEEDING (except in mid and late summer) |
|---|---|---|---|---|---|
| *Berberis* | Early to mid-spring | Sub-branches: after flowering. Shoots: after flowering but before early autumn. Branches: growing season | Possible throughout the year on woody branches for 4–6 months | Copiously in hot weather; allow to dry out; dislikes damp; mist in summer | After flowering in mid- to late autumn |
| *Camellia* | Late spring to early | Sub-branches: when flowers have withered | Late spring to late winter for 3–4 months; protect with raffia | Copiously in summer; allow to wilt before flowering; mist except when when in flower | After flowering and in autumn |
| *Chaenomeles* | Mid-autumn or after flowering | Sub-branches: after flowering. Branches: early summer to early autumn | From spring to late summer for 4 months | Regular, moderate before flowering; mist in summer | Sparingly after flowering until early autumn |
| *Cotoneaster* | Early spring | Shoots: early summer. Sub-branches: early autumn. Structure: late winter | Before bud break; protect with raffia | Seldom but moisten thoroughly and allow to dry out; mist regularly | Spring and autumn |
| *Crataegus* | Early spring to early autumn | Shoots: when hardened. Sub-branches: early to midsummer. Branches: before flowering | From spring to autumn; protect with raffia | Copiously and frequently; mist in hot, dry weather | After spring growth and in autumn |
| *Enkianthus* | Early spring | Sub-branches: after flowering but before new shoots have hardened | From spring to autumn | Copiously from appearance of leaves until autumn | Spring and autumn |
| *Ilex* | Early spring | Shoots and sub-branches: growing season Branches: early spring. Structure: late winter | Spring to summer; protect with raffia | Copiously once flowers have opened until fruit appears; allow soil to dry out; mist frequently | Spring and autumn |
| *Jasminum* | Before flowers in late winter or after flowers fall | Shoots: spring and midsummer Sub-branches: after flowering. Structure: midwinter | From spring to summer | Copiously; allow to dry out between waterings | After flowering and in autumn |
| *Lespedeza* | Early to mid-spring | Sub-branches: early spring to early autumn Structure: late winter | Spring to late summer; | More copiously when flower buds are forming; otherwise moderately | More in spring than in autumn |
| *Malus* | Early to mid-spring | Shoots: after growth. Sub-branching: after flowering in midsummer. Branches: early to mid-spring | Spring to autumn; protect with raffia | Moderately then more copiously when flower buds are forming | After flowering in spring and autumn |
| *Millettia reticulata* | Early spring | Sub-branches: after flowering but before shoots appear. Branches: autumn | Spring to summer | Copiously; can be soaked; mist regularly | More in spring than in autumn |
| *Morus* | Mid-spring | Shoots: spring to autumn. Sub-branches: after flowering. Branches: before bud break | Spring to summer; | Copiously but allow to dry out between waterings; mist except while flowering | More in spring than in autumn |
| *Parthenocissus* | Early spring | Sub-branches: after leaf buds form | Spring and summer | Copiously; mist except while flowering | Spring to autumn |
| *Prunus* | After flowering | Shoots, sub-branches and branches: after flowering | Mid-spring to mid-autumn | Copiously in bud and in summer; less while flowering | After flowering and in autumn (with phosphate) |
| *Prunus dulcis* | Early spring or after flowering | Sub-branches: after flowering. Branches: late summer and mid-autumn | Spring and summer | Copiously before flowering; mist after flowering | Spring and autumn unless in flower |
| *Prunus mume* | After flowering | Sub-branches: after flowering Branches: 1 month after flowering | From late spring to autumn | Copiously when budding and in flower; mist after flowering | After flowering in spring and autumn |
| *Pyracantha* | Early to mid-spring | Sub-branches: after flowering and in autumn. Branches: late winter | All year; do not leave on for more than 6 months | Copiously before and after flowering | Spring and autumn |
| *Rhododendron* | After flowering | Sub-branches: after flowering Branches: when repotting | Spring to autumn | Frequently; keep slightly moist; mist regularly | Except when in flower; spring and autumn |
| *Spiraea* | Early to mid spring | Sub-branches: after flowering | Do not wire | Copiously | Except when in flower; spring and autumn |
| *Syringa* | After flowering | Sub-branches: after flowering; early spring and late autumn | Spring to summer | Copiously in summer; reduce when in flower; mist in summer | Copiously; after flowering; autumn |
| *Wisteria* | Immediately after flowering | Sub-branches: after flowering and autumn Branches: after flowering | Spring to autumn | Copiously; mist after flowering | Copiously; spring and autumn |

# INDOOR BONSAI

| GENUS AND SPECIES | REPOTTING (every 2–3 years depending on age and species) | PRUNING (remove yellow leaves and faded flowers) | WIRING | WATERING AND MISTING (mist daily) | FEEDING (every fortnight; alternate liquid and granular forms) |
|---|---|---|---|---|---|
| *Aralia* | Mid-spring | Sub-branches: spring to autumn Branches: spring | Rare; possible throughout the year but best in warm weather | Copiously | Spring to autumn; once in winter |
| *Araucaria* | Mid- to late spring | Shoots: mid- to late spring Branches: when growth begins | Possible all year; do not leave wire for more than 4 months | Regularly; allow to dry between waterings | Spring and autumn |
| *Bambusa* | From late spring to early autumn | Offshoots: spring | During initial formation but not otherwise | Copiously and frequently | Apply lawn fertilizer in s spring and autumn |
| *Carmona* | Mid-spring | Sub-branches: spring to autumn Branches: late winter | Rarely used; can be done at any time of yeasr for 2–3 months on stems that have not hardened | Copiously; allow to dry out between waterings | Early spring to early summer; early autumn |
| *Cycas* | Mid-spring | Cut off withered leaves | Not used | Little in winter; moderately in summer, mist in summer | Spring and autumn |
| *Eugenia* | Early to late spring | Sub-branches: early spring to mid-autumn Branches: early to mid-spring | Possible all year; wire for no more more than 3 months | Copiously in summer and winter; less in spring and autumn | Spring and autumn; once in winter |
| *Ficus* | Mid- to late spring | Sub-branches: growing season Branches: late winter. Leaves: early summer | At any time on hardened wood; wire for no more than 2 months | Moderately; more in summer than winter | Spring and autumn; once in winter |
| *Murraya* | Mid- to late spring | Sub-branches: growing season Branches: spring | Possible all year; wire for no more than 10 weeks | Regularly; must have damp soil | Spring and autumn; once in winter |
| *Podocarpus* | Late spring | Shoots: growing season Sub-branches: after a growth spurt | At any time on hardened wood; wire for no more than 8–10 weeks | Regularly but moderately | Spring and autumn; once in winter |
| *Portulacaria* | Mid- to late spring | Shoots and sub-branches: growing season Branches: mid-spring to mid-autumn | Rarely done; for 6 weeks on hardened wood | Little in winter; moderately in summer; mist infrequently | Late spring, early summer and early autumn |
| *Rhapis* | Early to mid-spring | Main stem if offshoots occur; | Do not wire | Infrequently | Spring and autumn |
| *Sageretia* | Mid- to late spring | Sub-branches: growing season Branches: early spring | At any time on hardened wood; leave wire for 6–8 weeks | Regularly; more often in summer than winter | Spring to autumn |
| *Schefflera* | Early spring | Sub-branches and branches: spring | Rarely done | Infrequently; mist occasionally | Spring to autumn |
| *Serissa* | Early to mid-spring | Sub-branches: mid-spring to mid-autumn unless in flower. Structure: early 3 years in late winter | Early summer to early autumn | More often in summer than winter; allow to dry out between waterings | Spring and autumn |

# CONSERVATORY BONSAI

| GENUS AND SPECIES | REPOTTING (every 1–2 years depending on age and species) | PRUNING | WIRING (except in mid- to late summer) | WATERING AND MISTING | FEEDING |
|---|---|---|---|---|---|
| *Ampelopsis* | Mid-spring | Sub-branches: after emergence of leaves Leaves: summer; Structure: midwinter | From spring to summer | Little when leaves have fallen; regularly; | Spring to autumn |
| *Bougainvillea* | Mid- to late spring | Shoots and sub-branches: after flowering Branches: mid- to late winter | When branches have turned woody for 3–5 months | Frequently, regularly and moderately; every day in summer | After flowering and in in autumn |
| *Buxus* | Mid- to late spring | Sub-branches: growing season | On woody branches for no more than 2 months | Copiously; allow to dry between waterings | Spring and autumn; once in winter |
| *Caragana* | Mid-spring | Sub-branches: after flowering and throughout growing season | On woody branches for 6 weeks | Moderately | Spring and autumn |
| *Gardenia* | Late spring | Sub-branches: after flowering until early autumn | When branches have hardened | Little in winter; moderately in summer; more before flowering | After flowering and in autumn |
| *Lagerstroemia* | Early to mid-spring | Shoots: after flowering Sub-branches: late winter | From spring for 6 months | Copiously from spring to summer; moderately in autumn; less in winter | Spring and autumn |
| *Ligustrum* | Early to mid-spring | Sub-branches: growing season Branches: late winter | Any time of year for no more than 3 months | Frequently in summer and winter; otherwise, mist often in winter | Spring and autumn; once in winter |
| *Nandina* | Mid-spring | Sub-branches: growing season | Rare but spring and summer | Moderately and regularly | Spring and autumn |
| *Olea europaea* | Mid-spring | Sub-branches: early spring to late autumn Branches: early to mid-spring | Any time of year for no more than 3 months | Moderately in spring and autumn; less in summer and winter | Spring and autumn; once in winter |
| *Pistacia* | Mid-spring | Shoots: early spring. Sub-branches: early spring to late autumn Branches: early to mid-spring | Any time of year for no more than 3 months | Moderately in spring and autumn; less in summer and winter; mist in dry weather | Spring and autumn |
| *Punica granatum* | When leaves unfurl | Shoots: early spring to late autumn Sub-branches: after flowering until autumn | End of spring to summer | Copiously in summer; less in winter; mist except when flowering | Spring to autumn except when in flower |
| *Quercus* | Mid-spring | Shoots: early spring Sub-branches: early spring to late autumn | Any time of year for no more than 3 months | Moderately in spring and autumn; less in summer and winter; | Spring and autumn |
| *Ulmus parvifolia* | Early to late spring | Sub-branches and branches: end of winter | Any time of year for no more than 4 months | Copiously in summer; less in winter; mist frequently in winter | Spring and autumn; once in winter |

# INDEX

# GLOSSARY

**Achene** Of a fruit, one that is small, dry and single-seeded and that does not split to release the seed.

**Acicular** Needle shaped (as in the foliage of pine trees) and usually rounded in cross-section.

**Acuminate** A leaf or perianth segment that tapers to a point and has slightly convex sides.

**Acute** A leaf or perianth segment that tapers to a point and has slightly concave sides.

**Adventitious** Occurring in an unusual place, such as roots on aerial stems or buds on leaves.

**Anthracnose** A name given to several fungal diseases of plants, all of which are characterized by the appearance of dark, sunken spots on leaves.

**Apomictic** Asexual reproduction.

**Auriculate** A leaf or petal with an ear-shaped lobe.

**Axil** The acute angle formed by a branch growing out from a stem or by leaf growing from a branch.

**Bract** A leaf, often modified, or leaf-like structure that bears a flower in its axil and is apparently part of the flowerhead. In many cases, such as *Euphorbia*, the flowers themselves are insignificant and the bracts are conspicuous and brightly coloured.

**Calcifuge** A lime-hater; a plant, such as *Erica*, that is unable to thrive in alkaline soil.

**Cambium layer** The living cells found immediately beneath the bark of a tree and at the growing tips of roots and shoots. The cambium layer adds tissue, thus increasing the diameter of a trunk or root.

**Catkin** A spike or spike-like inflorescence, usually, but not always, pendulous. *Corylus* (hazel) bears pendulous catkins; *Salix caprea* (pussy willow) has erect catkins.

**Chitting** The process of sprouting tubers before planting or germinating seeds before sowing.

**Chlorosis** The yellowing or whitening of leaves, usually caused by lack of chlorophyll, which arises through a deficiency of minerals but may be caused by a virus.

**Clone** A plant produced by vegetative means (budding, layering, cutting and so on) from a single parent. The new plants are genetically identical to the parent plant.

**Conifer** A tree or shrub, usually evergreen and having needle-like or linear needles, and usually bearing seeds in cones. *Pinus* (pine) and *Picea* (spruce) bear cones; *Ginkgo biloba* does not.

**Contact** A type of pesticide or weedkiller that kills by coming into contact with the target. See also SYSTEMIC.

**Corymb** An inflorescence, usually flat topped or convex, in which the outer flowers open first. See also CYME.

**Culm** The stem, which is usually hollow, of a grass or a bamboo.

**Cultivar** A cultivated variety as distinct from a naturally occurring variety.

**Cycad** A member of an order of primitive GYMNOSPERMS, related to conifers but resembling ferns and palms.

**Cyme** A dome-shaped or flat-topped flowerhead; usually, the central or terminal flower opens first. See also CORYMB.

**Dentate** Toothed; usually used to describe the edges of leaves.

**Dioecious** A species that produces male and female flowers on separate plants. Some fruit trees and some willow and holly trees are dioecious. See also MONOECIOUS.

**Dormant** Of a plant, resting and having temporarily stopped growing, usually in winter.

**Epicormic** Of branches or buds, developing on or from a trunk. The growth may be latent or adventitious. Also sometimes known as water shoots.

**Ericaceous** Compost that is lime free; also plants, such as *Erica*, that prefer acid soil.

**Etiolated** Growth that has become pale, thin and straggly, with extended internodes, through lack of light.

**Eye** An immature growth bud.

**Fastigiate** Of a tree, with an erect habit of growth and appressed branches.

**Glabrous** Hairless but not necessarily perfectly smooth.

**Glaucous** The word used to describe the grey-blue colour of some plants; also, covered with a powdery bluish or greenish bloom.

**Gymnosperm** A member of a lower or primitive group of seed plants, whose seeds are not enclosed in an ovary. Conifers are gymnosperms.

**Indehiscent** Of a fruit, one that does not open or split to release the seeds contained within.

**Inflorescence** A branching stem or axis that bears a flower or flower; a flower cluster.

**Lanceolate** Of a leaf, shaped like the point of a lance – that is, tapering at both ends, longer than it is wide and wider below the centre.

**Lateral** A stem or shoot that arises in the leaf axil of a large stem.

**Loam** Fertile soil, containing moderate amounts of sand and clay (but not too much of either) and plenty of humus.

**Marcescent** Leaves that wither or die but do not fall until replaced by the next season's growth. *Fagus* (beech) leaves, for example, dry out in autumn, stay on the tree in winter and fall in spring when the new buds break.

**Monoecious** A plant producing separate male and female flowers that are borne on the same plant. *Corylus avellana* (common hazel) and *Chamaecyparis* spp. (false cypress) are monoecious. See also DIOECIOUS.

**Monocarpic** A plant that dies after flowering and setting seed. The word is most often used to describe plants such as annuals and biennials, some perennials, such as bromeliads and sempervivums, die after flowering.

**Node** The point, often swollen, where a leaf is attached to a stem. The joint from which young leaves and side-shoots arise.

**Obovate** or **obovoid** Of a leaf, OVATE but with the widest point above, rather than below, the middle point; narrowest towards the base.

**Ovate** Of a leaf, roughly oval in outline but with the widest part nearest the stalk. See also OBOVATE.

**Panicle** An inflorescence with several branches, which may be alternate or opposite. A branched raceme.

**Petiolate** A leaf on a stalk (a petiole).

**Pilose** A leaf that is covered with soft, fine hairs.

**Pinnate** A compound leaf that is feather-like, with the parts arranged in pairs on both sides of a central stem. The leaves of *Fraxinus* (ash) and of *Wisteria* are pinnate.

**Pubescent** Covered with short, fine, soft hairs; like down.

**Raceme** An unbranched and usually long inflorescence, composed of flowers on stems the same, or almost the same, length and carried on an unbranched stalk.

**Rachis** or **rhachis** An axis bearing flowers or leaflets. The axis of a pinnate leaf or frond.

**Reticulate** Marked with fine veins that form a network.

**Rootstock** A plant upon which another, compatible plant is grafted, usually the lower part of the trunk of a fruit tree, which is used for its roots. See also SCION.

**Samara** A dry, usually one-seeded, INDEHISCENT, winged fruit, like that of the elm, ash, sycamore and maple. Similar to a winged ACHENE.

**Scarify** To score or roughen the hard casing of a seed before sowing to assist the absorption of water and thus hasten germination.

**Scion** The detached bud, shoot or cutting that is grafted onto a ROOTSTOCK of another variety.

**Simple** A leaf or other part of a plant that is not compound. It is not divided into secondary units, such as leaflets or branches.

**Stoma** (pl. stomata) A minute, mouth-like opening in the epidermis of the green parts of a tree or other plant through which gases pass out of and into the plant from the atmosphere. They are usually, but not always, found on the undersurface of leaves.

**Stratify** To place hard seeds in layers of coarse sand or vermiculite and encourage germination by breaking the dormancy of the seeds by exposing them to cold weather or even by placing them in the refrigerator. It is a technique often used with plants that are native to cold areas such as some species of *Pinus* (pine).

**Sucker** A shoot that arises from below ground, usually from the roots of plant.

**Systemic** A pesticide or weedkiller that is absorbed into a plant's structure and circulates in the sap. A systemic insecticide thus destroys only sap-sucking insects. See also CONTACT.

# ACKNOWLEDGEMENTS

Jacket photographs: Octopus Publishing Group Ltd/Peter Myers. Alain Draeger: pages 6 (left), 25, 26, 30, 39, 43 (left), 45, 47, 48, 51, 59, 63, 65, 69, 73, 75, 76, 81, 85, 91, 92 (right), 93, 95, 97, 99, 107, 111, 118, 119, 120, 121, 129, 133, 137, 139, 145, 153, 155, 157, 163, 164, 166, 171, 172, 173, 174, 175, 177, 179, 184, 185, 187. Jeanbor/Photeb: page 7 (above). Daniel Lévy: page 24. MAP/François Gages pages 4-5. MAP/N. and P. Mioulane: pages 147 and 181. Christian Pessey: pages 7 (below), 17, 18, 19, 21, 23, 40, 41, 43 (right), 92, 140, 141, 145, 186, 187. Isabelle Samson: pages 6 (right), 8, 9, 10, 14, 15, 16, 28, 31, 36-7, 49, 53, 55, 57, 61, 67, 71, 77, 79, 82, 83, 87, 89, 100-101, 103, 105, 109, 113, 115, 117, 123, 125, 127, 131, 132, 135, 143, 149, 151, 159, 161, 169, 183, 186.

Jacket design and execution: Peter Burt